Politics in Contempor

In *Politics in Contemporary Indonesia*, Ken M.P. Setiawan and Dirk Tomsa analyse the most prominent political ideas, institutions, interests and issues that shape Indonesian politics today. Guided by the overarching question whether Indonesia still deserves its famous label as a 'model Muslim democracy', this book argues that the most serious threats to Indonesian democracy emanate from the fading appeal of democracy as a compelling narrative, the increasingly brazen capture of democratic institutions by predatory interests and the narrowing public space for those who seek to defend the values of democracy. In so doing, the book answers the following key questions:

- What are the dominant political narratives that underpin Indonesian politics?
- How has Indonesia's institutional framework evolved since the onset of democratisation in 1998?
- How do competing political interests weaken or strengthen Indonesian democracy?
- How does declining democracy affect Indonesia's prospects for dealing with its main policy challenges?
- How does Indonesia compare to other Muslim-majority states and to its regional neighbours?

Up-to-date, comprehensive and written in an accessible style, this book will be of interest to both students and scholars of Indonesian politics, Asian Studies, Comparative Politics and International Relations.

Ken M.P. Setiawan is Lecturer in Indonesian and Asian Studies at the Asia Institute, the University of Melbourne, Australia. She is also Associate at the Centre for Indonesian Law, Islam and Society (CILIS) at the Melbourne Law School. Her research interests include globalisation and human rights, particularly focusing on the promotion of human rights at national and local levels. She has widely published on the politics of human rights in contemporary Indonesia, including *Promoting Human Rights: National Human Rights Institutions in Indonesia and Malaysia* (2013).

Dirk Tomsa is Associate Professor in the Department of Politics, Media and Philosophy at La Trobe University, Australia. His main research interests focus on Indonesian and comparative Southeast Asian politics, especially in the areas of democratisation and democratic decline, electoral and party politics, institutional change and environmental politics. His publications include *Party Politics and Democratization in Indonesia: Golkar in the Post-Suharto Era* (Routledge, 2008) as well as two co-edited volumes and numerous journal articles and book chapters on Indonesian and Southeast Asian politics.

Politics in Contemporary Indonesia

Institutional Change, Policy Challenges and Democratic Decline

Ken M.P. Setiawan and Dirk Tomsa

Routledge
Taylor & Francis Group

LONDON AND NEW YORK

Cover image @ Nur Taufik Zamari

First published 2022
by Routledge
4 Park Square, Milton Park, Abingdon, Oxon OX14 4RN

and by Routledge
605 Third Avenue, New York, NY 10158

Routledge is an imprint of the Taylor & Francis Group, an informa business

© 2022 Ken M.P. Setiawan & Dirk Tomsa

British Library Cataloguing-in-Publication Data
A catalogue record for this book is available from the British Library

Library of Congress Cataloging-in-Publication Data
A catalog record has been requested for this book

ISBN: 978-1-138-62606-5 (hbk)
ISBN: 978-1-138-62608-9 (pbk)
ISBN: 978-0-429-45951-1 (ebk)

DOI: 10.4324/9780429459511

Typeset in Times New Roman
by Deanta Global Publishing Services, Chennai, India

Contents

Illustrations

Boxes

Acknowledgements

This book would not have been possible without the assistance and encouragement of a great number of colleagues and friends. We would like to thank our colleagues at La Trobe University and the University of Melbourne for providing supportive academic environments and valuable support networks. At La Trobe University, Dirk Tomsa was particularly grateful for stimulating discussions with Dina Afrianty, Nicholas Herriman, James Leibold and Gavin Height. At the University of Melbourne, Ken Setiawan would like to thank Rachael Diprose, Michael Ewing, Vedi Hadiz, Edwin Jurriëns, Kate McGregor, Dave McRae, Andrew Rosser, Justin Wejak and Hellena Souisa. In addition, a number of other colleagues and friends offered valuable advice, suggestions, recommendations and assistance. In particular, we would like to acknowledge Burhanuddin Muhtadi for conducting a public opinion survey that provided data for Chapter 11. We would also like to express special thanks to everyone in Indonesia who offered feedback at a time when the country was facing extraordinary hardship because of the Covid-19 pandemic.

At Routledge, we thank Dorothea Schaefter and Alexandra de Brauw, as well as Saraswathy Narayan and Joanna Hardern for their support and patience during the process of writing this book. Some sections of the book have appeared in other publications. Parts of Chapter 1, for instance, build on Tomsa (2018), 'Regime resilience and presidential politics in Indonesia', *Contemporary Politics,* vol. 24, no. 3, pp. 266-285. In Chapter 4, small sections were part of Tomsa (2015), 'Toning down the big bang: the politics of decentralisation during the Yudhoyono years', in E Aspinall, M Mietzner & D Tomsa (eds), *The Yudhoyono Presidency: Indonesia's Decade of Stability and Stagnation*, ISEAS, Singapore, pp. 155-174, while Chapter 6 includes scattered extracts from Tomsa (2019), 'Islamism and party politics in Indonesia', in P Djupe, MJ Rozell & T Jelen (eds), *Oxford Research Encyclopedia of Politics*. Oxford University Press. doi: http://dx.doi.org/10.1093/acrefore/9780190228637.013.1157. Chapter 10 builds on earlier publications by Setiawan, including 'The Human Rights Courts: embedding impunity', in M Crouch (ed.), *The Politics of Court Reform: Judicial Change and Legal Culture in Indonesia*, 2019, pp. 1-28; 'Shifting from international to 'Indonesian' justice measures: two decades of addressing past human rights violations', *Journal of Contemporary Asia*, vol. 49, no. 5, pp. 837-861 (2019, co-authored with Katharine McGregor); and 'A state of surveillance? Freedom of expression under the Jokowi Presidency', in T Power & E Warburton (eds), *Democracy in Indonesia: From Stagnation to Regression?*, ISEAS-Yusof Ishak Institute, Singapore, 2020, pp. 254-274. Chapter 11 includes data published in Setiawan & Tomsa, 'Covid-19, Public Ignorance and Democratic Decline: Three Forces Chipping Away at Indonesia's Poor Environmental Conservation', *The Conversation*, 16 June 2021.

Finally, both authors owe immense gratitude to their partners and families for their consistent support. As large parts of the book were written during the Covid-19 pandemic, we extend our thanks to Edwin, Wulan, Setia, Raphael and Hanna for allowing us to finish the project in between lockdowns, home schooling and seemingly endless online meetings.

Map 1 reproduced with the permission of CartoGIS Services, Scholarly Information Services, The Australian National University.

Glossary

abangan	Syncretic Muslims
ACCT	ASEAN Convention on Counter Terrorism
AGO	Attorney General's Office
AJI	Aliansi Jurnalis Independen, Alliance of Independent Journalists
AILA	Aliansi Cinta Keluarga, Family Love Alliance
akil baligh	Mental and physical maturity (Arabic)
APJII	Asosiasi Penyelenggara Jasa Internet Indonesia, Indonesian Internet Service Provider Association
Apkindo	Asosiasi Panel Kayu Indonesia, Indonesian Wood Panel Association
ASEAN	Association of Southeast Asian Nations
azas kekeluargaan	Family principle (New Order)
Bawaslu	Badan Pengawas Pemilu, Election Oversight Agency
bhinneka tunggal ika	Unity in diversity
bissu	Third sex (South Sulawesi)
BLT	Bantuan Langusung Tunai, Direct Cash Assistance
BPD	Badan Permusyawaratan Desa, Village Consultative Body
BPJS	Badan Penyelenggara Jaminan Sosial, Social Security Agency
BNPT	Badan Nasional Penanggulan Terorisme, National Counter Terrorism Agency
Cultivation System	19th-century Dutch-imposed revenue system
dakwah	Proselytisation
Densus 88	Detachment 88, counterterrorism unit
DOM	Daerah Operasi Militer, Military Operation Zone
DPD	Dewan Perwakilan Daerah, Regional Representative Council
DPR	Dewan Perwakilan Rakyat, People's Representative Council (also known as the House of Representatives and as parliament)
DPRA	Dewan Perwakilan Rakyat Aceh, Aceh People's Representative Council

DPRD I	Dewan Perwakilan Rakyat Daerah I, Regional People's Representative Council I (provincial parliament)
DPRD II	Dewan Perwakilan Rakyat Daerah II, Regional People's Representative Council I (district or municipal parliament)
DSI	Dewan Syariat Islam, Office for Syariat Islam
dwifungsi	Dual function of the military
EIU	Economist Intelligence Unit
Ethical Policy	Official policy of the Dutch government (1901-1942) to enhance living conditions
EODB	Ease of Doing Business Index
fatwa	Legal opinion issues by Islamic scholars
FPI	Front Pembela Islam, Islamic Defenders Front
Gafatar	Gerakan Fajar Nusantara, Archipelagic Dawn Movement
GAM	Gerakan Aceh Merdeka, Free Aceh Movement
GDP	Gross Domestic Product
Gerindra	Gerakan Indonesia Raya, Greater Indonesia Movement
Gerwani	Gerakan Wanita Indonesia, Women's organisation affiliated with the PKI
Golkar	Golongan Karya (Functional Groups)
golput	To Abstain from voting
gotong royong	Mutual assistance
GP Ansor	Nahdlatul Ulama (NU) youth wing
hajj	Islamic pilgrimage
halal	Lawful/permitted in Islam
HDI	Human Development Index
HTI	Hizbut Tahrir Indonesia
ICCPR	International Covenant on Civil and Political Rights
ICESCR	International Covenant on Economic, Social and Cultural Rights
ICMI	Ikatan Cendekiawan Muslim Indonesia, Indonesian Association of Muslim Intellectuals
ICW	Indonesia Corruption Watch
ijtihad	Religious interpretation
ILO	International Labour Organisation
ISIS	Islamic State of Iraq and Sham
ITE Law	Electronic Information and Transactions Law
IUCN	International Union for Conservation of Nature
JAD	Jamaah Ansharut Daulah
JIL	Jaringan Islam Liberal, Liberal Islam Network
JKN	Jaminan Kesehatan Nasional, National Health Insurance Scheme
jilbab	Islamic headscarf
keris	Ceremonial dagger

khalwat	Unmarried/unrelated individuals of different sexes being together in isolated spaces
kiai	Islamic scholar
KJS	Kartu Jakarta Sehat, Jakarta Health Card
KKN	Korupsi, Kolusi, Nepotisme – Corruption, Collusion, Nepotism
Komnas HAM	Komisi Nasional Hak Asasi Manusia, National Human Rights Commission
Komnas Perempuan	Komisi Nasional Anti Kekerasan Terhadap Perempuan, National Commission on the Elimination of Violence Against Women
Korpri	Korps Pegawai Negeri Republic Indonesia, Civil Servants' Corps of the Republic of Indonesia
Konstituante	Constitutional Assembly
Kostrad	Komando Strategi Angkatan Darat, Army Strategic Reserve Command
KPI	Komisi Penyiaran Indonesia, Indonesian Broadcasting Commission
KPK	Komisi Pemberantasan Korupsi, Corruption Eradication Commission
KPU	Komisi Pemilihan Umum, General Election Commission
KY	Komisi Yudisial, Judicial Commission
LBH	Lembaga Bantuan Hukum, Legal Aid Foundation
LGBT	Lesbian, Gay, Bisexual, Transgender
LIPI	Lembaga Ilmu Pengetahuan Indonesia, Indonesian Institute of Sciences
Masyumi	Modernist Muslim party
MK	Mahkamah Konstitusi, Constitutional Court
MMR	Maternal Mortality Rate
MNC	Media Nusantara Citra, media company
MPR	Majelis Permusyawaratan Rakyat, People's Consultative Assembly
MPU	Majelis Permuyawaratan Ulama, Ulama Consultative Assembly in Aceh
MRP	Majelis Rakyat Papua, Papuan People's Council
mudik	Annual migration of Muslims related to Ramadan
Muhammadiyah	Islamic mass organisation
MUI	Majelis Ulama Indonesia, Indonesian Council of Ulama (Islamic Scholars)
NGO	Non-governmental Organisation
NKRI	Negara Kesatuan Republic Indonesia, Unitary Republic of Indonesia
NLD	National League for Democracy
NU	Nahdlatul Ulama, Islamic mass organisation
OPM	Organisasi Papua Merdeka, Free Papua Organisation

otonomi daerah	Regional autonomy
Otsus	Otonomi Khusus, special autonomy
PAP	People's Action Party
PAN	Partai Amanat Nasional, National Mandate Party
Pancasila	Indonesian state ideology, literally 'five pillars'
Partai NasDem	Partai Nasional Demokrat, National Democratic Party
pasal karet	Rubber clause, broadly formulated regulations
PD	Partai Demokrat, Democratic Party
PDI	Partai Demokrasi Indonesia, Indonesian Democratic Party
PDI-P	Partai Demokrasi Indonesia-Perjuangan, Indonesian Democratic Party-Struggle
pembantu	Domestic helper
pemekaran	Blossomming; the process of creating new administrative entities at the subnational level
pesantren	Islamic boarding school
Perda	Peraturan Daerah, Regional Regulation
Permesta	Piagam Perjuangan Semesta, Universal Struggle Charter
Perppu	Peraturan Pemerintah Pengganti Undang-Undang, Government Regulation in Lieu of Law
PHDI	Planetary pressures-adjusted HDI
Pilkada	Direct local elections
PK	Partai Keadilan, Justice Party, predecessor of PKS
PKB	Partai Kebangkitan Bangsa, National Awakening Party
PKI	Partai Komunis Indonesia, Indonesian Communist Party
PKS	Partai Keadilan Sejahtera, Prosperous Justice Party
PNI	Partai Nasional Indonesia
PPP	Partai Persatuan Pembangunan, United Development Party
Prolegnas	Program Legislasi Nasional, National Legislative Program
PSBB	Pembatasan Sosial Berskala Besar, large-scale social restrictions put in place in response to the Covid-19 pandemic
PSHK	Pusat Studi Hukum dan Kebijakan Indonesia, Indonesian Centre for Law and Policy Studies
PSI	Partai Sosialis Indonesia, Indonesian Socialist Party
puskesmas	Health care posts
qanun	Laws and regulations enacted by a government, intended to supplement Islamic law in matters that are believed to be insufficiently regulated
reformasi	Reform, term used for the period after the fall of Suharto in 1998
RRI	Radio Republik Indonesia, Radio of the Republic of Indonesia

santri	Orthodox Muslims
Sarekat Islam	Islamic League
SDGs	Sustainable Development Goals
State Ibuism	New Order gender ideology
Supersemar	Surat Perintah Sebelas Maret, 11th of March Order
tarbiyah	Education (Arabic)
TII	Transparency International Indonesia
TRC	Truth and Reconciliation Commission
TVRI	Televisi Republik Indonesia, Television of the Republic of Indonesia
UDHR	Universal Declaration of Human Rights
ulama	Islamic scholar
ummah	Islamic community of believers
UMNO	United Malays National Organisation
UNDP	United Nations Development Programme
VOC	Vereenigde Oostindische Compagnie, United East Indies Company
WH	Wilayatul Hisbah, Sharia Police (Aceh)
WHO	World Health Organization

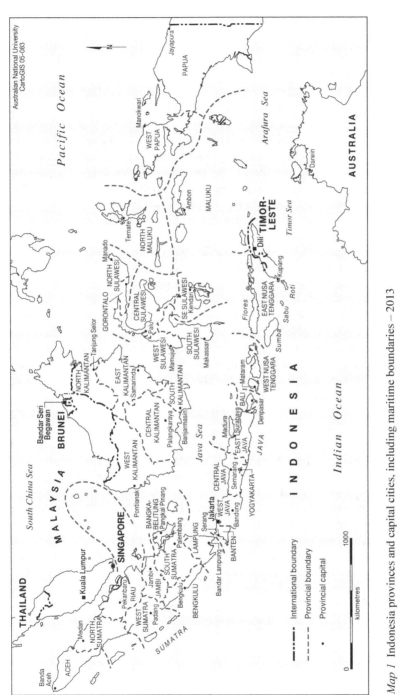

Map 1 Indonesia provinces and capital cities, including maritime boundaries – 2013

'Two of the foremost scholars of Indonesia, Ken Setiawan and Dirk Tomsa, have teamed up to write the most authoritative and comprehensive overview of that country's dynamic democracy, and to explain the myriad forces that are responsible for that democracy's resiliency and blemishes, in years. If one wants to grasp what has been happening since this large and strategic archipelagic nation-state started down its bumpy road to democracy nearly twenty-five years ago, and why careening off that road seems increasingly likely, start by reading this capably written, tightly organized, and exhaustively researched book.'

Jamie S. Davidson, *National University of Singapore*

'*Politics in Contemporary Indonesia* is a rich and highly readable assessment of current affairs in Indonesia, which offers a first-rate analysis of Indonesia's democratic decline and the forces behind that. Rather than focusing only on election outcomes and party politics, attention is directed to a much wider set of political issues that are shaping Indonesia's present and future, including human rights, social justice, gender, political Islam, and ecology. The COVID-19 pandemic receives special attention, not least as it has exacerbated many existing drawbacks. Setiawan and Tomsa offer long-term observers a highly plausible interpretation of contemporary Indonesia, but also succeed in making Indonesia more accessible to newcomers.'

Antje Missbach, *Bielefeld University, Germany*

'*Politics in Contemporary Indonesia* presents an excellent overview of Indonesian politics today. Written in an accessible style by two authors who know both the country and the scholarship superbly well, this volume takes readers through an even-handed and authoritative account of the major issues and themes driving contention in contemporary Indonesia. With chapters that provide deeply researched yet lightly written succinct overviews of key issues, and locates these within a broader framework of debates about the nature and depth of Indonesian democracy, this is a book that will provide readers with a strong grounding in Indonesian politics. Highly recommended for students of Indonesia, or for anyone seeking an introduction to, or update on, the politics of this fascinating country.'

Edward Aspinall, *Australian National University*

1 Trends and Features of Contemporary Indonesian Politics

Introduction

On 22 December 2020, Indonesian president Joko Widodo, better known as Jokowi, reshuffled his cabinet. Little more than a year after commencing his second and final term, Jokowi dismissed 6 out of 34 ministers, in a desperate attempt to lift his cabinet's performance in battling the Covid-19 pandemic, which by December 2020 had cost more than 20,000 Indonesian lives and driven the country into its first recession since the onset of democracy in 1998. Given Indonesia's poor track record in handling the pandemic, the reshuffle had been widely anticipated, especially the dismissal of controversial Health Minister Terawan Agus Putranto, who early on in the pandemic had made international headlines when he suggested that prayers would keep Indonesians safe from Covid-19 (Lindsey & Mann 2020). Throughout 2020, Terawan had faced constant criticism for his failure to implement any effective measures to contain the pandemic, so his replacement was widely regarded as an overdue reaction to consistent policy failure and ongoing public pressure. More broadly, however, the reshuffle also offered notable insights into some general trends and features of contemporary Indonesian politics.

First, it illustrated President Jokowi's belief in technocratic solutions for complex political, and in the case of the pandemic, scientific challenges. To be sure, the replacement of Terawan was overdue and hardly surprising. But Jokowi's choice of a former banker, Budi Gunadi Sadikin, as new Health Minister seemed to suggest a conviction, not uncommon among Indonesian presidents, that a professional with managerial skills from the corporate world would be best suited to overcome challenges that are inherently political. Yet, while such an approach may have helped the government address some of the organisational inefficiencies in Indonesia's underdeveloped public health system, Sadikin's appointment was hardly the kind of drastic measure required to tackle deeper political issues that had prevented a more effective response to Covid-19, such as populist anti-science attitudes, religious polarisation and endemic corruption (Mietzner 2020a).

Corruption, in fact, was the second key feature of Indonesian politics that left its mark on this cabinet reshuffle. Despite modest advances in Transparency International's Corruption Perception Index (CPI) in the years before the pandemic

DOI: 10.4324/9780429459511-1

hit (Transparency International 2020), Indonesia remains a highly corrupt country, so it was hardly surprising that two of the six ministers who were replaced in the reshuffle had only just been named suspects in large-scale corruption cases. President Jokowi therefore had virtually no choice but to appoint new ministers for these portfolios. What was particularly embarrassing for the president was that one of the two ministers, Social Affairs Minister Juliari Batubara, was accused of embezzling money from the aid budget that had been designated for Indonesians hit hardest by Covid-19. In the wake of these and other recent high-profile corruption cases, Indonesia's CPI score promptly dropped again in 2020 by three points.

Batubara's replacement, the former mayor of Indonesia's second largest city Surabaya, Tri Rismaharini, represents the third important feature of contemporary Indonesian politics, namely the importance of local politics as a catalyst for a career at the national level. Since the beginning of regional autonomy for provinces, municipalities and districts in the early 2000s, local leadership positions such as governor, mayor or district head have become important pathways to power, especially for politicians from outside established party networks. Jokowi epitomised this new crop of leaders when he rose from mayor of the small town of Solo (2005-2012) to become governor of the capital Jakarta (2012-2014) and eventually president (2014-2024). Several other ambitious local leaders have been regularly touted for higher office in recent years, including as potential successors of Jokowi.

Fourth, the reshuffle highlighted the persistence of a particular kind of transactional politics by which Indonesian presidents have long co-opted political opponents into coalitions of power. When Jokowi won his first presidential term in 2014, he had initially pledged to end this practice, labelled 'promiscuous powersharing' by Slater and Simmons (2013). But he soon abandoned that campaign promise and, just like his predecessors had done, appointed leading representatives of opposition parties to cabinet posts. After winning the 2019 election, he went a step further and made the very person who had run against him in both 2014 and 2019, Prabowo Subianto, the Defence Minister. With the 2020 reshuffle, Jokowi completed the set when he appointed Prabowo's running mate from the 2019 election, Sandiaga Uno, the Minister of Tourism and Creative Economy.

Finally, the appointment of Yaqut Cholil Qoumas as Religious Affairs Minister cemented the formidable political influence of Indonesia's largest Islamic organisation, the Nahdlatul Ulama (NU). For Jokowi, NU has long been an important ally in his fight against Islamic radicalism (Nuraniyah 2020), and in 2019, he won his second term in office with senior NU cleric Ma'ruf Amin as his vice-presidential running mate. But he then broke with protocol when he appointed a retired military general to lead the Religious Affairs Ministry, which has traditionally been held by a member of one of Indonesia's two largest mass organisations, NU and Muhammadiyah. The 2020 reshuffle rectified this by putting Yaqut, the leader of NU's youth wing GP Ansor, in charge of the ministry.

This short analysis of the 2020 cabinet reshuffle illustrates some of the key features of contemporary Indonesian politics. Though often hailed as Southeast Asia's largest democracy, Indonesia's current democratic regime is in fact laden with democratic deficits and, as many observers have noted, these deficits have become more plentiful and more severe in recent years (Diprose, McRae & Hadiz 2019, Mietzner 2020b, Warburton & Aspinall 2019). While promiscuous powersharing and corruption have been characteristic traits of Indonesian politics throughout the democratic period that began in 1998, other issues have only recently become more prevalent, prompting scholars to speak of the advent of a democratic regression (Power & Warburton 2020). Among the most concerning indicators of this regression are the spread of nationalist and religious populism, discrimination against religious and sexual minorities, as well as the governments' heavy-handed use of laws and state institutions to silence critics.

This book aims to build on the various recent assessments of Indonesian politics and further enhance our understanding of the reasons behind Indonesia's democratic decline. At the same time, it aims to provide readers with little prior knowledge of the country with some basic background about the most prominent political ideas, institutions, interests and issues that shape political dynamics in Indonesia today. Guided by the overarching question whether Indonesia still deserves its famous label as a 'model Muslim democracy', the book argues that the most serious threats to Indonesian democracy emanate from the fading appeal of democracy as a compelling narrative, the increasingly brazen capture of democratic institutions by predatory interests and the narrowing public space for those who seek to defend the values of democracy. But the book goes beyond a mere assessment of democratic quality. By linking various democratic deficits to a range of public policy issues, it also highlights how the declining democratic quality diminishes prospects for Indonesia to successfully confront its most pressing policy challenges in the areas of public health, gender equality, human rights and environmental conservation.

The remainder of this introductory chapter will review the vast literature on Indonesian politics and outline the main contours of Indonesia's current democratic regime. With frequent references to the key arguments presented in the following chapters, the discussion will interrogate how the complex interplay between ideas, interests and institutions has shaped the country's democratic trajectory. The chapter will end by highlighting some of the key policy implications of Indonesia's democratic decline.

The State of Indonesian Democracy: Resilient, but Increasingly Vulnerable

Indonesia democratised in 1998, after many decades of authoritarian rule under the country's first two presidents, Sukarno and Suharto. Chapter 2 will provide a brief summary of the key periods in Indonesian history that led up to the regime change from Suharto's New Order to democracy, underlining the adverse conditions under which the country commenced its political transformation. Not only was Indonesia in the midst of a severe financial crisis, but the pro-democracy forces that led the charge in 1998 also had to contend with a heavily politicised military, entrenched corruption and a spate of separatist, ethnic and religious violence at the margins of the archipelago. Moreover, as the largest Muslim-majority country in the world – about 90 percent of Indonesia's 270 million people are Muslims – Indonesia faced difficult questions about the place of religion in politics and public life.

Against the odds, however, the transition to a democratic regime proceeded remarkably well. Within less than ten years, the military retreated from politics, collective violence in most provinces subsided and demands from Islamists to turn Indonesia into a sharia-based Islamic state were rejected during deliberations about constitutional amendments. To address the problem of corruption, a new Corruption Eradication Commission (Komisi Pemberantasan Korupsi, KPK) was established. Yet, as Aspinall (2010, p. 21) pointed out, the irony of the successful transition was that 'spoilers have been accommodated and absorbed into the system rather than excluded from it, producing a trade-off between democratic success and democratic quality'. Thus, Indonesia never evolved into a consolidated liberal democracy. Instead, the country has been described as a 'patronage democracy' (Van Klinken 2009, Simandjuntak 2012), an 'electoral democracy' (Davidson 2009, Tomsa 2009) or, especially in more recent assessments, an 'illiberal democracy' (Hadiz 2017, Warburton & Aspinall 2019, Wilson 2015).

The range of different labels points to the variety of analytical lenses through which scholars of Indonesian politics have analysed the trajectory of Indonesia's post-authoritarian regime. While structural political economists consistently emphasise the pre-eminence of material wealth as a source of power, others have stressed the agency of social and political actors, including both elite and non-elite actors, or the influence of institutions in shaping political outcomes. In this introductory chapter, we canvass insights from these various approaches and integrate them into a broader regime-based framework that considers ideational, institutional and structural factors as complementary rather than contradictory features of Indonesian politics.

A political regime can be defined as a prevailing set of ideas, interests and institutional arrangements that provide a framework of opportunities and constraints for political actors, including the top decision-makers at the helm of government (Skowronek 1997). Indonesia has had four distinct regimes since independence. In the 1950s, the first regime of the post-colonial era was democratic but politically and economically unstable and therefore short-lived (1949-1957). It was replaced by Sukarno's nationalist-authoritarian Guided Democracy regime in 1957. Then, following an attempted coup and mass killings of 500,000 to 1 million people in 1965-1966 (McGregor, Melvin & Pohlman 2018), Suharto replaced Sukarno and established his developmentalist-authoritarian New Order regime which lasted for more than 30 years. Finally, in May 1998, the Asian financial crisis and mass student protests forced the resignation of Suharto and led to the transition to a new democratic regime which persists until today, even if its dominant ideas, interests and institutions have been subject to some noticeable changes in recent years. The following section will sketch the key contours of this regime and explain how important parameters have shifted over time.

Ideas and Narratives: *Reformasi* and Its Discontents

In 1998, one of the most drastic changes to the preceding Suharto regime became manifest in the realm of ideas where the New Order's authoritarian developmentalism was replaced by a popular narrative of *reformasi* (democratic reform). Though nostalgia for the old regime remained noticeable and other political ideas, especially Islamism, also resonated with sizeable segments of the population, it was the promise of democracy and good governance that captured the public imagination most forcefully, making it the new dominant political narrative in 1998.

While its commitment to open political processes and new institutions constituted a sharp break with the most recent authoritarian past, the new narrative's underlying values such as pluralism and tolerance actually fit neatly into key tenets of Indonesia's inclusivist state ideology Pancasila (Five Pillars) and the associated meta-narrative of *bhinneka tunggal ika* (unity in diversity), the country's national motto. Driven by students, non-governmental organisations and the media, the power of this new narrative first compelled interim president B.J. Habibie, who had taken over from Suharto in May 1998, to instigate some quick reforms and then prompted parliament to elect the liberal Muslim leader Abdurrahman Wahid as president in an indirect presidential election in 1999 (Crouch 2010). Wahid, however, soon lost the support of those who had elected him, and in 2001 he was impeached and replaced by his vice-president Megawati Sukarnoputri, the daughter of first president Sukarno and another symbolic figure of the reform movement.

For Megawati's supporters, her eventual rise to the presidency was the deserved reward for her role in the anti-Suharto opposition and the strong result for her Indonesian Democratic Party-Struggle (Partai Demokrasi Indonesia-Perjuangan, PDI-P) in the 1999 parliamentary election where PDI-P had won a third of the votes. As only the fourth female leader of a Muslim-majority state, she also symbolised the hopes of the women's movement for greater gender equality after decades of state-imposed patriarchal gender norms (see Chapter 9). But Megawati's popularity waned quickly. By the time direct presidential elections were held for the first time in 2004, she no longer represented the hopes and expectations of what the reform movement had struggled for. A former army general and minister under Megawati, Susilo Bambang Yudhoyono, exploited this situation adroitly. After a campaign that aligned effectively with key themes of the *reformasi* narrative (especially anti-corruption), Yudhoyono won the 2004 election and became the first directly elected president of Indonesia (see Chapter 3).

The peaceful transfer of power to the moderate ex-general who during the final months of the New Order had sought the dialogue with democracy activists confirmed the enduring appeal of the reform narrative six years after the fall of Suharto. Indeed, by mid-2004 public support for democracy as the best form of government had surged from a respectable 55 percent before the 1999 election to an enthusiastic 87.9 percent (Mujani & Liddle 2015, p. 215). When Yudhoyono was re-elected in 2009, it was still extremely high, indicating ongoing strong support

Table 1.1 Public support for democracy in Indonesia, 2004-2014

April 2004	July 2004	April 2009	July 2009	December 2010	June 2012	December 2012	April 2013	April 2014	July 2014
70.6	87.9	77.5	81.7	74.3	56.0	55.0	57.7	58.0	57.3

Source: Tomsa (2018, p. 272)

for the democratic ideals of the reform movement. Following Yudhoyono's re-election, former US ambassador to Indonesia Paul Wolfowitz (2009) wrote in the Wall Street Journal that 'Indonesia Is a Model Muslim Democracy'.

During Yudhoyono's second term, however, the numbers dropped back to more modest figures (see Table 1.1). Initially, this trend may just have reflected a 'normalization of politics' (Aspinall 2005), but over time it also signalled a growing public sentiment that the ideals of the reform movement were being abandoned by self-interested elites. Early indications of democratic stagnation and, in some policy fields, regression, included a never-ending stream of corruption cases, a deteriorating human rights situation, failure to overhaul the security sector, as well as the government's long-pursued but ultimately aborted plan to end direct local elections for governors, mayors and district heads (Aspinall, Mietzner & Tomsa 2015). As a consequence, alternative narratives that challenged the foundations of the reform narrative grew in strength.

In particular, conservative Islamist ideas, which had been marginalised in the early transition phase after a failed attempt to turn Indonesia into a sharia-based Islamic state via a constitutional amendment, became increasingly integrated into mainstream public discourse, as discussed in detail in Chapter 6. The most obvious expressions of this religious turn were the adoption of the Anti-Pornography Law in 2008, the retention of the controversial Blasphemy Law in 2010 and a growing number of attacks on religious minorities during Yudhoyono's second term. Menchik (2014) labelled the new religious assertiveness 'godly nationalism', arguing that it actually unites all six formally recognised religions – Islam, Protestantism, Catholicism, Hinduism, Buddhism and Confucianism – in joint opposition against deviant faiths. But while so-called deviant groups like Ahmadiyah or Shi'i Muslims were certainly frequent targets of religious intolerance, recognised minorities, such as Christians, also suffered increasing discrimination at the hands of the majority, giving the conservative religious turn a distinctly Islamic note.

While religion became more conspicuous in public discourse, debates on politics and the economy also took on more and more nationalistic tones during the Yudhoyono years. Thus, the two most prominent alternative narratives that emerged to compete with the *reformasi* narrative were moulded out of the classic social cleavage in Indonesian society between secular pluralist nationalists and devout Muslims. This cleavage has shaped Indonesian politics since independence and even though dealignment has taken its toll on partisan loyalties in the post-1998 regime, traditional affiliations with the ideational baselines remain deeply rooted in many parts of Indonesia (Fossati 2016). Significantly, however, the new political narratives that have sought to tap into these long-existing cleavage structures differ from the Islamism and the nationalism of the 1950s as they possess neither the ideological rigour nor the intellectual underpinnings that had characterised these political streams in the early independence period. As Aspinall (2016, p. 72) noted for the new nationalism, 'Indonesian nationalism today has few ideologues but many recyclers of old tropes and promoters of base emotional appeals'.

In the 2014 presidential election, the two candidates Jokowi and Prabowo Subianto both fit into Aspinall's description as promoters of base emotional appeals. But it was Prabowo who most forcefully sought to challenge the reform narrative as he mixed aggressive anti-foreign rhetoric with some inherently anti-democratic ideas, for instance when he labelled elections a Western import unsuitable for Indonesia (Aspinall 2015). Prabowo's campaign resonated with large parts of the Indonesian electorate, yet the reform narrative proved remarkably resilient. In the end, the former general lost the election, partly at least, because his opponent at the time epitomised widely held hopes that the reform narrative could not only be upheld but be actively revitalised after Yudhoyono's lacklustre second term. Although Jokowi's 2014 campaign was vague, his promises on the campaign trail certainly aligned with the reform narrative.

During his first term in office, however, Jokowi failed to fulfil the expectations of democracy activists. Rather than tackling corruption, addressing past and present human rights violations and strengthening democratic institutions, Jokowi commenced his presidency by focusing primarily on developmentalist policy issues such as health and education and, above all, the expansion of infrastructure. He also produced some highly nationalistic programmes and policies like destroying foreign fishing vessels or executing foreign drug convicts (see Chapter 12), in an apparent attempt to take some steam out of Prabowo's aggressive nationalism. What Jokowi did not do, however, was to articulate a broader overarching vision for Indonesian society that could provide the basis for a strong new political narrative. As Warburton (2016, p. 318) observed, 'Jokowi is changeable – even unpredictable – and something of a blank slate'.

In this kind of political environment, where the old narrative is losing traction, but the president is yet to offer a compelling new narrative, the space for alternative political ideas is expanding. Jokowi's political opponents realised this in late 2016 when they started their first moves to exploit this space. Building on the growing tide of religious conservatism that had swept across Indonesia for more than a decade (see Chapter 6), they turned to Islamism as the basis for their challenge. Using politically charged blasphemy allegations against the Christian ethnic Chinese governor of Jakarta and Jokowi ally Basuki Tjahaja Purnama (then better known as Ahok) as a pretext for mobilisation, opportunistic elite politicians like Prabowo Subianto and Susilo Bambang Yudhoyono joined forces with Islamist hardliners and organised a series of huge mass demonstrations in Jakarta (Fealy 2016).

The rallies had their intended polarising effect. Not only was Ahok convicted and jailed, but anti-Chinese sentiment and religious intolerance increased (see Chapter 10) while public support for radical Islamist groups surged. For example, the Islamic Defenders Front (Front Pembela Islam, FPI), an organisation many observers had long dismissed as a bunch of criminal thugs with good connections to political elites but little public support, suddenly recorded higher approval ratings in public opinion surveys than mainstream conservative Islamic parties (Mietzner & Muhtadi 2018). For the first time since the formation of the democratic regime, it seemed that Islamism was manifesting itself as a potent new challenge to the hitherto dominant narrative of democratic reform.

Jokowi could have responded to this challenge by lifting his own democratic credentials, but instead he resorted to 'fighting illiberalism with illiberalism' (Mietzner 2018a). In the run-up to the 2019 election, he initiated a range of coercive measures aimed primarily at radical Islamists, but also at other government critics, including those from pro-democratic civil society organisations who slammed the president's general assault on dissent (Setiawan 2020). At the same time, Jokowi sought to build a new campaign to protect and revitalise the Pancasila as the basic pluralist foundation of the Indonesian state. Thus, despite early indications that the 2019 election might simply be fought over socio-economic issues, the poll eventually took place in an intensely polarised atmosphere shaped by ideology-infused narratives about the place of religion in public life. In the shade of this aggressive contest between Islamism and pluralism, the *reformasi* narrative faded into the background, kept alive only by a small group of activists who promoted abstaining from the ballot as the only defence of democratic values.

Articulating Interests: Oligarchy and Other Strategic Groups

Pro-democracy activists did not only struggle to gain wider public attention in the run-up to the 2019 election. For many years now, they have faced stiff competition in public discourse and behind-the-scenes lobbying from other, often better-resourced interest groups, including business associations and religious organisations as well as trade unions (Caraway & Ford 2020). Interests in young and precarious democracies like Indonesia, however, are not only articulated through formally organised interest groups. Thompson (2014, p. 446) has therefore suggested to extend the analysis of interest articulation in young democracies to so-called strategic groups (Evers & Gerke 2009), which can be defined as powerful extra-electoral veto actors who seek to secure access to resources and control over their distribution. Support or resistance from such groups can have a significant impact on a regime's trajectory. Yet, it is important to note that while members of strategic groups share the common goal of resource appropriation, they do not necessarily form a monolithic block. In fact, relations between as well as within these groups can fluctuate between conflict and cooperation.

Arguably, the most influential strategic group in Indonesia is what has become known simply as the oligarchy, a somewhat amorphous assemblage of business tycoons, bureaucrats and politicians who have captured the new democratic institutions and continued the New Order practice of fusing the bases of economic and political power (Hadiz & Robison 2013, p. 38). Proponents of the thesis that oligarchs are the most dominant political force in Indonesia argue that 'the wealth power of oligarchs shapes and constrains Indonesia's democracy far more than democracy constrains the power of wealth' (Winters 2013, p. 12).

Though the patterns of oligarchy originated during the authoritarian New Order regime, the post-Suharto period has produced its fair share of new oligarchs as well. Just like their adaptable counterparts who survived from the New Order days, these new oligarchs have embraced the procedures of democracy, but not its values. In fact, oligarchs have thrived in the democratic period because the new regime has allowed them to use political institutions as a facade to defend and further expand their wealth. Through their enormous material resources, leadership of political parties and ownership of media conglomerates, they have extraordinary influence over both elected politicians as well as public opinion (see Chapters 3 and 7).

Accommodating the interests of oligarchs through cabinet representation, access to patronage and other financial perks is therefore crucial to any Indonesian president, while local leaders need to consider the growing class of small-scale oligarchs who have come to dominate local economies and party branches in the wake of Indonesia's decentralisation programme (see Chapter 4). Although it remains contested to what extent oligarchs can ultimately dictate the process of interest articulation in contemporary Indonesia (Ford & Pepinsky 2014), even critics of the oligarchy thesis acknowledge that their influence on Indonesian politics is immense. Among the various predicaments of Indonesian politics that have been blamed on the pervasive influence of oligarchs are rampant corruption and vote buying as well as the poor institutionalisation of political parties, many of whom are dependent on the financial support from oligarchic backers (Tomsa 2010).

Oligarchs, however, are not the only strategic group that has shaped the current regime. One other important group that has used its powers to extract favours from elected leaders is the military. Like in any other new democracy transitioning out of military-backed authoritarianism, presidents in Indonesia have had to provide incentives for the armed forces to refrain from coups or other destabilising actions. Aspinall (2010, p. 22) has described 'the effective sidelining of the military from the commanding heights of political power' as the 'greatest achievement of Indonesian democratisation'.

But while sidelined, the armed forces never really returned to the barracks. No president of the post-Suharto era, for example, has dared dismantle the notorious territorial structure which runs parallel to the political institutions at all administrative levels from the province to the village level (Laksmana 2019). Civilian control over the armed forces remains elusive, and towards the end of the Yudhoyono years, military personnel were once again participating in essentially civilian tasks, such as infrastructure development (Institute for Policy Analysis of Conflict 2015). Significantly, these programmes have gained further pace under current president Jokowi who cultivated links with some of the most conserva-tive factions in the military soon after taking office. For Jokowi, close ties with the military are particularly important not only because his partisan base is weak (Mietzner 2018b), but also because the military can be easily mobilised to assist with projects in his main policy priority, the development of Indonesia's dilapi-dated infrastructure.

The third important strategic group comprises organisations that can be loosely subsumed under the banner of political Islam. Chapter 6 provides a detailed dis-cussion of political Islam which comprises a heterogeneous array of groups that range from relatively moderate yet conservative mainstream mass organisations like Nahdlatul Ulama (NU) and Muhammadiyah to archconservative movements like Hizbut Tahrir and Islamist groups like the Islamic Defenders Front (both controversially banned in 2017 and 2020, respectively). Endowed with a mix of moral and mobilisational capital, these groups not only represent powerful inter-ests, but also endeavour to shape or, in some cases, replace the dominant regime narrative. Political Islam, in other words, operates within both the realm of ideas and the realm of interests. While all but a few extremist fringe groups have aban-doned the goal of establishing a formal Islamic state based on sharia law, most groups are steadfast in pursuing their mission to impose conservative Islamic val-ues on Indonesia's multicultural society.

To achieve this overarching goal, many Islamic organisations have forged extensive ties with political actors in parties, parliament and the bureaucracy, making it risky for elected presidents to move against these groups (Buehler 2016). Especially during the Yudhoyono presidency, political Islam steadily expanded its influence over policymaking, as was evident in high-level admin-istrative support for anti-pluralist organisations like the FPI or the Indonesian Council of Ulama (Majelis Ulama Indonesia, MUI), the appointment of conserva-tive Islamic figures to important government positions and the passing of a range of discriminatory laws and decrees (Bush 2015).

What is striking about this conservative religious turn in Indonesian politics is that these extra-electoral groups extended their influence precisely at a time when most Islamic parties were performing poorly at the ballot box (Tomsa 2019). Current president Jokowi was first confronted with the new assertiveness of this social force in late 2016 when Islamist demonstrations derailed the re-election campaign of Jakarta's former Christian governor and Jokowi ally Ahok. Since then, Jokowi has embarked on an aggressive campaign against the most radical groups while at the same time trying to appease the largest mainstream organisa-tion, NU, through the generous distribution of patronage and by offering the vice-presidency to NU cleric Ma'ruf Amin (Aspinall & Mietzner 2019).

The only strategic group of the post-Suharto era whose interests have been directly aligned with the *reformasi* narrative is the diverse and fragmented cohort of liberal and progressive civil society groups (see Chapter 7). That the ideals of the *reformasi* movement remained resonant with so many Indonesians for so long is to a large extent a result of the intense efforts by the activists that comprise this strategic group (Dibley & Ford 2019). Especially during the second Yudhoyono term, when anti-democratic elites became increasingly assertive in their push for a democratic rollback, civil society activists made their presence felt, for example by mobilising large-scale support for the embattled KPK, preventing the planned politicisation of the election commission and ensuring that direct elections for local executives, one of the key pillars of Indonesia's decentralisation programme, would not be abolished again (Mietzner 2012).

In the run-up to the 2014 presidential election, pro-democracy activists again played a decisive role when they defended the *reformasi* narrative against the neo-authoritarian threat posed by Prabowo Subianto and spearheaded an unprecedented mass mobilisation of volunteers to help Jokowi defeat his rival in the race for the presidency (Tomsa & Setijadi 2018). During Jokowi's first term in office, however, pro-democracy activists became increasingly marginalised as Jokowi abandoned his democratic credentials in his efforts to counter the alliance between Prabowo and radical Islamists. In the run-up to the 2019 election, some activists sought to capture public attention with a new *golput* (abstain from voting as a sign of protest) campaign (Mudhoffir & A'yun 2019), but the appeals to abstain failed to strike a chord with a deeply polarised population mobilised to vote for one of the two candidates.

The Institutional Framework: Multiparty Presidentialism

The contentious interplay between narratives and interests in Indonesia takes place within the institutional framework of a multiparty presidential system which has its origins in rather hastily concluded electoral reforms during the Habibie interregnum (see Chapter 3). Back in 1998-1999, these reforms were negotiated by old regime elites inside parliament, but they were heavily influenced by public pressure for democracy from outside the legislature. One of the key institutional outcomes of these early crisis-driven reforms was the retention of Proportional Representation (PR) as the electoral system for parliamentary elections. Predictably, once the New Order restrictions on party formation were removed, this electoral system produced an extremely fragmented party system which, despite some adjustments to the electoral rules in the years that followed, has remained a key characteristic of Indonesia's institutional landscape (Tomsa 2014).

Beyond the party system, the other institutional pillars of Indonesia's democratic regime, including a Constitutional Court, a constitutionally anchored human rights framework and a strengthened presidency, were shaped in four rounds of constitutional amendments that took place between 1999 and 2002 (Horowitz 2013). During the early rounds of these amendments, the new institutional framework was effectively a semi-presidential system in which the presidency was significantly weakened in its powers vis-à-vis the parliament. But after the controversial impeachment of President Abdurrahman Wahid in 2001, the powers of the president were strengthened again and by the time the constitutional amendments were completed in 2002, the new system had struck the balance reasonably well. In fact, balance appeared to have been a key consideration during the constitutional reform process, as epitomised in the stipulation (Article 20 (2)) that legislation must be passed by 'joint agreement' between the president and the People's Representative Council (Dewan Perwakilan Rakyat, DPR). Beyond its participation in law-making, parliament exercises its influence vis-à-vis the executive primarily through its right to question ministers.

By and large, however, despite the formally enshrined balance between the two arms of government, the president has substantial leverage over the legislature. Apart from the effective veto power provided by the 'joint agreement' provision, the executive also has the exclusive right to issue a range of presidential regulations and decrees (Kawamura 2010, p. 14) as well as implementing regulations for legislation that has been passed in parliament. Last but not least, the president has the prerogative right to appoint cabinet ministers, deputy ministers and commissioners at state-owned enterprises. All of these positions are highly sought after by the parties represented in parliament as they offer access to lucrative patronage resources which the parties rely on for their organisational survival.

Faced with this institutional framework, Indonesian presidents have resorted to the tools of 'coalitional presidentialism' (Chaisty, Cheeseman & Power 2014) to secure stable executive-legislature relations. Most prominent among these tools has been the establishment of huge coalition cabinets. Initially formed by Abdurrahman Wahid in an ultimately futile attempt to keep parliament tame, his successors Megawati Sukarnoputri and especially Susilo Bambang Yudhoyono, institutionalised this 'promiscuous powersharing' (Slater & Simmons 2013), even though constitutional amendments put in place after the Wahid impeachment meant that presidents were now much safer from being removed from office than Wahid had been.

Yudhoyono's successor Jokowi initially pledged to discontinue the practice of rainbow cabinets and to emancipate the highest political office from the patronage demands of the party oligarchs and other strategic groups. When he took office, his coalition only comprised four out of ten parties, representing 37 percent of parliamentary seats. Jokowi's departure from the practices of promiscuous powersharing did not last long, however. When he reshuffled his cabinet in 2016, he appointed a number of ministers from parties previously excluded from cabinet, so that his new line-up comprised parties holding around two thirds of the parliamentary seats. Then, after his re-election in 2019, Jokowi took promiscuous powersharing to new heights when he first offered his main political rival of the last two elections, Prabowo Subianto, a position in cabinet, before eventually appointing Prabowo's running mate Sandiaga Uno as well. Thus, by 2020 Jokowi had well and truly re-established the regime's well-documented 'accountability trap' (Slater 2004).

Given the collusive pattern of executive-legislature relations, the democratic robustness of Indonesia's institutional framework depends to a large extent on other checks and balances such as the judiciary, the media and other state and non-state institutions that can enforce accountability, for example the Corruption Eradication Commission, the Human Rights Commission and the National Commission on Violence Against Women. Many of these institutions have performed admirably throughout the years, but their effectiveness has also been hampered by a broad range of problems.

Large parts of the judiciary, for example, remain mired in corruption and opaque recruitment patterns, as we discuss in Chapter 5. To bypass these deeply entrenched problems, a Constitutional Court was established effectively outside the regular court system in 2003. Thanks to its institutional independence, this court has been relatively immune from the tentacles of what Butt and Lindsey (2011) have called the 'judicial mafia'. Despite accusations of politicisation and occasional scandals – two Constitutional Court judges have been caught up in corruption cases since 2013 – the court has been instrumental in upholding horizontal accountability in Indonesia (Dressel 2019).

An even more important island of integrity has been the Corruption Eradication Commission, widely known by its Indonesian acronym KPK. Since its establishment in 2002, the KPK has detained hundreds of politicians, businesspeople and bureaucrats, with many of them receiving hefty jail sentences from specialised anti-corruption courts. The bolder the KPK became over the years, however, the more frequent became the attempts to weaken it, and in 2019, political elites eventually succeeded in pushing through legislation that took away many of the commission's powers (McBeth 2020). Other institutions such as the National Commission on Violence Against Women and the Human Rights Commission have been less influential but have nevertheless also made important contributions to defending human rights in Indonesia (see Chapters 9 and 10).

Democratic Decline and Policy Challenges

All in all, Indonesia's democratic regime has proven remarkably resilient since its inception in 1998. In the last few years, however, it has become increasingly vulnerable as the reform narrative has faded and counter-democratic interests have intensified their assault on the country's formal democratic institutions. The revision of the KPK law in 2019 was a particularly severe blow to Indonesian democracy, but since then more controversial legislation has been passed which further accentuates the prevailing trend. Most prominently, the Omnibus Bill on Job Creation, passed into law on 5 October 2020, has been widely criticised by democracy activists because it restricts the rights of workers and indigenous groups (Human Rights Watch 2020). It also dismantles many environmental protections and is therefore likely to result in more deforestation and other environmental problems in Indonesia (see Chapter 11).

Significantly, President Jokowi has actively aided this erosion of democratic regime foundations. While he occasionally pays lip service to the virtues of democracy, he has in fact repeatedly undermined it, especially after the resurgence of religious identity politics in the wake of the Ahok crisis. Some observers even detected an 'authoritarian turn' (Power 2018) in the president's determination to silence dissent. Ominously, the growing illiberalism has continued in the wake of the Covid-19 health emergency in 2020 when the government's poorly coordinated response elicited widespread criticism (see Chapter 8). As Power and

Warburton (2020: 2) note, by early May 2020 'more than 100 Indonesians had been arrested for spreading what authorities deemed "hate speech" or "misinformation" relating to Covid-19'.

These developments pose a serious threat to the overall future of Indonesia's democratic regime. They not only dilute the democratic reform narrative, but they have also had an enormous impact on civil society's ability to act as the last bastion of *reformasi*. As mentioned earlier, civil society has long been the only strategic group aligned with the reform narrative but heightened socio-political polarisation and growing state repression as well as fragmentation and tensions between different activist circles have made it increasingly difficult for civil society groups to mobilise behind common goals (Mietzner 2021).

The following chapters will provide a more detailed analysis of these various trends sketched out in this brief introduction. Taken together, they will provide a comprehensive overview of all major features of Indonesia's increasingly precarious democratic regime. Moreover, they will demonstrate how this regime trajectory affects Indonesia's ability to tackle some of its most pressing policy challenges.

After a succinct review of historical events that preceded the establishment of democracy in 1998 in Chapter 2, the following three chapters introduce Indonesia's main political institutions in more detail. Chapter 3 focuses on the country's presidential and multiparty systems, whereas Chapter 4 outlines the main contours of local politics. Chapter 5 then turns to the judiciary and other legal institutions, highlighting the important accountability function of the Constitutional Court and (semi-)independent commissions. Up next are two chapters that analyse the influence of strategic interests such as Islamic groups (Chapter 6) and pro-democratic civil society groups (Chapter 7).

The final part of the book then shifts attention to some of Indonesia's most pressing policy challenges. Chapter 8 assesses the state of human development and public health in Indonesia, with particular reference to the effects of Covid-19. Chapter 9 then analyses questions of gender equality, while Chapter 10 focuses on human rights more broadly. Chapters 11 and 12 examine environmental challenges and Indonesia's place in the world. Lastly, the book concludes with a comparative analysis of Indonesia's democratic trajectory in Chapter 13.

References

Aspinall, E 2005, 'Elections and the normalization of politics in Indonesia', *South East Asia Research*, vol. 13, no. 2, pp. 117–156.

Aspinall, E 2010, 'The irony of success', *Journal of Democracy*, vol. 21, no. 2, pp. 20–34.

Aspinall, E 2015, 'Oligarchic populism: Prabowo Subianto's challenge to Indonesian democracy', *Indonesia*, vol. 99, no. 1, pp. 1–28.

Aspinall, E 2016, 'The new nationalism in Indonesia', *Asia and the Pacific Policy Studies*, vol. 3, no. 1, pp. 72–82.

Aspinall, E & Mietzner, M 2019, 'Nondemocratic pluralism in Indonesia', *Journal of Democracy*, vol. 30, no. 4, pp. 104–118.

Aspinall, E, Mietzner, M & Tomsa, D (eds) 2015, *The Yudhoyono presidency: Indonesia's decade of stability and stagnation*, Institute of Southeast Asian Studies, Singapore.

Buehler, M 2016, *The politics of shari'a law: Islamist activists and the state in democratizing Indonesia*, Cambridge University Press, Cambridge.

Bush, R 2015, 'Religious politics and minority rights during the Yudhoyono presidency', in E Aspinall, M Mietzner & D Tomsa (eds), *The Yudhoyono presidency: Indonesia's decade of stability and stagnation*, Institute of Southeast Asian Studies, Singapore, pp. 239–257.

Butt, S & Lindsey, T 2011, 'Judicial mafia: the courts and state illegality in Indonesia', in E Aspinall & G van Klinken (eds), *The state and illegality in Indonesia*, KITLV Press, Leiden, pp. 189–213.

Caraway, TL & Ford, M 2020, *Labor and politics in Indonesia*, Cambridge University Press, Cambridge.

Chaisty, P, Cheeseman, N & Power, T 2014, 'Rethinking the 'presidentialism debate': conceptualizing coalitional politics in cross-regional perspective', *Democratization*, vol. 21, no. 1, pp. 72–94.

Crouch, H 2010, *Political reform in Indonesia after Soeharto*, Institute of Southeast Asian Studies, Singapore.

Davidson, JS 2009, 'Dilemmas of democratic consolidation in Indonesia', *The Pacific Review*, vol. 22, no. 3, pp. 293–310.

Dibley, T & Ford, M (eds) 2019, *Activists in transition: progressive politics in Indonesia*, Cornell University Press, Ithaca and London.

Diprose, R, McRae, D & Hadiz, VR 2019, 'Two decades of reformasi in Indonesia: its illiberal turn', *Journal of Contemporary Asia*, vol. 49, no. 5, pp. 691–712.

Dressel, B 2019, 'Prabowo challenges Indonesia's poll result at Constitutional Court but doubts its impartiality. New research confirms the Court's fairness', *The Conversation*, 11 June, viewed 11 March 2021, <https://theconversation.com/prabowo-challenges-indonesias-poll-result-at-constitutional-court-but-doubts-its-impartiality-new-research-confirms-the-courts-fairness-113486>.

Evers, HD & Gerke, S 2009, *Strategic group analysis*, ZEF Working Paper Series, No. 34, University of Bonn, Center for Development Research (ZEF), Bonn.

Fealy, G 2016, 'Bigger than Ahok: explaining the 2 December mass rally', *Indonesia at Melbourne*, 7 December, viewed 13 December 2019, <http://indonesiaatmelbourne.unimelb.edu.au/bigger-than-ahok-explaining-jakartas-2-december-mass-rally/>.

Ford, M & Pepinsky, TB (eds) 2014, *Beyond oligarchy: critical exchanges on political power and material inequality in Indonesia*, Cornell University Press, Ithaca.

Fossati, D 2016, 'Partisan affiliations remain strong in Indonesia', ISEAS Perspective 52, ISEAS-Yusof Ishak Institute, Singapore.

Hadiz, VR 2017, 'Indonesia's year of democratic setbacks: towards a new phase of deepening illiberalism?', *Bulletin of Indonesian Economic Studies*, vol. 53, no. 3, pp. 261–278.

Hadiz, VR & Robison, R 2013, 'The political economy of oligarchy and the reorganisation of power in Indonesia', *Indonesia*, vol. 96, pp. 35–57.

Horowitz, DL 2013, *Constitutional change and democracy in Indonesia*, Cambridge University Press, Cambridge.

Human Rights Watch 2020, *Indonesia: new law hurts workers, indigenous groups*, viewed 11 March 2021, <https://www.hrw.org/news/2020/10/15/indonesia-new-law-hurts-workers-indigenous-groups>.

Institute for Policy Analysis of Conflict 2015, *The expanding role of the Indonesian military*, IPAC Report No. 19, IPAC, Jakarta.

Kawamura, K 2010, *Is the Indonesian president strong or weak?* IDE Discussion Paper No. 235, Institute of Developing Economies, Chiba.

Laksmana, EA 2019, 'Reshuffling the deck? Military corporatism, promotional logjams and post-authoritarian civil-military relations in Indonesia', *Journal of Contemporary Asia*, vol. 49, no. 5, pp. 806–836.

Lindsey, T & Mann, T 2020, 'Indonesia was in denial over coronavirus. Now It may be facing a looming disaster', *The Conversation*, 9 April, viewed 11 March 2021, <https://theconversation.com/indonesia-was-in-denial-over-coronavirus-now-it-may-be-facing-a-looming-disaster-135436>.

McBeth, J 2020, 'End of an anti-corruption era in Indonesia', *Asia Times*, 7 January, viewed 11 March 2021, <https://asiatimes.com/2020/01/end-of-an-anti-corruption-era-in-indonesia/>.

McGregor, K, Melvin, J & Pohlman, A (eds) 2018, *The Indonesian genocide of 1965: causes, dynamics and legacies*, PalgraveMacmillan and Springer International, Cham.

Menchik, J 2014, 'Productive intolerance: godly nationalism in Indonesia', *Comparative Studies in Society and History*, vol. 56, no. 3, pp. 591–621.

Mietzner, M 2012, 'Indonesia's democratic stagnation: anti-reformist elites and resilient civil society', *Democratization*, vol. 19, no. 2, pp. 209–229.

Mietzner, M 2018a, 'Fighting illiberalism with illiberalism: Islamist populism and democratic deconsolidation in Indonesia', *Pacific Affairs*, vol. 91, no. 2, pp. 261–282.

Mietzner, M 2018b, 'The Indonesian armed forces, coalitional presidentialism and democratization: from praetorian guard to imagined balance of power', in RW Hefner (ed.), *Routledge handbook of contemporary Indonesia*, Routledge, London and New York, pp. 140–150.

Mietzner, M 2020a, 'Populist anti-scientism, religious polarisation, and institutionalised corruption: how Indonesia's democratic decline shaped its COVID-19 response', *Journal of Current Southeast Asian Affairs*, vol. 39, no. 2, pp. 227–249.

Mietzner, M 2020b, 'Authoritarian innovations in Indonesia: electoral narrowing, identity politics, and executive illiberalism', *Democratization*, vol. 27, no. 6, pp. 1021–1036.

Mietzner, M 2021, 'Sources of resistance to democratic decline: Indonesian civil society and its trials', *Democratization*, vol. 28, no. 1, pp. 161–178.

Mietzner, M & Muhtadi, B 2018, 'Explaining the 2016 Islamist mobilisation in Indonesia: religious intolerance, militant groups and the politics of accommodation', *Asian Studies Review*, vol. 42, no. 3, pp. 479–497.

Mudhoffir, AM & A'yun, RQ 2019, 'Can *golput* save Indonesian democracy?', *Indonesia at Melbourne*, 30 January, viewed 3 March 2021, <https://indonesiaatmelbourne.unimelb.edu.au/can-golput-save-indonesian-democracy/>.

Mujani, S & Liddle, RW 2015, 'Indonesia's democratic performance: a popular assessment', *Japanese Journal of Political Science*, vol. 16, no. 2, pp. 210–226.

Nuraniyah, N 2020, 'Divided Muslims: militant pluralism, polarisation and democratic backsliding', in T Power & E Warburton (eds), *Democracy in Indonesia: From stagnation to regression?*, ISEAS-Yusof Ishak Institute, Singapore, pp. 81–100.

Power, T 2018, 'Jokowi's authoritarian turn and Indonesia's democratic decline', *Bulletin of Indonesian Economic Studies*, vol. 54, no. 3, pp. 307–338.

Power, T & Warburton, E 2020, 'The decline of Indonesian democracy', in T Power & E Warburton (eds), *Democracy in Indonesia: From stagnation to regression?*, ISEAS-Yusof Ishak Institute, Singapore, pp. 1–20.

Setiawan, KMP 2020, 'A state of surveillance? Freedom of expression under the Jokowi presidency', in T Power & E Warburton (eds), *Democracy in Indonesia: From stagnation to regression?*, ISEAS-Yusof Ishak Institute, Singapore, pp. 254–274.

Simandjuntak, D 2012, 'Gifts and promises: patronage democracy in a decentralized Indonesia', *European Journal of East Asian Studies*, vol. 11, no. 1, pp. 99–126.

Skowronek, S 1997, *The politics presidents make: leadership from John Adams to Bill Clinton*, Belknap Press, Cambridge, MA.

Slater, D 2004, 'Indonesia's accountability trap: party cartels and presidential power after democratic transition', *Indonesia*, vol. 78, pp. 61–92.

Slater, D & Simmons, E 2013, 'Coping by colluding: political uncertainty and promiscuous powersharing in Bolivia and Indonesia', *Comparative Political Studies*, vol. 46, no. 11, pp. 1366–1393.

Thompson, MR 2014, 'The politics Philippine presidents make', *Critical Asian Studies*, vol. 46, no. 3, pp. 433–460.

Tomsa, D 2009, 'Electoral democracy in a divided society: the 2008 gubernatorial election in Maluku, Indonesia', *South East Asia Research*, vol. 17, no. 2, pp. 229–259.

Tomsa, D 2010, 'The Indonesian party system after the 2009 elections: towards stability?', in E Aspinall & M Mietzner (eds), *Problems of democratisation in Indonesia: elections, institutions and society*, Institute of Southeast Asian Studies, Singapore, pp. 141–159.

Tomsa, D 2014, 'Party system fragmentation in Indonesia: the sub-national dimension', *Journal of East Asian Studies*, vol. 14, no. 2, pp. 249–278.

Tomsa, D 2018, 'Regime resilience and presidential politics in Indonesia', *Contemporary Politics*, vol. 24, no. 3, pp. 266–285.

Tomsa, D 2019, 'Islamism and party politics in Indonesia', in *Oxford Research Encyclopedia of Politics*, Oxford University Press, https://oxfordre.com/politics/view/10.1093/acrefore/9780190228637.001.0001/acrefore-9780190228637-e-1157, viewed 13 March 2021.

Tomsa, D & Setijadi, C 2018, 'New forms of political activism in Indonesia: redefining the nexus between electoral and movement politics', *Asian Survey*, vol. 58, no. 3, pp. 557–581.

Transparency International 2020, *Indonesia's score over time*, viewed 9 January 2021. <https://www.transparency.org/en/cpi/2019/results/idn>.

Van Klinken, G 2009, 'Patronage democracy in provincial Indonesia', in O Törnquist, N Webster & K Stokke (eds), *Rethinking popular representation*, PalgraveMacmillan, New York, pp. 141–160.

Warburton, E 2016, 'Jokowi and the new developmentalism', *Bulletin of Indonesian Economic Studies*, vol. 52, no. 3, pp. 297–320.

Warburton, E & Aspinall, E 2019, 'Explaining Indonesia's democratic regression: structure, agency and popular opinion', *Contemporary Southeast Asia*, vol. 41, no. 2, pp. 255–285.

Wilson, C 2015, 'Illiberal democracy and violent conflict in contemporary Indonesia', *Democratization*, vol. 22, no. 7, pp. 1317–1337.

Winters, JA 2013, 'Oligarchy and democracy in Indonesia', *Indonesia*, vol. 96, pp. 11–33.

Wolfowitz, P 2009, 'Indonesia is a model Muslim democracy', *Wall Street Journal*, 17 July.

2 The Road to Democracy

Introduction

> I don't want to be a dictator because it is contrary to my own conscience. I am a democrat, but I don't desire democratic liberalism. On the contrary I want a guided democracy [...] I have a conception of my own which I will put at the disposal of the party leaders if required.
>
> (Sukarno, 30 October 1956, cited in Kahin & Kahin 1997, p. 53)

> The democracy that we live by is Pancasila democracy [...], the principle of people's sovereignty inspired by and integrated with the other principles of Pancasila. [...] Pancasila democracy originates from an understanding of family values and mutual cooperation. [...] Indeed opposition groups found in liberal democracies are unknown in the life of Pancasila democracy. Pancasila democracy recognises only consensual decision-making.
>
> (Suharto 1967, cited in Bourchier & Hadiz 2003, pp. 38–39)

The quotes above from Sukarno and Suharto – Indonesia's first and second presidents, who together were in power for more than 50 years – underline that from the early independence period, Indonesian leaders have used the term 'democracy' when describing the country's political system, but not in the sense of a liberal democracy. Instead, they have been highly critical of liberalism, arguing in favour of a system where shared values, mutual support and reaching decisions through consensus are prioritised. In practice, however, both Sukarno's Guided Democracy and Suharto's Pancasila democracy amounted to authoritarian rule.

This chapter will outline the key features of these authoritarian periods in order to highlight how much historical baggage Indonesia brought along when it democratised in 1998. It focuses on how, across time, governance was organised in the territory that we know as Indonesia today. In so doing, the chapter pays attention to recurring debates on central and decentralised government, the role of the military in politics, the position of political Islam, spaces for oppositional politics, the emergence of a powerful oligarchy, as well as corruption. While some of these factors, such as corruption, became particularly pronounced during the New

DOI: 10.4324/9780429459511-2

Order regime (1966–1998), others – including the role of the military in politics and the position of political Islam – can be traced back to earlier times, including the colonial period.

Following this brief introduction, the chapter is chronologically divided into three parts. It begins with an overview of Indonesia's first encounters with the outside world and experiences of European colonialism, as well as its struggle for independence. The chapter then segues to the period from independence to 1965, in which Indonesia shifted from a nation pursuing liberal democratic values to more authoritarian forms of governance. The last section of this chapter addresses the rise, establishment and fall of the New Order regime. The chapter concludes with a reflection upon the legacies of authoritarianism and how these are manifested in Indonesian politics today.

External Encounters and the Colonial State

Indonesia, the world's largest archipelagic state, has been exposed to external influences through seas and oceans from early times. Some scholars have suggested that migrations from the mainland into island Southeast Asia occurred as early as 2000 BCE. Over time, these maritime corridors brought new faiths, goods, knowledge and technologies. Buddhism came to the islands through Indian merchants in the 3rd century CE (Taylor 2003). Similarly, Islam came to Indonesia through trade, as early as the 8th or 9th century. From the 13th century, the growing presence of Muslim traders and teachers started influencing the sociocultural fabric of the archipelago (Ricklefs 2001, p. 16). As mosques were built and Islamic communities were established, Islam linked people of various backgrounds, and conversions to Islam increased throughout the 15th and 16th centuries (Taylor 2003, p. 73).

It was in this context that European traders entered the archipelago in the early 16th century. The Portuguese were the first Europeans to arrive, followed by the Spanish. While some local rulers converted to Christianity, in general society was less receptive to European ideas in comparison to its earlier acceptance of Islam. Illegal trade by Portuguese officials, limited human resources and inability to work with local rulers, as well as rivalries with other European powers led to the decline of Portuguese influence in the region (Cribb & Kahin 2004, p. 353). The Dutch arrived in the late 16th century, and over time emerged as the most powerful European actor in Indonesia.

Dutch presence was governed by the United East Indies Company (Vereenigde Oostindische Compagnie or VOC), a government-directed union of Dutch trading companies. In 1619, the VOC established its headquarters in Jayakarta, which was subsequently renamed Batavia, and is now known as Jakarta. In expanding its possessions, the VOC took advantage of rivalries between local rulers (Locher-Scholten 2004, p. 44). However, by the late 18th century, the power of the VOC declined and the Company was formally dissolved, with the Dutch government taking control of all its possessions (Ricklefs 2001, p. 144).

The end of the VOC in 1800 signalled the gradual formation of the Dutch colonial state in Indonesia. This process, however, was interrupted and influenced by the Napoleonic Wars in Europe (1803–1815), which saw brief periods of French and British rule in the archipelago. During the British interregnum (1811–1816), land rent taxes were imposed on Javanese farmers. In having to pay these to local rulers, who were agents of the British government, a system of indirect rule was introduced (Brown 2003, pp. 73–75). After the Dutch regained control, indirect rule became a main feature of its way of governing the colony.

The Dutch saw the Indies as a source for revenue and state policies were moulded around this idea. In 1830, the so-called Cultivation System required villages in Java to set aside one-fifth of their rice fields to produce a crop nominated by the government. While the system was a financial success for the Dutch government, in Java it led to corruption in local village governments and the exploitation of farmers. Following public outrage in the Netherlands, the Cultivation System was gradually dismantled (Brown 2003, pp. 83–86).

Between 1870 and 1900, there was increased movement of private capital to Indonesia. For most Indonesians, and particularly farmers, these decades were characterised by a decline in living standards (Brown 2003, pp. 89). Once again, these developments caused concern in the Netherlands, where another shift in colonial policy was introduced in 1901. Under the so-called Ethical Policy, the Dutch explicitly stated that they had a moral responsibility to colonial subjects and new programmes were introduced including in the fields of agriculture, public administration and education. This approach, however, was geared towards improving the lives of colonial subjects, rather than creating a path to self-sufficiency (Cribb 1994).

Against this backdrop of changing colonial policies in which the Dutch sought to emphasise benevolence towards its subjects, the Dutch also turned to military conquest to expand and consolidate its possessions. Perhaps the most violent example of this was the Aceh War (1873–1904), where the Dutch eventually defeated the Acehnese despite fierce resistance from the sultanate (Reid 2005). The Aceh War served as a blueprint for the training of the colonial army (Limpach 2016, p. 61) and between 1901 and 1910, the Dutch took control over smaller kingdoms, including in Sumatra, Maluku, Borneo and Sulawesi, as well as Bali. In the 1920s, at the other end of the archipelago, the Dutch took full control over the western part of the island of New Guinea (Vickers 2013, pp. 10–14).

While conquered areas were initially placed under military rule, the modus operandi of the Dutch in its colony was indirect rule, whereby the indigenous aristocracy was placed under the hierarchy of Dutch officials. Indirect rule was both a way to preserve tradition, through which the colonial state could be secured, and a strategy to minimise costs as it did not require the establishment of an entirely new bureaucracy (Vickers 2013, p. 15). Many local rulers readily collaborated with the Dutch, and even at the start of the revolutionary period (1945), the indigenous ruling class showed little dissatisfaction with the system (Van Klinken 2018, p. 117).

Closely related to the principle of indirect rule was the establishment of a dual legal system, whereby a sharp distinction was made between Europeans and those who had equal legal status, on the one hand, and Indonesians on the other (Otto 2010). In this system, the Indonesian elites were subjected to Dutch law because of their close alliance with the colonial administration. However, not everyone in the colony was classified as either European or Indonesian. Chinese Indonesians, considered 'economically important and useful but otherwise unpopular' (Lev 1985, p. 62), were classed as a third group: 'foreign Orientals', meaning they were treated as Indonesians in criminal law but as Europeans in commercial law. While discrimination of and violence against Chinese Indonesians predates the colonial state (Purdey 2006), the special status accorded to this group did little to counter widespread sentiments that considered Chinese Indonesians as 'foreign'.

Rising Nationalism

While there was localised opposition to Dutch colonial conquest across the islands, a nationalist movement – especially in comparison to those in other colonised territories elsewhere in the world – was slow to develop. In part, this was because the colonial state itself was established relatively late (Vickers 2013, p. 75), but also because the combination of indirect rule and economic exploitation had effectively disabled opposition to the Dutch colonisers (Kahin 2003, p. 41).

Eventually though, in the early 20th century, nationalist sentiments were driven by indigenous elites who were dissatisfied with the limited education opportunities extended to them. More broadly, the social discrimination Indonesians were subjected to – as encapsulated by the dual legal system – was a constant source of irritation (Kahin 2003, pp. 52–54). Despite the late emergence of nationalism, shared colonial experiences, administration, language and currency all contributed to the imagining of a post-colonial state (Anderson 1983).

The first nationalist organisation with a clear political orientation was the Islamic League (Sarekat Islam). Established in 1912, in less than ten years, it developed a following of two and a half million people. Its programme was unequivocally committed to complete independence (Kahin 2003, p. 76). Within the Islamic League, various strands of nationalism emerged, including more radical forms of Islamism, but also, despite its atheist foundations, communism. The Islamist groups were focused on the establishment of an independent Islamic state, whereas communists worked from within the League to advance their goal of freedom from Dutch colonialism and capitalism. Over time, the differences between the two became more pronounced, eventually leading to a walkout of the Islamic right in 1919 (Vickers 2013, pp. 79–81).

Despite the split within the Islamic League, the common goal of ending colonial rule ensured that nationalism continued to grow, although the movement lacked organisational power and was very diffuse. In 1927, the Indonesian National Party (Partai Nasional Indonesia, PNI) was established by the nationalist Sukarno. The PNI advocated for Indonesian independence, opposed imperialism and capitalism and supported secularism and unity among the different ethnicities in the colony (Ricklefs 2001). Other prominent nationalists included Mohammad

Hatta and Sutan Sjahrir, who both hailed from Sumatra and came to represent the non-Javanese in nationalist circles.

It was in this context of binding a diverse range of interests together that the term 'Indonesia' emerged in nationalist discourse. In October 1928, young nationalists gathered at a congress in Jakarta gave the movement a new impetus when they declared 'one homeland, one people and one language' in their famous Youth Pledge (Foulcher 2000). At this congress, the national anthem (Indonesia Raya or Great Indonesia) was also played for the first time. The congress provided a crucial moment in Indonesian nationalism. Many new political organisations mushroomed in its aftermath, although none garnered the mass following of the Islamic League. The one party that threatened to do so – the PNI led by Sukarno – was successfully repressed by the colonial government. Sukarno and other leaders were arrested in 1929 and the PNI was dissolved two years later (Vickers 2013, p. 84).

Without their most prominent leaders, the nationalists struggled to maintain momentum. In 1942, this changed as the Japanese invaded the archipelago. Initially, Indonesians welcomed the arrival of the Japanese, impressed by their military prowess. However, these sentiments quickly evaporated as everyday life for Indonesians became more difficult, with many subjected to forced labour (Ricklefs 2001). Europeans were interned in camps, where they were subjected to cruel conditions, including sexual slavery of women (McGregor 2016). While experiences of Japanese occupation in Indonesia varied highly, the commonality shared was that Europeans were eliminated from governance and everyday life (Taylor 2003, p. 311).

By March 1945, it became apparent that the Japanese would lose the war. This shifted Japanese policy, and the occupying forces established a committee to discuss the independence of Indonesia. Dominated by Sukarno and his allies, this committee developed the basic foundations of governance and politics for the independent era. The contestation of liberal democratic ideas became apparent, as an idea that gained traction was that of a so-called integralist state, one that espoused harmony and reciprocity between rulers and ruled. Proponents argued that this was suitable for the independent nation because it was inherent to Indonesian traditions. In emphasising the organic unity of all groups in society, the notion of the integralist state also excluded the concept of individual rights (Bourchier 2015, p. 2).

The most contentious debate in the committee, however, revolved around the place of religion, and particular Islam, in the new Indonesian state. Sukarno and his allies favoured a secular and nationalist republic as they believed this would support the unity of a highly pluralist society. Sukarno outlined his vision in a speech on 1 June 1945 where he introduced his idea of a new state ideology called Pancasila (five pillars). But the idea of a secular state was fiercely contested by conservative Muslims in the committee, who put forward the so-called Jakarta Charter to the draft constitution. Crucially, this Charter amended the Pancasila by stipulating that Muslims in Indonesia must follow sharia law and the head of state must be Muslim (Brown 2003, p. 153). Following the capitulation of the

Japanese armed forces on 14 August 1945, Sukarno and Hatta were pressured by youth groups to declare Indonesia's independence. They did so three days later on 17 August. The following day the Constitution was launched and at the very last minute, the Charter was removed from the Constitution's preamble, much to the chagrin of the Islamist members of the committee (Elson 2009). Instead, the principles that were finally adopted in the preamble were those of the Pancasila:

- The belief in one almighty god (*ketuhanan yang maha esa*);
- A just and civilised humanity (*kemanusiaan yang adil dan beradab*);
- The unity of Indonesia (*persatuan Indonesia*);
- A nation led by the people through consensus (*kerakyatan yang dipimpin oleh hikmat kebijaksanaan, dalam permusyawaratan perwakilan*);
- Social justice for all Indonesians (*keadilan sosial bagi seluruh rakyat Indonesia*).

The independence committee then appointed Sukarno as president and Hatta as vice-president (Brown 2003). At the time, Sukarno envisaged a one-party state, and administrative structures were very much derived from Japanese principles. This was strongly opposed by other influential nationalist figures, led by Sjahrir. In addition to concerns around the nature of the state, Sjahrir argued that the proposed system was unlikely to receive support from the Allied forces, whose approval was crucial for the new state to gain international legitimacy and support (Bourchier 2015, p. 86–88). Sukarno responded by postponing the idea of a one-party state, and in October 1945, Hatta issued a decree that ended the period of direct presidential rule. A month later, Sukarno's cabinet resigned and a new cabinet was formed by Sjahrir in which he was prime minister.

Independence and Parliamentary Democracy, 1945–1955

The development of Indonesia's post-colonial state was not straightforward. One challenge was Dutch opposition to Indonesia's independence claims and the instability of the subsequent revolutionary period (1945–1949). While among Indonesian politicians there were differing views on how to secure sovereignty, Sukarno and Hatta favoured a diplomatic approach, as was illustrated in the way the government responded to the Dutch. During the independence war, the Dutch initiated two major military offensives against the revolutionaries in 1947 and 1948. During these offensives, the Dutch won significant territory, but also attracted increasing international criticism. Indonesian nationalists used this to leverage more international support for their claims to independence (Ricklefs 2001).

In the context of rising global tensions between the United States and the Soviet Union, Sukarno and Hatta also sought to bolster the non-communist credentials of Indonesian nationalists. When in August 1948 leftist factions in the Indonesian military seized control over the city of Madiun in East Java, Sukarno and Hatta responded by declaring it an illegal uprising (Reid 2011). In so doing, they rallied popular support against the left. Aided by Islamic militias, the attack was opened on the communists and the leftist revolutionaries were crushed. This gained Indonesian nationalists important support from non-communist powers, who in turn put pressure on the Dutch to give up their colony (Ricklefs 2001).

Not only did the Indonesian state struggle with international recognition and formal independence from the Netherlands, but it also faced challenges at home. The war had left Indonesia's economy in dire straits and with a weak state apparatus. Establishing central authority proved difficult for the government, particularly in outer regions, illustrating tensions between leaders on Java and other islands. This was not only because of the complexities of geographical distance but also because regional elites were distrustful towards the dominance of Java and the Javanese. The unity of the Indonesian state was also contested. One group that launched a rebellion was the Darul Islam movement that emerged in West Java in 1948 with the aim of establishing an Islamic State (Elson & Formichi 2011). The government responded to movements such as Darul Islam by deploying the armed forces against them, thereby pushing the army to the forefront of the modern Indonesian state.

In December 1949, the Dutch finally transferred sovereignty to Indonesia, but as a concession they demanded the creation of a federal state known as the 'Republic of the United States of Indonesia'. This included the entire territory of the former colony with the exception of Netherlands New Guinea, sovereignty over which was retained by the Netherlands until further negotiations. The Constitution of 1949 that underpinned this federal system provided for democratic government, human rights and judicial review. Indonesian nationalists were not in favour though, believing that a federal system would leave the state fragmented and weak. However, in order to secure independence, the nationalists complied with this and other Dutch demands, including that Indonesia took over Netherlands Indies debt (Ricklefs 2001, p. 284).

The federal state was considered by many Indonesians as an attempt by the Dutch to retain some control over the new nation and an impediment to the unity of the nation. As such, the government moved quickly to dismantle it and in early 1950, the state governments that had been set up by the Dutch were dissolved, followed by the federal state in August. This resulted in a new (interim) constitution which retained many aspects of the 1949 Constitution, including a largely democratic system. It was determined that the government was run by a cabinet, chaired by a prime minister, and the government was answerable to the People's Representative Council (Dewan Perwakilan Rakyat, DPR) that would be elected democratically. There were provisions of civil and political rights, as well as the separation of powers (Lubis 1993).

Indonesia's period of parliamentary democracy in the 1950s was characterised by the emergence of a fragmented party system. The country was governed by a number of coalition cabinets dominated by three parties: the secular (PNI), the modernist Muslim party Masyumi and Nahdlatul Ulama (NU), a traditionalist Muslim party. The PNI had a popular base linked to the old aristocracy and radical nationalists, while Masyumi had its base among the Islamic middle class in urban areas and outside of Java and was strongly anti-communist. NU had its supporter base mainly in rural areas in Java. In addition to these parties, the Indonesian Communist Party (Partai Komunis Indonesia, PKI) emerged as a political force. With its strong connections to the independence struggle, the PKI had a large following among landless peasants and urban workers, mainly on Java as well as Sumatra (Vickers 2013). Cabinets in this period did not last long and the diversity of parties also illustrated that there were deep divisions, both politically and socially, along religious, class and ethnic lines.

Indonesia's first general elections were held in 1955, which also included elections for a Constitutional Assembly (Konstituante) to draft a permanent Constitution (Lubis 1993). It was hoped that these elections would bring much needed stability to the political landscape. Indonesians enthusiastically took part in the elections, with 91 percent of eligible voters participating, and the elections were widely regarded as free and fair. However, only four parties managed to secure 16 or more percent of the vote: Masyumi, NU, PNI and the PKI. Of these, only Masyumi won votes across Indonesia, with the other three almost getting all their votes from Java. This outcome was therefore unlikely to bring stability to the political landscape (Brown 2003).

Rising Authoritarianism, 1955–1965

For Sukarno, who from the outset was ambivalent towards parliamentary democracy, the results of the 1955 elections were evidence that multiparty democracy was incompatible with Indonesian political culture and the main reason for its instability (Brown 2003, p. 186). In response, Sukarno called for the establishment of a new form of governance, Guided Democracy, which he argued was better suited to Indonesia and based on mutual cooperation (*gotong royong*) between major parties and so-called functional groups, the membership of which would be drawn from youth, workers, peasants and women, to name just a few. While some parties including the PNI and PKI approved of these ideas, others such as Masyumi did not (Ricklefs 2001, pp. 309–310). Sukarno's increasing interference with the constitutional system ultimately led to Vice-President Hatta's resignation at the end of 1956, which was a particular shock to non-Javanese Indonesians.

Sukarno's proposals also deepened the regional divide between Java and the other islands. An inter-regional anti-Jakarta movement, known as Permesta (Piagam Perjuangan Semesta, Universal Struggle Charter), emerged from military commanders outside Java who were dissatisfied with the central authority from Java on economic and political power. On 2 March 1957, Permesta proclaimed a counter-government. In response, Sukarno declared martial law in 1957 which benefited both his objectives and those of the military command in Jakarta, which was able to seize control all over the country and address its internal divisions (Ricklefs 2001, p. 310). Meanwhile, Sukarno could end parliamentary democracy and put in place Guided Democracy, which included the reinstatement of the 1945 Constitution, with far-reaching powers for the president. It also enabled

Sukarno to move against his political opponents, with Masyumi and the Socialist Party (Partai Sosialis Indonesia, PSI) both banned in 1960 (Brown 2003, pp. 188–189).

The period of Guided Democracy was characterised by the centrality of Sukarno in political life, the army's rise as a major political force and a minimal role for political parties (Lev 1966). The exception to this was the PKI, which Sukarno increasingly courted to counterbalance the growing power of the army (McGregor 2013, p. 135). By the mid-1960s, the PKI was the largest communist party in the world outside of the Soviet Bloc and China and claimed 3.5 million members and a mass support base of 20 million others (Mortimer 1974, p. 366). Globally, this rise was of increasing concern to anti-communist powers that feared Indonesia would 'fall' to communism, thereby jeopardising Western economic interests (Simpson 2008).

The anti-communist bloc was also uncomfortable with Sukarno's increasing closeness to communist countries in the region and his evermore aggressive anti-Western stance. In the early 1960s, Western countries tried to appease Sukarno when the Indonesian government sought control over West New Guinea, which at the time was still in the hands of the Dutch. Negotiations between Indonesia and the Netherlands about this territory had stagnated. The Dutch had no intention to hand West New Guinea to Indonesia. For Sukarno and Indonesian nationalists, however, the Netherlands New Guinea should be a part of Indonesia. The rapid growth of the PKI meant that Sukarno received support from Western powers, notably the United States (Ricklefs 2001, p. 328). It was hoped that by settling this matter in Indonesia's favour, further alignment of Indonesia with the communist bloc could be avoided. This appeasement of Indonesia had severe consequences for Papuans, who were sidelined in debates on the future of their territory. In 1962, the New York Agreement signed between the Netherlands and Indonesia determined that the Dutch transferred the territory to an interim UN administration, which in turn handed over administration to Indonesia (Chauvel & Bhakti 2004).

Sukarno's focus on the integration of New Guinea – or Irian Jaya, as Indonesians called it at the time – into Indonesia also was meant to divert attention from increasing sociopolitical tensions. In the 1960s, the concurrent rise of the army and the PKI as major political forces led to increasing polarisation between Islamic, communist and 'developmentalist' groups that advocated capitalist policies from the colonial era. The latter found particular support among nationalist groups and the army. Each of these streams saw themselves as the 'rightful heir' to the Indonesian state. There was deep distrust between the three, but it was especially pronounced between the military and the PKI (Cribb 2001). At the same time, Indonesia's economy deteriorated swiftly. By the mid-1960s, the Indonesian economy 'settled into permanent hyper-inflation' (Ricklefs 2001, p. 328) and more and more Indonesians suffered from poverty and starvation. This combination of sociopolitical polarisation and economic downturn is widely regarded as precursor to the mass violence that unfolded in 1965–1966 and led to a dramatic regime change (McGregor, Melvin & Pohlman 2018, p. 7).

The Rise and Fall of the New Order, 1966–1998

On 30 September 1965, a group of middle-ranking military officers supportive of Sukarno kidnapped and killed six generals and a lieutenant. This group, who called themselves the 30th of September Movement, then announced the establishment of a Revolutionary Council to protect President Sukarno (Roosa 2006). The movement was quickly crushed by the Army Strategic Reserve under the leadership of Major-General Suharto, who blamed the movement on the PKI. The army used propaganda to depict PKI members and supporters as dangerous internal enemies of the Indonesian people that had to be eliminated. This incited widespread civilian participation in mass violence against PKI members and sympathisers, which was well underway by mid-October 1965. Many anti-communist countries, such as the United States, the United Kingdom and Australia, encouraged these repressions as their leaderships feared a communist takeover in Indonesia (Melvin 2018).

The army established a military structure to coordinate the attack on the Indonesian Left, assisted by military-backed civilian militias. While the exact number of victims of the violence is unknown, it is estimated that from late 1965 to mid-1966 approximately 500,000 men, women and children were killed, largely in Central Java, East Java and Bali. In addition, over a million people were arrested and detained, often for lengthy periods of time, without trial. In the context of the Cold War, there was very little international scrutiny of the violence. Most political prisoners were released in the late 1970s, but even after that they experienced systemic discrimination and were denied an array of civil rights, such as the right to vote or to work in certain sectors (McGregor, Melvin & Pohlman 2018).

The violence perpetrated against members of the Indonesian Left was complemented by a military takeover of the Indonesian state led by Suharto. As Suharto seized state power gradually and in a manner that projected an image of legality, Roosa (2006, p. 4) dubbed the change of power from Sukarno to Suharto a 'creeping coup'. This was essential for the legitimacy of the new government, as despite deep polarisation and economic downturn, Sukarno remained highly popular among many Indonesians and therefore a total break with the past was not desirable. And thus, Suharto took power slowly. In March 1966, Sukarno gave executive power to Suharto through a letter that became known as Supersemar (Surat Perintah Sebelas Maret, 11th of March Order). Yet, even though this handover effectively marked the end of Sukarno's authority, the annihilation of the Left and the consolidation of the army as the main political force in the country (Robinson 2018, p. 65), it was not before the following year that Suharto was appointed as acting president and only in 1968 was he formally made president. Two years later, in 1970, Sukarno died under house arrest (Robinson 2018).

Suharto called his regime the New Order to distinguish it from Sukarno's Old Order. This New Order regime was characterised by at least three key features. The first of these was anti-communism. The violent crushing of the PKI and its affiliated organisations immediately after the events of 1965, and more broadly the annihilation of the Indonesian Left as a social and political force, resulted in a 'complete reorientation of Indonesian society' (McGregor, Melvin & Pohlman 2018, p. 15). A fear of communism was inherent in this and throughout the New Order, the 'latent danger of communism' (Roosa 2006, p. 12) was used to justify the crushing of dissent. This perceived threat of communism also was at the basis of Indonesia's response to the imminent independence of (then Portuguese) East Timor, where leftist political parties had become influential and were moving the territory towards independence. Jakarta had little interest in a socialist state on its doorstep and, with support from Western powers, the Indonesian military invaded East Timor in December 1975. Half a year later, East Timor was declared Indonesia's 27th province (Ricklefs 2001, p. 364).

The second key feature of the New Order was an aversion to party politics and the insistence on political stability, the latter entrenching the military as a dominant social and political force. In this vein, the New Order upheld the 1945 Constitution, including the state ideology Pancasila. In fact, the system of governance put forward was called 'Pancasila Democracy' to indicate that Suharto's New Order was merely undertaking a correction of the path that Indonesia was already on since independence (Bourchier 2015). In this system, the executive yielded strong powers and there was very limited protection of individual rights (Lubis 1993).

While under the New Order elections were held every five years, Suharto never restored the parliamentary system that Indonesia knew before 1957. In 1971, the first general elections of the New Order period were held. These elections were carefully designed to ensure the victory of Golkar, the new government vehicle, to provide legitimacy to the New Order. While Golkar secured more than 60 percent of the vote, the government did not regard this as a sign to relax political controls. Rather, the outcome was used to justify the merger of existing political parties, with Islamic parties pressured into the Partai Persatuan Pembangunan (PPP or United Development Party) and non-Islamic parties into the Partai Demokrasi Indonesia (PDI or Indonesian Democracy Party) (Ricklefs 2001, p. 361).

During the New Order, all elections were won by Golkar, thanks to the systematic weakening of political opponents – particularly political Islam – and widespread coercion to vote for Golkar. Civil servants, for instance, were not allowed to join any political party and were pressured to join Golkar, while business owners were 'reminded' of the advantages to vote for the party. While Indonesians voted for representatives in the DPR, part of the DPR was also made up of army representatives appointed by the government. Similarly, the army was also represented in the People's Consultative Assembly (Majelis Permusyawaratan Rakyat, MPR), a kind of super-parliament which officially 'elected' the president, though this election was always a foregone conclusion (Ricklefs 2001, Vickers 2013). As such, while under the New Order Indonesia maintained the appearance of a formal democracy, the political institutions merely served to entrench the dictatorship.

The presence of military appointees in the legislature illustrated the prominent role of the armed forces in politics. For President Suharto, this raised the need for an ideological justification which he called *dwifungsi*, or dual function. The military presented its political involvement as a natural consequence of its role in securing Indonesia's independence. By the early 1970s, the armed forces were firmly entrenched in all aspects of political, economic and social life (Mietzner 2009, p. 52), which greatly hindered the development of a strong civilian bureaucracy.

The third key feature of the New Order was modernisation and economic development as an overriding priority. Considering the dire economic situation that Indonesia found itself in in the mid-1960s, it was unsurprising that economic development was at the core of the New Order regime. In order to restore the economy, Indonesia realigned with the West and welcomed overseas investment. The revenue from this was spent on infrastructure and social services. In the 1970s, Indonesia's economy boomed in part because of rising global oil prices, which assisted the government's Western-educated 'technocrats' in economic reforms (Vickers 2013). Rapid economic growth was evident in the real GDP annual growth rate, which between 1971 and 1981 averaged 7.7 percent (Ricklefs 2001, p. 366).

However, swift economic development also saw the emergence of a powerful politico-bureaucratic oligarchy. This was not simply a group of military and civilian officials that extracted financial benefits, but was 'a broad and complex political class of officials and their families, political and business associates, clients and agents who fused political power with bureaucratic authority, public office with private interest' (Robison & Hadiz 2004, pp. 53–54). This oligarchy included high-ranking military officials and their companies, often with strong links to Chinese Indonesian entrepreneurs, as well as those close to the Suharto family. Unsurprisingly, the concentration of economic power in the hands of a few gave rise to corruption. By the end of the 1970s, the scale of corruption became more publicly known and it was estimated that it took around 30 percent of international aid and government expenditure (Ricklefs 2001, p. 368).

By the 1980s, despite increased reports of corruption and systematic human rights abuses (Lubis 1993), the New Order had firmly established itself. It had the country under control and enjoyed close relationships with Western countries that seemed quite comfortable with accepting Suharto's authoritarianism as a price to be paid for development. However, by the 1990s, the stability of the New Order was increasingly contested. Young Indonesians in particular started questioning their inability to establish political groups, and there was increasing attention for human rights issues (Vickers 2013).

The end of the Cold War placed pressure on the Suharto government. Its anti-communist stance no longer shielded Indonesia from criticism on its human rights record, particularly where it concerned the conduct of the military in East Timor (Setiawan 2013). The government responded to this by announcing a brief period of economic and social liberalisation. It also changed its handling of Islam, with Suharto and his family taking on a more overtly Islamic public profile and granting greater space for Islamic intellectuals to set the tone of politics (Vickers 2013, pp. 204–205). At the same time, however, cracks started to appear in the economy: while growth rates remained high, interest rates soared and the Indonesian

Rupiah was declining in value. Foreign investment decreased, while government debts were high and social tensions increased (Ricklefs 2001, p. 398).

In 1996, the New Order government came under intense pressure when Megawati Sukarnoputri – the daughter of first president Sukarno and leader of the opposition party PDI – gained increasing influence. The military attempted to halt Megawati's rise by appointing Suryadi, who was considered less of a threat, as the party's leader. The order to remove Megawati came directly from Suharto (Aspinall 2005, p. 183). Despite a crackdown on Megawati supporters in the aftermath (McGregor & Setiawan 2019), Megawati's breakaway party PDI-P (Partai Demokrasi Indonesia-Perjuangan, Indonesian Democracy Party-Struggle) continued to gain ground.

The following year, large parts of Southeast Asia plunged into a deep economic crisis. Indonesia's poorly structured economy was not able to withstand the pressure and slumped into recession. Matters were only made worse as the worst drought of the 20th century reduced rice production and increased forest fires. More and more Indonesian businesses collapsed and the number of registered poor more than doubled (Suryahadi & Sumarto 2003). This also meant that a key legitimising pillar of the New Order started crumbling down.

In popular discourse, the causes of the crisis were dubbed corruption, collusion and nepotism – *Korupsi, Kolusi, Nepotisme*, or KKN. As the economic crisis deepened, calls for change amplified. These protests were mainly led by students in major cities (Brown 2003, p. 229), who demanded 'total reform' (*reformasi total*). While at the 1997 general elections, Golkar once again won in a landslide victory, gaining just over 74 percent of the vote (Ricklefs 2001, p. 404), this came about in a context of increased opposition and public discontent. The economic crisis swiftly turned into a political crisis, as well as heightened tensions between ethnic groups.

In May 1998, while Suharto was on a visit to Egypt, the protests against the regime reached their climax. Cornered, the regime reacted with oppression and intimidation. A number of student leaders were abducted and on 12 May, four students were shot dead by security forces at Trisakti University. The killing of the students triggered a wave of violence across Jakarta and other cities in Indonesia (McGregor & Setiawan 2019). During this violence, which was largely directed against Chinese Indonesians who were seen as scapegoats for the crisis, the security forces were either absent or inactive. An estimated 1,000 people died, and many women were sexually assaulted and raped (Purdey 2006). In the days after the violence, the pressure on Suharto became so intense that he finally resigned on 21 May 1998 and handed power to his deputy, B.J. Habibie.

Conclusion

Suharto's 1998 resignation marked a shift in Indonesian political history. It heralded the start of the *reformasi* (reform) era after long periods of authoritarian rule. This chapter has sketched various distinct phases of this authoritarian history, from the colonial era to Sukarno's Guided Democracy and Suharto's New

Order. Strikingly, prior to 1998, Indonesia had experienced less than ten years of democracy. This kind of history was always going to pose significant challenges for the development of democracy after the end of the New Order. This chapter has identified several legacies of the past that influence and impact upon Indonesia's political system today.

First, corruption emerged in the colonial era and became deeply entrenched during the New Order. Closely related to this was the rise of a powerful politico-bureaucratic oligarchy. These networks permeated across a broad range of different sectors, encompassing the civil service, the security forces and the business elite, with the Suharto family firmly at the core. This legacy continues to haunt democracy in contemporary Indonesia, not least because much of the New Order regime remained in place after Suharto's resignation (Purdey, Missbach & McRae 2020, p. 59).

Second, more than three decades of authoritarian rule had severe impacts on patterns of political participation. Under the New Order's 'Pancasila democracy', leftist political organisations were banned and stigmatised so systematically that the Left remains conspicuously absent from Indonesian politics until today. Moreover, only three political parties were allowed to contest elections during the Suharto years, a policy that significantly undermined the development of institutionalised parties. Similarly, civil society was subject to strict controls, leading to an almost complete demobilisation of society up until the emergence of the protest movement that brought down President Suharto in 1998. Once political space opened up around the time of the democratic transition, participation in politics increased dramatically, but as the New Order regime had long thwarted the organic growth of parties and non-government organisations, both the party system and civil society became heavily fragmented.

A third notable legacy of the past is the enduring significance of the social cleavage between proponents and opponents of a greater role for Islam in politics. The origins of this issue can be traced back to the revolutionary period and the last-minute removal of the Jakarta Charter from the Constitution, which significantly reduced the role of Islam in political and social life (Elson 2009, p. 105). While in the years that followed various parties and movements sought to expand the influence of Islam in politics, the Indonesian state successfully put a halt to these efforts. Particularly under the New Order, political Islam was considered a major threat to the state, resulting in its further marginalisation. The freedoms of the post-1998 era, however, allowed for the resurgence of political Islam, with significant implications for contemporary Indonesian politics.

A fourth legacy of Indonesia's past is manifested in recurrent debates on the relationship between the government in Jakarta and those in the regions. This can be traced back to the revolutionary period: when in 1945 Indonesia proclaimed its independence from the Dutch, the new government pursued a unitary and cohesive state. This was not merely a nationalist cry but reflected what political leaders believed to be necessary for binding the religiously and ethnically diverse nation together. However, over time, conflicts between political elites and resistance from the regions contested this centralised system of governance, which then influenced Indonesia's regression into more authoritarian forms of governance from the late 1950s onwards. Under the New Order, Indonesia remained a highly centralised state, resulting in an accumulation of local grievances which in some areas turned into violent insurgencies. After 1998, addressing these grievances became a key driver for Indonesia's decentralisation process (Buehler 2010), but this has not meant a definite end to tensions between Jakarta and the regions.

A fifth legacy of Indonesia's authoritarian history is the political role of the military. This too finds its roots in the first two decades after independence when the nationalist government regularly deployed the army to crush regional rebellions. From the late 1950s, the army's political influence continued to grow as the country descended into authoritarianism. The military then played a key role in the mass violence of 1965–1966 (Melvin 2018) that laid the foundations of Suharto's presidency. During the New Order, the political role of the military was secured through *dwifungsi* and was crucial in repressing dissent. While after 1998 the military formally rescinded its political role, it remained a political force to be reckoned with.

With the combined burden of these legacies, Indonesia entered its new era of democracy under inauspicious circumstances. The following chapters will analyse how the country overcame these to establish a democratic regime that has demonstrated remarkable resilience in the face of sustained adversity. However, the book will also highlight that this democratic regime has become increasingly vulnerable in recent years, partly at least because it has been unable to adequately address the legacies of the past.

References

Anderson, B 1983, *Imagined communities: reflections on the origin and spread of nationalism*, Verso, London.

Aspinall, E 2005, *Opposing Suharto: compromise, resistance and regime change in Indonesia*, Stanford University Press, Stanford.

Brown, C 2003, *A short history of Indonesia: the unlikely nation*, Allen & Unwin, Crows Nest.

Bourchier, D 2015, *Illiberal democracy in Indonesia: the ideology of the family state*, Routledge, London & New York.

Bourchier, D & Hadiz, VR 2003, *Indonesian politics and society: a reader*, Routledge, London & New York.

Buehler, M 2010, 'Decentralisation and local democracy in Indonesia: the marginalisation of the public sphere', in E Aspinall & M Mietzner (eds), *Problems of democratisation in Indonesia: elections, institutions and society*, Institute of Southeast Asian Studies, Singapore, pp. 267–287.

Chauvel, R & Bhakti, IN 2004, *The Papua conflict: Jakarta's perceptions and policies*, East-West Center, Washington DC.

Cribb, R (ed.) 1994, *The late colonial state in Indonesia: political and economic foundations of the Netherlands Indies: 1880–1942*, KITLV Press, Leiden.

Cribb, R 2001, 'Genocide in Indonesia, 1965-1966', *Journal of Genocide Research*, vol. 3, no. 2, pp. 219–319.

Cribb, R & Kahin, A 2004, *Historical dictionary of Indonesia*, 2nd edn, Scarecrow Press, Lanham etc.

Elson, RE 2009, 'Another look at the Jakarta Charter controversy of 1945', *Indonesia*, no. 88, pp. 105–130.

Elson, RE & Formichi, C 2011, 'Why did Kartosuwiryo start shooting? An account of Dutch-Republican-Islamic forces interaction in West Java, 1945–49', *Journal of Southeast Asian Studies*, vol. 42, no. 3, pp. 458–486.

Foulcher, K 2000, 'Sumpah Pemuda: the making and meaning of a symbol of Indonesian nationhood', *Asian Studies Review*, vol. 24, no. 3, pp. 377–410.

Kahin, GM 2003, *Nationalism and revolution in Indonesia*, SEAP Publications, Ithaca.

Kahin, A & Kahin, GM 1997, *Subversion as foreign policy: the secret Eisenhower and Dulles debacle in Indonesia*, University of Washington Press, Washington.

Lev, DS 1966, *The transition to guided democracy: Indonesian politics 1957–1959*, Modern Indonesia Project, Ithaca.

Lev, DS 1985, 'Colonial law and the genesis of the Indonesian state', *Indonesia*, no. 40, pp. 57–74.

Limpach, R 2016, *De brandende kampongs van Generaal Spoor*, Boom, Amsterdam.

Locher-Scholten, E 2004, *Sumatran sultanate and colonial state: Jambi and the rise of Dutch imperialism, 1830–1907*, Southeast Asia Program, Ithaca.

Lubis, TM 1993, *In search of human rights: legal-political dilemmas of Indonesia's New Order 1966–1990*, Gramedia Pustaka Utama, Jakarta.

McGregor, K 2013, 'Mass violence in the Indonesian transition from Sukarno to Suharto', *Global Dialogue*, vol. 15, no. 1, pp. 133–144.

McGregor, K 2016, 'Emotions and activism for former so-called "comfort women" of the Japanese occupation of the Netherlands East Indies', *Women's Studies International Forum*, vol. 54, pp. 67–78.

McGregor, K, Melvin, J & Pohlman, A 2018, 'New interpretations of the causes, dynamics and legacies of the Indonesian genocide', in K McGregor, J Melvin & A Pohlman (eds), *The Indonesian genocide of 1965: causes, dynamics and legacies*, Palgrave Macmillan, Cham, pp. 1–26.

McGregor, K & Setiawan, K 2019, 'Shifting from international to "Indonesian" justice measures: two decades of addressing past human rights violations', *Journal of Contemporary Asia*, vol. 49, no. 5, pp. 837–861.

Mietzner, M 2009, *Military politics, Islam and the state in Indonesia: from turbulent transition to democratic consolidation*, ISEAS, Singapore.

Melvin, J 2018, *The army and the Indonesian genocide: mechanics of mass murder*, Routledge, London & New York.

Mortimer, R 1974, *Indonesian communism under Sukarno: ideology and politics, 1959–1965*, Cornell University Press, Ithaca.

Otto, JM 2010, 'Sharia and national law in Indonesia', in JM Otto (ed.), *Sharia incorporated: a comparative overview of the legal systems of twelve Muslim countries in past and present*, Leiden University Press, Leiden, pp. 433–490.

Purdey, J 2006, *Anti-Chinese violence in Indonesia 1996–1999*, National University of Singapore Press, Singapore.

Purdey, J, Missbach, A & McRae D 2020, *Indonesia: state and society in transition*, Lynne Rienner Publishers, Boulder & London.

Reid, A 2005, *An Indonesian frontier: Acehnese and other histories of Sumatra*, NUS Press, Singapore.

Reid, A 2011, *To nation by revolution: Indonesia in the 20th century*, NUS Press, Singapore.

Ricklefs, M 2001, *A history of modern Indonesia since c. 1200*, 3ʳᵈ edn, Stanford University Press, Stanford.

Robison, R & Hadiz, VR 2004, *Reorganising power in Indonesia: the politics of oligarchy in an age of markets*, RoutledgeCurzon, London & New York.

Robinson, GB 2018, *The killing season: a history of the Indonesian massacres 1965-66*, Princeton University Press, Princeton & Oxford.

Roosa, J 2006, *Pretext for mass murder: the September 30ᵗʰ Movement and Suharto's coup d'etat in Indonesia*, University of Wisconsin Press, Madison, Wis.

Setiawan, KMP 2013, *Promoting human rights: National Human Rights Institutions in Indonesia and Malaysia*, Leiden University Press, Leiden.

Simpson, BR 2008, *Economists with guns: authoritarian development and U.S.-Indonesian Relations, 1960–1968*, Stanford University Press, Stanford.

Suryahadi, A & Sumarto, S 2003, 'Poverty and vulnerability in Indonesia before and after the economic crisis', *Asian Economic Journal*, vol. 17, no. 1, pp. 45–64.

Taylor, JG 2003, *Indonesia: peoples and histories*, Yale University Press, New Haven.

Van Klinken, G 2018, 'Citizenship and local practices of rule in Indonesia', *Citizenship Studies*, vol. 22, no. 2, pp. 112–128.

Vickers, A 2013, *A history of modern Indonesia*, 2ⁿᵈ edn, Cambridge University Press, Cambridge.

3 Political Institutions

Multiparty Presidentialism and Electoral Politics

Introduction

On 17 April 2019, Indonesians went to the polls to elect their president. Like in the previous election in 2014, there were only two, and the same, candidates to choose from, Joko Widodo (Jokowi) and Prabowo Subianto. This limited choice for voters stood in stark contrast to the bewildering number of candidates competing in the multi-layered elections for national, provincial and district parliaments all held on the same day. All in all, more than 245,000 candidates ran for more than 20,000 parliamentary seats in the lower and upper house as well as the various local parliaments in Indonesia's 34 provinces and 514 municipalities and districts.

The election thus neatly encapsulated two seemingly contradictory features of Indonesian politics. On the one hand, Indonesia remains what Aspinall (2013) once described as 'a nation in fragments', where a multitude of barely distinguishable political parties and legislative candidates compete in highly personalistic campaigns driven primarily by the quest for patronage. At the same time, this fragmentation is complemented by a basic socio-religious cleavage which has long divided Indonesian politics into proponents and opponents of a greater role for Islam in public life. Although this cleavage had been somewhat dormant in the early 2000s, the narrow choices in the last two presidential elections have revitalised and arguably further accentuated its relevance, thereby facilitating rising polarisation around the competing narratives of secular pluralism and Islamism.

Institutionally, the two trends of fragmentation and polarisation are channelled through a political system characterised by a presidential executive and a fragmented legislature. Governance in such multiparty presidential systems is often said to be difficult, so this chapter will analyse how the country has coped with the various challenges of multiparty presidentialism. It shows that all elected presidents since 1999 have responded to the nature of the institutional framework by building large oversized rainbow coalitions with as many parties as possible. This has facilitated cabinet stability, but it has also compromised accountability and effectiveness of governance. The chapter then goes on to show that while elections have been mostly free and fair, the highly personalistic voting system for parliamentary elections has progressively undermined the role of political parties and led to an explosion in vote buying and other forms of money politics. Presidential

DOI: 10.4324/9780429459511-3

elections, meanwhile, have contributed to increased polarisation, which in turn threatens social cohesion. Thus, Indonesian elections have produced a number of unintended side effects that are in need of reform.

In developing these arguments, the chapter will begin with an overview of the constitutional and partisan powers of the executive, before sketching the key features of Indonesia's bicameral parliament. It then proceeds to examine the party system and the main parties currently represented in parliament. The last section looks at Indonesia's electoral history since 1999 and highlights important trends in electoral politics.

The Executive in Indonesia's Political System

Indonesia has been a presidential republic for most of its independent history. Only in the 1950s did the country briefly experiment with a parliamentary form of government, but the dual forces of political fragmentation and socio-religious polarisation, coupled with resistance from the politicised military and the revolutionary fervour of first President Sukarno, who only held a ceremonial role in this system, led to the 'decline of constitutional democracy in Indonesia' (Feith 1962). As outlined in Chapter 2, Sukarno disbanded parliament in 1957 and established 'Guided Democracy', during which he banned most political parties and decreed a return to the 1945 Constitution (Lev 1966). What followed were decades of authoritarian rule, first under Guided Democracy (1957-1965) and then under Suharto's New Order regime (1966-1998).

Both of Indonesia's first two presidents exploited the relative vagueness of the Constitution to concentrate enormous power in the office of the president. At the same time, other formal political institutions such as parliament, parties and the judiciary were systematically weakened. In fact, during Guided Democracy no national elections took place at all. When Suharto took power, he eventually reintroduced legislative elections for the People's Representative Council (Dewan Perwakilan Rakyat, DPR) in 1971, but these polls were so heavily rigged that the regime party Golkar won every election with a comfortable majority (see Table 3.1).

Suharto himself was then elected unopposed by the People's Consultative Assembly (Majelis Permusyawaratan Rakyat, MPR), a kind of super-parliament that comprised the members of the DPR and hundreds of appointed Suharto loyalists. Though formally the highest organ of the state, the MPR was merely a rubber stamp institution, completely subordinate to Suharto.

Once Indonesia democratised in 1998, the political system was thoroughly overhauled. Over the course of four rounds of constitutional reforms (1999-2002) and several changes to the election and party laws, a new institutional framework eventually took shape, which has provided the basis for Indonesia's political system ever since (Horowitz 2013). Executive power within this system still rests with the president, who remains both Head of State and Head of Government. In contrast to the New Order, however, the president is now directly elected by the people once every five years. There is a term limit of two consecutive terms, and to guard against politically motivated attempts from parliament to remove

Table 3.1 Parliamentary election results, 1971-1997 (in percent)

	1971	1977	1982	1987	1992	1997
Golkar	62.8	62.1	64.3	73.2	68.1	74.5
PPP	27.1*	29.3	27.8	16.0	17.0	22.4
PDI	10.1*	8.6	7.9	10.9	14.9	3.1

*The total percentage of votes obtained by Islamic parties (NU, Parmusi, PSII and Perti) that merged into the PPP and the total percentage of votes obtained by the PNI, the IPKIP, Murba, Partai Katolik and Parkindo, which merged into the PDI (Haris 2004, p. 31).

a president from office, impeachment requires the consent of the Constitutional Court rather than just the legislature. This requirement was added during the constitutional amendments after the first president of the reform era, Abdurrahman Wahid, was removed from office in a chaotic and politically driven impeachment process in parliament in 2001.

A key aim of the constitutional change process was to prevent a repeat of the authoritarian abuse of the presidential office, as had happened during the Sukarno and Suharto years. To achieve this, parliament was strengthened and a greater balance between the executive and the legislature was established. According to Article 20 (2) of the Constitution, new laws in Indonesia must be passed by 'joint agreement' between the president and the House of Representatives. Nevertheless, the president has substantial leverage over the legislature. In fact, the 'joint agreement' provision effectively amounts to an informal veto power for the president as parliament can only pass a bill into law with the approval of the president. However, this effective veto power is restricted to the time when a bill is being deliberated. Once the DPR has passed it, the president can no longer veto it as any bill passed by the parliament will automatically become law after 30 days even if the president no longer wants to endorse it (Kawamura 2013, p. 164).

Still, even then the president has a chance to reimpose his authority as the Constitution grants the executive the right to issue a presidential decree called a Government Regulation in Lieu of Law (Peraturan Pemerintah Pengganti Undang – Undang, Perppu). This is only allowed 'in case of emergency', but what exactly constitutes an emergency is not clearly defined. In reality, all Indonesian presidents have used Perppus to repeal legislation they no longer supported after the DPR had passed it, usually with little public attention. In some cases, however, the bills passed in parliament were so controversial that the public actually demanded that the president issue a Perppu, with mixed success. Prominent examples include the passing of a bill that would have abolished the direct elections for local leaders in 2014 (President Yudhoyono in this case did issue a Perppu) and the passing of a bill that weakened the Corruption Eradication Commission (KPK) in 2019 (in this case President Jokowi did not issue a Perppu).

In addition to the effective veto power derived from the joint agreement clause and the right to issue presidential decrees, another source of presidential power is the right to issue implementing regulations for legislation that has been passed in parliament. These regulations can be delayed almost indefinitely, giving the president or cabinet ministers the option of completely foiling the implementation of legislation they may not fully approve. Moreover, the executive also often dominates the law-making process because of its superior human and material resources. While the president and his ministers can fall back on an experienced and well-resourced apparatus of bureaucrats and advisors, the Indonesian parliament lacks comparable institutional capacity due to a smaller operational budget and a high proportion of inadequately qualified members among its ranks who have little to no experience in drafting or reviewing legislation (Hanan 2012, pp. 164–180). Finally, the president oversees the distribution of the most lucrative patronage resources through the cabinet formation process and appointments to state-owned enterprises and government-controlled agencies.

All in all then, the presidency represents the pinnacle of political power in Indonesia. However, there are a range of checks and balances in place that limit the ability of presidents to impose their will all too forcefully. These checks and balances include sub-national governments empowered by the introduction of regional autonomy in 1999 (see Chapter 4), an assertive Constitutional Court that was created in 2003 and a number of semi-independent institutions such as the KPK (see Chapter 5). Most importantly perhaps, the Indonesian parliament was endowed with new powers during the constitutional change process to act like an effective check on the executive. The following section will examine the role of the legislature more closely, arguing that despite its formal powers, the second arm of government only occasionally fulfils its role as a check on the executive.

Box 3.1: Indonesian Presidents

Indonesia has had seven presidents since independence, but only since 2004 have presidents been elected directly by the Indonesian people. The first two presidents – Sukarno and Suharto – held the highest office for several decades during the early post-colonial era and the authoritarian Guided Democracy and New Order regimes. In 1998, the transition to democracy resulted in a short period of political turbulence in which three presidents – Habibie, Wahid and Megawati – were replaced in quick succession. In 2004, the introduction of direct presidential elections eventually brought a period of political stability within a democratic institutional framework in which both Susilo Bambang Yudhoyono and Joko Widodo won two successive five-year terms in office:

1945-1967: Sukarno
1967-1998: Suharto
1998-1999: B.J. Habibie
1999-2001: Abdurrahman Wahid
2001-2004: Megawati Sukarnoputri
2004-2014: Susilo Bambang Yudhoyono
2014-2024: Joko Widodo

The Legislature in Indonesia's Political System

Indonesia has a bicameral parliament. It consists of the lower house, known as the DPR, and the upper house, called the Regional Representative Council (Dewan Perwakilan Daerah, DPD). Together, the two institutions make up the MPR, which used to be a super-parliament under the New Order, but whose role is now limited to considering constitutional amendments, swearing in newly elected presidents and vice-presidents and deciding on next steps in case the Constitutional Court approves an impeachment motion from the DPR.

In 2019, the DPR had 575 sitting members of parliament, whilst the DPD had 136 members. DPD members like to call themselves Senators, but in actual fact the DPD is a rather weak institution which has no legislative powers and can only act in an advisory role during the law-making process. In contrast to the DPR, members of the DPD are supposed to act above the partisan interests of political parties. With four representatives from each province, the DPD's main function is to represent the interests of all Indonesian provinces equally in Jakarta, regardless of size and population of the province (Sherlock 2006). Conversely, in the DPR, the number of seats per province is allocated based on population size. Thus, in the 2019-2024 period, there were 91 legislators from Indonesia's most populous province West Java, whilst thinly populated provinces like Bangka Belitung, North Kalimantan, Gorontalo, North Maluku and West Papua all just had three DPR members.

While geographic representation is engineered through electoral rules, the Indonesian parliament is far less representative of its population when it comes to socio-economic and gender factors. More than half of the DPR members are wealthy entrepreneurs, professionals or members of prominent families who tend to represent their own personal business interests more than those of their constituencies. By contrast, lower socio-economic segments of the population are poorly represented in the DPR (Muhtadi 2019, p. 256).

Moreover, despite some advances in promoting women's political rights in recent years (see Chapter 9), there is also a significant gender imbalance. In the current parliament elected in 2019, only 118 out of 575 legislators are women, which equates to about 21 percent (Halimatusa'diyah 2019). The proportion of female DPD members is slightly higher at just under 31 percent. Generally, female legislators in both houses are often members of prominent political families whereas competent female politicians without dynastic affiliations often struggle to win seats in parliament (Aspinall, White & Savirani 2021).

As mentioned before, the DPD has only very limited political influence, but the DPR does play a very prominent role in contemporary Indonesian politics. After decades of insignificance during the New Order years, its place within the political system was strengthened enormously after the fall of Suharto, as the constitutional reform process sought to restore a better balance between the executive and the legislature. Today, the DPR enjoys some notable powers in its relations with the executive, including, for example, budget approval powers, the right to question cabinet members and involvement in the appointment of key state officials

(Sherlock 2010, p. 163). Moreover, it is a key player in the law-making process. Even though most new bills originate in the executive, they can, as previously mentioned, only be passed into law by 'joint agreement' between the president and the DPR. Thus, the president always needs the support of a majority of parties in parliament in order to get new laws passed – not an easy feat when large numbers of parties are represented in the legislature and the president's own party has only a small share of the seats.

In Indonesia, this type of constellation has been the norm since the first post-New Order election in 1999. The largest party typically wins only about 20 percent of the vote, and in the last three parliamentary periods, the absolute number of parties in parliament fluctuated between nine and ten (see Table 3.2).

To deal with this fragmentation, successive presidents have built large rainbow coalitions of parties in the hope that these coalitions support the executive's agenda in parliament. This kind of coalitional presidentialism is fairly common in other multiparty presidential systems around the world (Chaisty, Cheeseman & Power 2014), but Indonesian presidents have taken coalition-building to extremes, often granting cabinet representation or other perks to all but one or two parties in parliament. Susilo Bambang Yudhoyono, for example, used cabinet appointments to secure 73 percent and 75 percent majorities in parliament during his two terms in office, while Jokowi even intervened in internal party affairs to secure a 69 percent majority in parliament in his first term (Mietzner 2016). In his second term, that majority swelled to 74 percent. According to Slater (2018), the resultant absence of meaningful opposition in Indonesia's parliament is a form of 'party cartelisation', as presidential coalitions have systematically eliminated vertical accountability between politicians and voters.

Table 3.2 Parliamentary election results, 1999-2019 (in percent), major parties only

Party	1999	2004	2009	2014	2019
Partai Demokrasi Indonesia-Perjuangan (PDIP)	33.7	18.5	14.0	18.9	19.3
Partai Golkar	22.4	21.6	14.5	14.8	12.3
Partai Kebangkitan Bangsa (PKB)	12.6	10.6	4.9	9.0	9.7
Partai Persatuan Pembangunan (PPP)	10.7	8.2	5.3	6.5	4.5
Partai Amanat Nasional (PAN)	7.1	6.4	6.0	7.6	6.8
Partai Keadilan Sejahtera (PKS)	1.4*	7.3	7.9	6.8	8.2
Partai Demokrat (PD)	-	7.5	20.9	10.2	7.8
Gerindra	-	-	4.5	11.8	12.6
Nasdem	-	-	-	6.7	9.1
Other	12.1	19.9	22.0	7.7	9.7
Total	100.0	100.0	100.0	100.0	100.0

* In 1999, PKS competed under the name PK (*Partai Keadilan*, Justice Party).
Sources: Aspinall and Berenschot (2019, p. 70) plus data from the Indonesian General Election Commission, available at https://www.kpu.go.id/

Large coalitions are not only detrimental to accountability, they also rarely correspond to effective governance. Even if parties officially support the government, their representatives in parliament often fail to toe the line and instead challenge government policy proposals in the influential parliamentary committees where bills are deliberated. The DPR has 11 committees (sometimes called commissions, from the Indonesian term *komisi*) whose subject areas correlate with the executive government bodies they oversee, but as Sherlock (2015) has demonstrated, these committees tend to have very peculiar power dynamics that can at times be completely removed from the directives of the party leadership boards. As a result, all Indonesian presidents have had to deal with opposition from inside parliament, irrespective of the size of their coalitions.

The need to find joint agreement between the executive and the legislature often leads to prolonged deliberations before a bill can be finally passed into law. Accordingly, legislative output has been very low over the years, with the DPR routinely failing to achieve the targets of its National Legislative Program (Program Legislasi Nasional, Prolegnas). Between 2009 and 2014, for example, the DPR had set an ambitious target of passing 247 bills into law, while the target for the 2014-2019 period was 220. On average, however, only about ten new laws were passed each year (Putri 2019, Ramadhani 2018).

Both the executive and the legislature are part of this process, but it is usually the DPR that slows down the negotiations as many legislators view committee work primarily as opportunities to extort favours from the government. Committees handling natural resource policy or transport and communication issues are regarded as particularly 'wet', which means that they provide the most lucrative prospects for rent-seeking and other illicit activities. The extent of the problem is reflected in the statistics of the KPK. Between 2014 and 2019, the anti-corruption commission declared 24 DPR members suspects in corruption cases, including prominent figures such as the speaker of the House, Setya Novanto, and one of his deputies, Taufik Kurniawan (CNN Indonesia 2019a). Both were convicted and sentenced to lengthy jail terms by the anti-corruption court.

The combined effects of rampant corruption, elitism and disregard for the day-to-day duties of an elected representative have shaped public perceptions of the Indonesian parliament over the years. In public opinion surveys, both DPR and DPD are usually listed among the least trusted public institutions in Indonesia. Tellingly, the only institutions that tend to receive even lower trust scores than the two houses of parliament are political parties, the very organisations responsible for recruiting candidates for parliament.

Political Parties and the Party System

Political parties are, despite their lack of popularity, an essential building block in Indonesia's political system. Parties are not only the main power brokers in parliament, but their support is also required by presidential candidates in order to receive an official nomination for the top job. According to Indonesia's electoral laws, only candidates nominated by political parties with at least 20 percent of seats in the DPR or 25 percent of the votes in the previous election can be registered with the General Election Commission (Komisi Pemilihan Umum, KPU). In other words, political parties are crucial gatekeepers to the highest political offices, including the presidency and the DPR. In addition, they perform similar roles at the local level, where most candidates for executive leadership positions also seek party nominations, even though independent candidatures are permitted here.

However, Indonesian parties are relatively weakly institutionalised, which means they often lack the organisational infrastructure, financial resources and mass membership base to recruit enough candidates from their own ranks (Tomsa 2010). Many candidates are therefore recruited from outside the party, based primarily on popularity ratings provided by public opinion surveys. Clientelistic ties between prospective candidates and power brokers within parties also help, as personal relationships often trump partisan loyalties. Muhtadi (2019, p. 255) has cited research by the Indonesian NGO Formappi, which showed 'that in the 2014 election, only 33% of the candidates could be classified as party cadres'. Once parties have signalled to a candidate that they are generally willing to nominate them, the parties usually ask the candidate to pay a hefty nomination fee, effectively abusing their pivotal position in the system to auction off candidatures to the highest bidders.

Despite the prevalence of clientelistic and non-partisan recruitment patterns, at least some Indonesian parties do have a relatively distinct socio-political identity that is directly linked to the country's most salient socio-cultural cleavage, the religious dividing line between secular pluralists and proponents of political Islam. Reflecting this schism, which dates back to the early days of state formation and the party system of the 1950s, contemporary Indonesian parties may not differ much in their stance on economic, social or foreign policy, but they do differ in their view on the role of Islam in Indonesian politics and society. Voters are well aware of this, although it remains unclear to what extent voting behaviour is influenced by the parties' religious identity (Aspinall & Sukmajati 2016; Fossati et al. 2020; Mujani, Liddle & Ambardi 2018).

Among the nine parties represented in the 2019-2024 parliament, up to five can be classified as secular pluralist, while four have a distinct Islamic identity. At the most secular pluralist end of the spectrum is the staunchly nationalist Indonesian Democratic Party-Struggle (Partai Demokrasi Indonesia-Perjuangan, PDI-P), the de facto successor party to the Indonesian National Party (Partai Nasional Indonesia, PNI) from the 1950s. Since its establishment in 1999, PDI-P has been led by Megawati Sukarnoputri, the daughter of Indonesia's first president Sukarno. With a relatively clearly defined voter base comprising large numbers of non-Muslims and secular Muslims who do not practice their faith in daily life (Mietzner 2012, p. 518), PDI-P is the party that is most adamantly opposed to a greater role of Islam in politics.

Another party that has often defended Indonesia's pluralist tradition is Golkar, the former New Order regime party which successfully adapted to competitive elections after the fall of Suharto (Tomsa 2008). Compared to PDI-P, Golkar tends to be more accommodative of Islamic interests, but usually more out of pragmatic opportunism rather than conviction. Instead of laying claim to represent the interests of a particular cleavage-based community, Golkar is linked to its support base primarily by its reputation as a natural government party that can reliably provide patronage to its members and supporters.

While Golkar has been able to retain a strong position in the party system after 1998, defections have taken their toll on the party as several prominent former Golkar members set up splinter parties over the years. These include the Democratic Party (Partai Demokrat, PD), the Greater Indonesia Movement (Gerindra) and the National Democratic Party (Nasdem), as well as several other smaller parties that failed to win seats in the 2019 election. The prime motivation for the establishment of these new parties was their founders' ambition to run for president or at least secure access to patronage through cabinet representation. Ideologically, these personalist parties are largely indistinguishable, although Nasdem is arguably the most secular pluralist of the three, whereas PD and Gerindra have been less reluctant to support Islamic issues or candidates (Mietzner 2013).

At the other end of the spectrum are four Islamic parties whose political identities are largely shaped by their goal to promote a greater role for Islam in public life. Despite their common religious identity though, these parties differ significantly in their voter base and level of piety. Two of these parties, the National Awakening Party (Partai Kebangkitan Bangsa, PKB) and the National Mandate Party (Partai Amanat Nasional, PAN), are relatively moderate in outlook and mainly represent the interests of two distinct streams in Indonesian Islam, the traditionalists and modernists (see Chapter 6). Both parties have close links to long-established religious mass organisations called Nahdlatul Ulama (NU, affiliated with PKB) and Muhammadiyah (somewhat more loosely affiliated with PAN) and, with the help of these organisations, have developed relatively solid roots in society.

At the most conservative end of the party spectrum, the United Development Party (Partai Persatuan Pembangunan, PPP) and the Prosperous Justice Party (Partai Keadilan Sejahtera, PKS) are sometimes labelled 'Islamist' parties because they used to struggle for sharia law to replace the secular-nationalist Pancasila as the ideological basis of the Indonesian state. Both parties have by now abandoned this formal goal and are perhaps more accurately described as conservative religious parties (Tomsa 2019). Though both PPP and PKS pursue similar religious goals, they have different constituencies. While the former is a remnant of the New Order era and mainly appeals to older rural Muslims, the latter emerged out of a student movement after the fall of Suharto and has its main support base among young urban professionals.

What unites all Indonesian parties regardless of their programmatic or ideological orientation is their huge appetite for patronage. As parties receive only tiny amounts of regular income from state subsidies or membership dues (Mietzner 2015), yet are faced with ever-increasing campaign costs and the need to maintain sprawling party apparatuses, they are in constant need to shore up new funds.

While in some parties these funds are generated from wealthy donors and the parties' own members of parliament, other parties are directly controlled by super-rich oligarchs who are not only bankrolling the party apparatus but, in some cases, have also taken charge of leadership boards. Nasdem with media tycoon Surya Paloh at its helm is the most blatant example of such a party, but others also rely on the personal wealth of leading party members. Arguably the most lucrative source of funds for all parties, however, is state patronage accessed through cabinet representation, parliamentary committees or positions in state-owned enterprises via fictitious projects, mark-ups and embezzlement (Mietzner 2013, pp. 77–80).

In order to seize these opportunities to access patronage resources, most parties willingly join the kind of presidential rainbow cabinets described above, even if they had opposed the winning presidential candidate prior to the election. Slater and Simmons (2013, p. 1370) have described this particular form of collusion as 'promiscuous powersharing', which they define as 'an especially flexible coalition-building practice, in which parties express or reveal a willingness to share executive power with any and all other significant parties after an election takes place, even across a country's most important political cleavages'. Throughout the post-New Order era, such promiscuous powersharing has been the norm, allowing parties to use state money for their own needs.

Increasingly, however, the patronage that used to fill party coffers is channelled away from parties and more directly to individual politicians who use it to recoup private investments they made during their election campaigns. If in the early post-New Order days a party leader like former Golkar chairman Akbar Tandjung was convicted for using embezzled state funds to strengthen his party's campaign finances (Tomsa 2006), a change in the electoral rules in 2009 – the introduction of an open list proportional representation electoral system – has weakened the role of political parties in elections so much that most patronage distribution today occurs outside formal party apparatuses. As Aspinall and Berenschot (2019, p. 9) note, the electoral system change shifted the focus of electoral campaigning from parties to candidates, so that 'political candidates had little to gain from coordinating their patronage distribution efforts through parties but had incentives to build personal teams, cultivate personal clienteles, and foster personal relationships with social networks'. Parties, in other words, are no longer the main beneficiaries of Indonesia's patronage democracy, even though, as Aspinall and Berenschot (2019, p. 8) also note, they 'are engaged in a long-term struggle to gain greater control over such resources'.

Elections for President and Parliaments

Elections are generally regarded as a hallmark of Indonesia's democracy. Held every five years, all elections of the post-Suharto period have been largely free and fair, despite enormous logistical challenges and widespread vote buying. The first parliamentary election after the end of the New Order was held in 1999, whereas the first direct presidential election followed five years later in 2004. In the most recent instalment in 2019, nine parties won seats in parliament, while Jokowi won the presidential election to secure a second term in office. According to the constitution, a president in Indonesia can serve only two terms, as is common in many other presidential democracies around the world.

Many Indonesians justifiably take pride in the fact that since the beginning of democratisation in 1998, the country has successfully conducted five legislative elections and four presidential elections. Voter turnout has been consistently high, averaging around 80 percent across all elections (79.3 percent for the presidential elections, 80.2 percent for legislative elections). By comparison, the average global voter turnout for parliamentary elections in the period 2011-2015 was only 66 percent (Solijonov 2016, p. 24). Contrary to widespread fears in the early days of the transition, all elections have been largely peaceful and there has been no systematic electoral fraud, even if some losing candidates have at times claimed the opposite. Whenever results have been challenged, the Constitutional Court has been an effective arbiter in electoral disputes (Dressel 2019), whilst the KPU has won plaudits for organising the complex elections professionally and in line with its constitutional mandate of being national, permanent and independent.

Indeed, Indonesian elections are a massive logistical challenge. In 2019, the country held no less than five different elections simultaneously on the same day. Elected were:

- The president and vice-president;
- The House of Representatives (DPR);
- The Regional Representatives Council (DPD);
- Provincial Legislatures (DPRD) in 34 provinces;
- Municipal and District Legislatures (DPRD II) in more than 500 cities and districts.

Nearly 193 million voters were registered to cast their votes, including around 80 million millennial voters. On voting day, more than 7 million election workers helped to ensure that voting at the more than 800,000 polling stations went smoothly. After the votes had been cast, a complex recapitulation process ensued during which votes were counted again repeatedly at the subdistrict, district and provincial level. More than a month later, the KPU finally announced the official results, but even then the election marathon was not over yet as more than 300 unsuccessful candidates, including presidential candidate Prabowo Subianto filed complaints with the Constitutional Court (CNN Indonesia 2019b). On 27 June, the court at last rejected Prabowo's case and declared Jokowi the winner of the election.

From an organisational perspective then, the 2019 elections were yet another success. But while the logistical challenges were mastered, these elections also revealed some serious democratic deficits in Indonesia's electoral process. Not all of these deficits were new, of course, but seen against the background of the country's broader political development, they cast a shadow over the reputation of elections as a main pillar of Indonesian democracy. In fact, as Aspinall and

Mietzner (2019, p. 104) have argued, 'the election continued the country's slow-motion slide toward democratic regression'.

Perhaps the most troubling aspect of the 2019 elections was the widespread use of illiberal tactics to silence political opponents, limit public space for debate and discredit the credibility of the election commission and professional polling institutes (Power 2020). This trend towards illiberalism in Indonesia had started more than two years earlier during the controversial election for Jakarta governor in 2017. Back then, Islamist opponents of the ethnic Chinese Christian governor Basuki Tjahaja Purnama (Ahok) had run a systematic smear campaign to prevent the incumbent's re-election after he had allegedly insulted the Qur'an during a campaign event. Following mass protests in the streets of Jakarta, Ahok was eventually charged with blasphemy and even though he still contested the election, he lost by a large margin and was later sentenced to two years in prison.

The shocking effectiveness of the anti-Ahok campaign spooked President Jokowi. Well aware that the same Islamist groups responsible for Ahok's downfall would support Prabowo Subianto in the 2019 presidential election, Jokowi decided to respond by 'fighting illiberalism with illiberalism' (Mietzner 2018). Merely two months after Ahok was convicted, the government banned prominent Islamist organisation Hizbut Tahrir, while the charismatic leader of the Islamic Defenders Front (Front Pembela Islam, FPI), Habib Rizieq Shihab, was effectively forced into exile after being threatened with pornography charges. Rizieq fled to Saudi Arabia, leaving the FPI without its most influential figure. In 2018, the campaign to silence government critics was extended well beyond Islamists as other prominent Prabowo supporters and even government critics not affiliated with the Prabowo camp were prosecuted (Setiawan 2020).

Apart from tightening the space for public discourse, the Jokowi government also moved to mobilise the state apparatus to campaign for him. Police and military officers, provincial governors and district heads were all roped in to pledge support for the incumbent. According to Aspinall and Mietzner (2019, p. 112), 'no other president since 1998 had sought so much backing from local leaders'. This style of campaigning stood in stark contrast to Jokowi's first campaign in 2014, when he had relied on enthusiastic volunteers to create an image of a down-to-earth, approachable politician who likes to mingle with ordinary people (Tomsa & Setijadi 2018). In 2019, only the most fanatic Jokowi supporters still believed in this image.

Thus, Jokowi was instrumental in tarnishing the 2019 election. But Prabowo and his supporters also contributed. Particularly prominent in the former general's campaign rhetoric were allegations that the electoral commission was biased against him and that polling companies were fabricating survey results to give the impression that he stood no chance in the election. Prabowo's brother Hashim Djojohadikusumo and several pro-Prabowo politicians also sought to intimidate the KPU by threatening mass protests, a legal challenge at the Constitutional Court and even a complaint to the United Nations (McRae & Tomsa 2019). By the time the election was held, many Prabowo supporters were so agitated in their rage against Jokowi that violent riots eventually broke out during protests against the election results. In short, the campaign left the Indonesian electorate deeply polarised and both camps shared the blame for this development.

It is important to note, however, that the polarisation that characterised the 2019 elections was neither entirely new nor was it only a product of broader socio-political trends. The electoral system for presidential elections also contributed to this polarisation which Davidson (2018, p. 41) had already described as a 'defining political feature' of Indonesian politics before the 2019 election. Back in 2004, when the first direct presidential election was held, nominations of presidential candidates were allowed for parties or coalitions of parties which had received just 5 percent of the vote or 3 percent of seats in the DPR. These low nomination thresholds enabled five candidates to run for president in 2004. But from 2009 onwards, only parties or coalition of parties that had won at least 25 percent of the vote or 20 percent of seats in the DPR could nominate candidates. The tightened rules reduced the number of candidates to contest presidential elections to three in 2009, and then only two in 2014 and 2019, with the same two candidates – Jokowi and Prabowo – facing off in the last two elections. Both of these elections saw deepening polarisation between the supporters of the two candidates and this has, at least to some extent, been a consequence of institutional engineering (Mietzner 2019).

Moreover, there are other problems with the electoral framework, especially with the regulations for the parliamentary elections. Since 2009, Indonesia has used an open list proportional representation system to elect the DPR and local parliaments. This means not only that all candidates on a party list are visible to the voter on the ballot paper, but also that a seat won by a party in a given constituency will be allocated to the candidate with the highest number of votes, regardless of that candidate's position on the list. In practice, this system turns candidates from the same party into direct rivals and incentivises highly personalistic campaigns. In order to distinguish themselves from other competitors, many candidates have resorted to increasingly excessive vote buying (Muhtadi 2019) and other forms of money politics, including the distribution of small gifts like clothes, prayer mats or household items, the provision of social services and the sponsoring or organisation of community events such as sports, fishing or bird-singing competitions (Aspinall & Sukmajati 2016).

Combined with the exploding costs for securing a candidature in the first place – as mentioned before, parties routinely charge a hefty fee from their candidates – and subsequent campaign-related activities such as hiring political consultants, the ubiquity of vote buying and money politics has turned running for political office in Indonesia into an extremely expensive undertaking. In 2019, candidates could expect to spend 1-2 billion rupiah (US\$ 70-140,000) to finance a campaign for a DPR seat (Kompas.com 2018). In this environment, competent and experienced candidates without sufficient financial resources are increasingly excluded. Women in particular are struggling as they often lack the financial clout to fund their own campaigns (Prihatini 2019). All in all, the open party list system, while superficially increasing choice for voters and establishing a more direct connection between candidates and voters, has effectively transformed the electoral arena into a playground for wealthy elites.

Conclusion

For a long time, Indonesia's reputation as a stable democracy rested to a great extent on its successful adaptation of a seemingly difficult institutional set-up and its proud record of organising multiple complex elections at various levels. Contrary to concerns at the beginning of the democratic transition in 1998, the combination of presidentialism and a fragmented multiparty system without any dominant parties did not cause institutional deadlock. Equally impressive, elections have been largely peaceful and orderly, despite the massive logistical challenges that come with a huge population scattered over a sprawling archipelagic state. Indonesia has deservedly earned a lot of global respect for this track record, especially because it remains an exception in a region that is otherwise characterised by the prevalence of non-democratic rule (see Chapter 13).

But there are also significant shortcomings in the institutional framework. The oversized rainbow coalitions which presidents have built in response to the fragmentation in the party system, for example, have been detrimental to accountability and representation. The parties' weak institutionalisation and susceptibility to corruption have led to high levels of public dissatisfaction with both parties and parliaments. And the electoral system has fostered personalisation and individualisation of electoral campaigning at the expense of programmatic platforms, not to mention an explosion in costs and expenses that has made it difficult for women and candidates from lower socio-economic backgrounds to compete.

What has been particularly concerning in recent years is that the accumulated effects of these problems have combined with broader socio-political trends such as polarisation and a widening gap between elites and ordinary citizens to have an increasingly negative impact on electoral integrity. This trend was first visible in 2014, when the first presidential contest between Jokowi and Prabowo exposed Indonesia to the risks of an aggressively populist election campaign. At the same time, the legislative election that year was marred by unprecedented vote buying. The 2017 Jakarta election then provided a new impetus for deepening polarisation, before the 2019 election exposed the socio-demographic fault lines once again.

Following the 2019 election, President Jokowi further added to the concerns about democratic quality when he took the tradition of rainbow cabinets to new levels by inviting his former foe Prabowo Subianto into the cabinet. With this new power constellation, it seems unlikely that the various democratic deficits in Indonesia's institutional set-up are going to be addressed any time soon. On the contrary, during Jokowi's second term, recurring debates about extending the presidential term limit or reviving the MPR's authority to determine the broad direction of national development strategy raised concerns that Indonesia's democratic institutions may be further weakened rather than strengthened in the near future.

References

Aspinall, E 2013, 'A nation in fragments: patronage and neoliberalism in contemporary Indonesia', *Critical Asian Studies*, vol. 45, no. 1, pp. 27–54.

Aspinall, E & Berenschot, W 2019, *Democracy for sale: elections, clientelism, and the state in Indonesia*, Cornell University Press, Ithaca and London.

Aspinall, E & Mietzner, M 2019, 'Non-democratic pluralism in Indonesia', *Journal of Democracy*, vol. 30, no. 4, pp. 104–118.

Aspinall, E & Sukmajati, M (eds) 2016, *Electoral dynamics in Indonesia: money politics, patronage and clientelism at the grassroots*, NUS Press, Singapore.

Aspinall, E, White, S & Savirani, A 2021, 'Women's political representation in Indonesia: who wins and how?', *Journal of Current Southeast Asian Affairs*, vol. 40, no. 1, pp. 3–27.

Chaisty, P, Cheeseman, N & Power, T 2014, 'Rethinking the 'presidentialism debate': conceptualising coalitional politics in cross-regional perspective', *Democratization*, vol. 21, no. 1, pp. 72–94.

CNN Indonesia 2019a, 'Infografis: daftar anggota DPR 2014–2019 terjerat korupsi', *CNN Indonesia*, 19 September, viewed 3 March 2021, <https://www.cnnindonesia .com/nasional/20190919085039-35-431798/infografis-daftar-anggota-dpr-2014-2019 -terjerat-korupsi>.

CNN Indonesia 2019b, 'Jumlah Sengketa Pemilu 2019 di MK Bertambah Jadi 340 Kasus', *CNN Indonesia*, 1 June, viewed 3 March 2021, <https://www.cnnindonesia.com /nasional/20190531134239-32-400029/jumlah-sengketa-pemilu-2019-di-mk -bertambah-jadi-340-kasus>.

Davidson, JS 2018, *Indonesia: twenty years of democracy*, Cambridge University Press, Cambridge.

Dressel, B 2019, 'Prabowo challenges Indonesia's poll result at Constitutional Court but doubts its impartiality. New research confirms the Court's fairness', *The Conversation*, 11 June, viewed 3 March 2021, <https://theconversation.com/prabowo-challenges -indonesias-poll-result-at-constitutional-court-but-doubts-its-impartiality-new -research-confirms-the-courts-fairness-113486>.

Feith, H 1962, *The decline of constitutional democracy in Indonesia*, Cornell University Press, Ithaca, NY.

Fossati, D, Aspinall, E, Muhtadi, B & Warburton, E 2020, 'Ideological representation in clientelistic democracies: the Indonesian case', *Electoral Studies*, vol. 63, pp. 1–12.

Halimatusa'diyah, I 2019, 'Semakin banyak perempuan di DPR, tapi riset ungkap kehadiran mereka mungkin tidak signifikan', *The Conversation*, 21 October, viewed 3 March 2021, <https://theconversation.com/semakin-banyak-perempuan-di-dpr-tapi -riset-ungkap-kehadiran-mereka-mungkin-tidak-signifikan-125013>.

Hanan, D 2012, *Making presidentialism work: legislative and executive interaction in Indonesian democracy*, PhD Thesis, Ohio State University, Columbus.

Haris, S 2004, 'General elections under the New Order', in H Antlöv & S Cederroth (eds.), *Elections in Indonesia: the New Order and beyond*, RoutledgeCurzon, London and New York, pp. 18–37.

Horowitz, DL 2013, *Constitutional change and democracy in Indonesia*, Cambridge University Press, Cambridge, UK.

Kawamura, K 2013, 'President restrained: effects of parliamentary rule and coalition government on Indonesia's presidentialism', in Y Kasuya (ed.), *Presidents, assemblies and policy-making in Asia*, PalgraveMacmillan, Houndmills, Basingstoke, pp. 156–193.

Kompas.com 2018, 'Ingin jadi caleg, berapa miliar dana dibutuhkan?' *Kompas.com* , 1 August, viewed 3 March 2021, <https://ekonomi.kompas.com/read/2018/08/01 /064607526/ingin-jadi-caleg-berapa-miliar-dana-dibutuhkan?page=all>.

Lev, DS 1966, *The transition to Guided Democracy: Indonesian politics, 1957–59*, Modern Indonesia Project, Cornell University, Ithaca, NY.

McRae, D & Tomsa, D 2019, 'Prabowo cries foul ahead of Indonesian elections', *East Asia Forum*, 14 April, viewed 3 March 2021, <https://www.eastasiaforum.org/2019/04/14/ prabowo-cries-foul-ahead-of-indonesian-elections/>.

Mietzner, M 2012, 'Ideology, money and dynastic leadership: the Indonesian Democratic Party of Struggle, 1998–2012', *South East Asia Research*, vol. 20, no. 4, pp. 511–531.

Mietzner, M 2013, *Money, power and ideology: political parties in post-authoritarian Indonesia*, NUS Press, Singapore.

Mietzner, M 2015, 'Dysfunction by design: political finance and corruption in Indonesia', *Critical Asian Studies*, vol. 47, no. 4, pp. 587–610.

Mietzner, M 2016, 'Coercing loyalty: coalitional presidentialism and party politics in Jokowi's Indonesia', *Contemporary Southeast Asia*, vol. 38, no. 2, pp. 209–232.

Mietzner, M 2018, 'Fighting illiberalism with illiberalism: Islamist populism and democratic deconsolidation in Indonesia', *Pacific Affairs*, vol. 91, no. 2, pp. 261–282.

Mietzner, M 2019, 'Indonesia's electoral system: why it needs reform', Discussion paper, viewed 3 March 2021, <www.newmandala.org/indonesia-electoral-reform>.

Muhtadi, B 2019, *Vote buying in Indonesia: the mechanics of electoral bribery*, PalgraveMacmillan, Houndmills, Basingstoke.

Mujani, S, Liddle, RW & Ambardi, K 2018, *Voting behaviour in Indonesia since democratisation: critical democrats*, Cambridge University Press, Cambridge.

Power, T 2020, 'Assailing accountability: law enforcement politicisation, partisan coercion and executive aggrandisement under the Jokowi administration,' in T Power & E Warburton (eds), *Democracy in Indonesia: from stagnation to regression?* ISEAS-Yusof Ishak Institute, Singapore, pp. 277–302.

Prihatini, ES 2019, 'Women's views and experiences of accessing national parliament: evidence from Indonesia', *Women's Studies International Forum*, vol. 74, May-June, pp. 84–90.

Putri, RD 2019, 'DPR 2014–2019: malas bekerja tapi boros anggaran', *Tirto*, 11 April, viewed 3 March 2021, <https://tirto.id/dpr-2014-2019-malas-bekerja-tapi-boros -anggaran-dlQ8>.

Ramadhani, NF 2018, 'House sets ambitious legislation target', *Jakarta Post*, 30 October, viewed 3 March 2021, <https://www.thejakartapost.com/news/2018/10/30/house-sets -ambitious-legislation-target-2019.html>.

Sherlock, S 2006, *Indonesia's Regional Representative Assembly: democracy, representation and the regions – a report on the Dewan Perwakilan Daerah (DPD)*, Center for Democratic Institutions, Canberra.

Sherlock, S 2010, 'The parliament in Indonesia's decade of democracy', in E Aspinall & M Mietzner (eds), *Problems of democratisation in Indonesia: elections, institutions, and society*, Institute of Southeast Asian Studies, Singapore, pp. 160–178.

Sherlock, S 2015, 'A balancing act: relations between state institutions under Yudhoyono', in E Aspinall, M Mietzner & D Tomsa (eds), *The Yudhoyono presidency: Indonesia's decade of stability and stagnation*, Institute of Southeast Asian Studies, Singapore, pp. 93–113.

Setiawan, KMP 2020, 'A state of surveillance? Freedom of expression under the Jokowi presidency', in T Power & E Warburton (eds.), *Democracy in Indonesia: from stagnation to regression?*, ISEAS Yusof Ishak Institute, Singapore, pp. 254–274.

Slater, D 2018, 'Party cartelisation, Indonesian-style: presidential power-sharing and the contingency of democratic opposition', *Journal of East Asian Studies*, vol. 18, no. 1, pp. 23–46.

Slater, D & Simmons, E 2013, 'Coping by colluding: political uncertainty and promiscuous powersharing in Bolivia and Indonesia', *Comparative Political Studies*, vol. 46, no. 11, pp. 1366–1393.

Solijonov, A 2016, *Voter turnout trends around the world*, International Institute for Democracy and Electoral Assistance (IDEA), Strömsborg.

Tomsa, D 2006, 'The defeat of centralized paternalism: factionalism, assertive regional cadres, and the long fall of Golkar chairman Akbar Tandjung', *Indonesia*, 81 (April), pp. 1–22.

Tomsa, D 2008, *Party politics and democratization in Indonesia: Golkar in the post-Suharto era*, Routledge, London and New York.

Tomsa, D 2010, 'The Indonesian party system after the 2009 elections: towards stability?' in E Aspinall & M Mietzner (eds.), *Problems of democratisation in Indonesia: elections, institutions and society*, Institute of Southeast Asian Studies, Singapore, pp. 141–159.

Tomsa, D 2019, 'Islamism and party politics in Indonesia', in *Oxford Research Encyclopedia of Politics*, Oxford University Press, https://oxfordre.com/politics/view/10.1093/acrefore/9780190228637.001.0001/acrefore-9780190228637-e-1157, viewed 13 March 2021.

Tomsa, D & Setijadi, C 2018, 'New forms of political activism in Indonesia: redefining the nexus between electoral and movement politics', *Asian Survey*, vol. 58, no. 3, pp. 557–581.

4 Local Government

Introduction

In 2005, a charismatic but politically inexperienced furniture trader ran for the post of mayor in the small town of Solo in Central Java. Despite his status as a political outsider, he won the election with a narrow margin. Once in office, the new mayor introduced a range of innovative policies that revitalised the once sleepy town by improving access to healthcare facilities and public spaces, cleaning up the notoriously inefficient bureaucracy and tackling corruption. The people of Solo were so impressed that in 2010 they re-elected their mayor with a massive 90 percent of the vote. The success story from Central Java soon grabbed the attention of savvy consultants from the capital Jakarta who approached the political newcomer and persuaded him to join the 2012 gubernatorial election in Jakarta as a candidate for the Indonesian Democratic Party-Struggle (PDI-P).

Without close links to PDI-P's powerful party elite or other segments of the Jakarta establishment, the man from Solo started his campaign as the clear underdog. But thanks to a highly effective campaign strategy based on frequent neighbourhood visits, volunteer activism and the use of social media, he pulled off an upset victory. Once inaugurated, the new governor brought many of his successful policies from Solo to Jakarta and devoted substantial efforts to sharpening his public image as a down-to-earth approachable man of the people. Within a year, he had become a media sensation and the firm favourite for the 2014 presidential election. And so, in July 2014, Joko Widodo, the former furniture trader from Solo now widely known as Jakarta Governor Jokowi, became Indonesia's first president from outside Jakarta's established elite.

The meteoric rise of Jokowi illustrates a pathway to power that only became possible in Indonesia after the introduction of the so-called regional autonomy programme, a comprehensive package of decentralisation policies that complemented other political reforms of the early 2000s. Prior to regional autonomy, local executive leaders had been elected indirectly through local parliaments and therefore owed their positions more to loyalty to party elites than to competence or popularity. In 2005, however, direct local elections (known as pilkada in Indonesian) were introduced and soon became a cornerstone of Indonesian democracy.

DOI: 10.4324/9780429459511-4

But the so-called big bang decentralisation (World Bank 2003) contained more than just direct elections for local leaders. In addition, it expanded the authority for district governments over a broad range of policy areas which previously had been determined by the central government in Jakarta. In order for the regions to fulfil these new responsibilities, the central government also allowed them to raise local taxes and issue local government regulations. Finally, new streams of financial assistance were channelled to district governments to help accelerate local development, especially in disadvantaged regions in the Eastern parts of Indonesia.

Within a few years after its introduction, regional autonomy had transformed Indonesia 'from a highly centralised state into one of the most decentralised in the world' (Buehler 2010, p. 268). This chapter will outline the main features of this multi-level system of government and evaluate some of the successes and shortcomings of regional autonomy. It argues that while local politics remains dominated by entrenched elites, elections at the provincial, municipal and district levels are highly competitive and open to the occasional challenge from maverick candidates. Furthermore, it will build on earlier assessments of Indonesia's decentralisation process (Bünte 2008, Buehler 2010, Tomsa 2015) to show that there continues to be significant contestation over the extent and nature of decentralisation between national and local governments.

The chapter begins with a brief overview of the historical legacy of centralised authoritarianism during the New Order, before proceeding to discuss the main pillars of regional autonomy, including fiscal decentralisation, direct elections and the authority for local governments to issue local legislation. The chapter also examines why some provinces have obtained special autonomy status that gives them the right to enact specific local regulations that would otherwise contravene Indonesian law. The last section then illustrates how assertive some local governments have become vis-à-vis the central government in Jakarta over the years.

Local Government before 1998

When Indonesia declared independence from the Dutch in 1945, the country's founding fathers envisaged a unitary republic with limited authority for local governments at the provincial and district level. The departing colonial power attempted to thwart the establishment of such a unitary state, but failed in its endeavour to impose a federal structure on the former colony. Thus, the newly independent state became formally known as the Unitary Republic of Indonesia (Negara Kesatuan Republik Indonesia, NKRI), whereas the concept of federalism was irreversibly discredited as a tool for Western interference in Indonesia's domestic affairs. The strong centralisation of power in Jakarta, however, soon caused resentment in some regions, resulting in armed rebellions in parts of Sumatra and Sulawesi in the late 1950s. Although these early rebellions were short-lived and the central government reacted with some concessions (for example the establishment of new provinces or the passing of a new local government law), bitterness about Jakarta's dominant role over the regions remained strong in some parts of the archipelago (Booth 2011).

When Suharto became president after the massacres of 1965-1966, he took the centralisation of power to unprecedented levels. By creating a new system of centrally allocated grants, he stripped local governments off their already limited financial autonomy and effectively reduced their function to implementing guidelines from Jakarta. Though the regime allowed elections for local parliaments from 1971 onwards, these elections were so blatantly rigged in favour of the new regime party Golkar that parliaments merely cast a semi-formal institutional shell around the authoritarian power structures and dense webs of clientelistic networks on which the New Order regime rested in the regions. Endowed with negligible authority, the local parliaments' main task was to elect provincial governors, mayors and district heads once every five years, but due to Golkar's overwhelming dominance in these parliaments, real contests for local leadership were exceptionally rare (Mietzner 2010, p. 175).

Beneath the veneer of highly ritualised formal politics, informal networks within local military commands, Golkar and the bureaucracy provided the main pathways to power at the local level. Throughout the New Order, President Suharto systematically developed these three regime pillars to tighten his grip over the regions. First, the army institutionalised its territorial structure and its 'dual function' (*dwifungsi*), a military doctrine that maintained that the armed forces were not only responsible for external defence but also had a role to play in domestic political affairs (Crouch 1988). In practical terms, this meant that the army was granted a powerful presence on every administrative level, not only through local military commands but also through appointed representatives in local parliaments.

Second, the regime built an expansive bureaucratic apparatus across the five tiers of administration (national, province, district/municipality, sub-district and village), which by the 1990s consisted of more than 4 million civil servants (Kristiansen & Ramli 2006, p. 215). In many areas outside the industrial centres of Java, Sumatra and Kalimantan, a job in the bureaucracy constituted the only viable employment opportunity outside the traditional agricultural sector. Moreover, the civil service provided easy access to lucrative sources of patronage that were distributed through the state apparatus.

Third, the Suharto regime made it compulsory for all military personnel and civil servants to become members of Golkar. As a de facto state party with direct institutional links to the armed forces and the newly created Civil Servants' Corps of the Republic of Indonesia (Korps Pegawai Negeri Republik Indonesia, Korpri), Golkar quickly became the 'greatest source of patronage, greatest provider of facilities, greatest distributor of offices, greatest procurer and supplier of finance' (Ward 1974, p. 83). Its hegemonic status in local politics was further underpinned by the introduction of the so-called floating mass concept which called for the depoliticisation of the population and prohibited all parties to establish branches below the district level (Ramage 1997). As a result, Golkar won all parliamentary elections during the New Order with a comfortable majority.

Taken together, Golkar, the military and the bureaucracy helped the Indonesian state spread its tentacles into almost every corner of the archipelago. In some parts of the country where the traditional authority of local notables was particularly strong, the co-optation of local elites into the New Order structure worked so well that the regime rarely needed to apply its coercive apparatus to demonstrate its power. But in other areas, resentment against Jakarta's control over the regions and the lack of political, cultural and financial autonomy was strong. Especially at the margins of the archipelago, this resentment turned into open hostility towards the central government, eventually erupting in armed separatist insurgencies that haunted the New Order regime for decades.

At the northern tip of Sumatra, for example, the resource-rich and famously pious province of Aceh became the site of a prolonged uprising when long pent-up grievances spawned the formation of the Free Aceh Movement (Gerakan Aceh Merdeka, GAM) in 1976. In its struggle for independence, GAM thrived on widespread local perceptions that the central government suppressed the province's unique cultural and religious heritage and exploited the region's natural resources (Aspinall 2009). Brutal military crackdowns that killed thousands of Acehnese further galvanised support for independence from Jakarta, helping to transform GAM 'from a small, armed organisation with an intellectual vanguard into a popular resistance movement' (Schulze 2004, p. viii).

Meanwhile, at the other end of the archipelago, separatist rebellions also broke out in Papua and East Timor. What distinguished these two rebellions from the GAM insurgency in Aceh, however, was that neither Papua nor East Timor had initially been part of Indonesia at the time of independence. Instead, Indonesia had annexed them by means of a staged referendum (Papua, in 1969) and a military invasion (East Timor, in 1975). Massive military operations were required to subdue the local populations after these annexations, but like in Aceh, the Indonesian state struggled mightily in its attempts to crush the rebellions.

Introducing Big Bang Decentralisation

When President Suharto eventually stepped down in 1998, the resistance movements in Aceh, East Timor and Papua saw the regime change as an unprecedented opportunity to achieve independence. At the same time, the power vacuum created by Suharto's resignation also triggered intense power struggles among local elites in other regions, which in some cases turned into violent ethnic and religious conflict (Bertrand 2004, Davidson 2009). According to conservative estimates, around 10,000 lives were lost in communal violence across Indonesia during the extended transition period between 1990 and 2003 (Van Klinken 2007, p. 4), with most of the casualties recorded after 1998 in West and Central Kalimantan, Maluku, North Maluku and Central Sulawesi. At the peak of the violence, some observers feared that Indonesia faced the prospect of national disintegration.

To pre-empt this, and concurrently gain support from the international community for his presidency, the embattled interim president B.J. Habibie decided to take the radical step of offering East Timor an independence referendum. This decision, however, drew the ire of the staunchly nationalist armed forces, who responded with a bloody intimidation campaign aimed at coercing people into voting for autonomy within Indonesia rather than independence. It was to no avail. On 30 August 1999, the overwhelming majority of East Timorese voted for independence (Schulze 2001).

Significantly, no other region was offered the prospect of an independence referendum. Instead, Habibie and his successor Abdurrahman Wahid attempted to address local grievances and rein in separatist tendencies through a mix of special autonomy deals for restive provinces like Aceh and Papua and a general decentralisation programme for the rest of the country. The two special autonomy packages encountered a range of challenges which delayed their implementation, but the broader decentralisation programme, dubbed the 'big bang' by the World Bank (2003) due to its sudden introduction and comprehensive scope, was passed into law in 1999 and put into practice in 2001.

Since then, the legislative framework for regional autonomy has undergone several revisions, but despite a tendency towards recentralisation in the 2010s (Tomsa 2015), the main pillars of regional autonomy have remained largely intact. Among the most important features are the following:

- The central government is required to transfer substantial proportions of its domestic revenue to sub-national governments who can use and allocate these funds without major restrictions;
- Sub-national governments enjoy extensive authority to formulate and implement policy for their own jurisdictions and to raise local taxes;
- The epicentre of local politics is the third administrative tier consisting of districts and municipalities, even though provincial governors regained some authority vis-à-vis the mayors and district heads in their provinces in later amendments to the regional autonomy framework;
- Governors, mayors and district heads are elected by direct popular elections (added to the framework in 2005)';
- Increased funding, greater administrative autonomy and new accountability mechanisms were introduced for Indonesia's more than 74,000 villages, especially after the passing of the 2014 Village Law.

Taken together, these reforms had direct implications for the governmental structure of the Indonesian state because the combined prospect of quick access to central government funds and unprecedented autonomy to allocate these funds incentivised the creation of ever smaller administrative regions at all levels. As a consequence, the number of provinces, municipalities, districts, sub-districts and villages grew enormously between 1998 and 2019 (see Table 4.1), a process known as *pemekaran* ('blossoming') in Indonesia.

Pathways to Local Power

Decentralisation not only triggered the creation of new administrative units, it also made governing these units more attractive than ever before. Accordingly,

Table 4.1 Growth in administrative entities, 1998-2019

Administrative Unit	Number in 1998	Number in 2006	Number in 2012	Number in 2019
Province	27	33	34	34
Municipality	65	91	98	98
District	249	349	399	416
Sub-district	4,028	5,656	6,793	7,230
Village	67,925	71,563	79,075	74,953

Sources: Menteri Dalam Negeri Republik Indonesia (2019, p. 6); Mietzner (2014, p. 58).

contests for local leadership positions have turned into fierce electoral battles in many regions, often involving high-profile candidates. As mentioned earlier and illustrated in Table 4.2, since 2005 the leaders of all the main sub-national administrative units except the sub-district are elected in direct popular elections held every five years. While village head elections were already conducted during the New Order (though these were neither free nor fair back then), governors, mayors and district heads had been elected indirectly through local parliaments prior to 2005. The switch to direct elections ended the widespread practice of vote buying inside parliament and opened up new opportunities for enhanced citizen participation, competition and accountability in local politics. Yet, despite modest achievements in these democratic qualities over the years, there have also been some significant problems in the conduct of the pilkada.

On the positive side, the pilkada have promoted citizen participation in local politics as candidates routinely assemble huge campaign teams that rely on clientelistic networks at the grassroots to mobilise support (Aspinall & Berenschot 2019). For a sub-national election, voter turnout has also been remarkably high in many pilkada (see Table 4.3) and voters have often embraced the opportunity to hold local leaders accountable for their performance in office. While incumbency has provided an enormous advantage due to high name recognition, easy access to patronage and opportunities to mobilise support from the bureaucracy (McRae & Zhang 2015), many challengers have also emerged victorious. In the 2018 round of elections, for example, about two-thirds of the 171 pilkada were won by non-incumbents, even though this included elections in which incumbents were no longer eligible to run because of the two-term limit (Azanella & Dewi 2018).

However, while citizens have a chance to vote and be part of campaign teams, the actual electoral competition is effectively off limits for large parts of the population because over time the cost of campaigning has exploded. Pilkada are strongly personalistic elections in which the popularity of a candidate usually matters more than party affiliation or policy agenda, so aspiring candidates need to invest heavily in professional political consultants to enhance name recognition and develop a positive public image (Trihartono 2014). During the campaign, vote buying is rampant, and many candidates believe that refusal to distribute generous amounts of money and gifts to voters and local community groups would disadvantage

Table 4.2 Indonesia's governmental structure

Level of government	Heads of executive government	Legislative body
National	President and vice-president, directly elected	People's Representative Council (DPR)
Provinces	Governor and deputy governor, directly elected	Regional People's Representative Council I (DPRD I)
Districts and municipalities	District heads and mayors plus their deputies, directly elected	Regional People's Representative Council II (DPRD II)
Sub-districts	Sub-district head, appointed civil servant	-
Villages and small urban precincts	Village head, directly elected; *lurah*, appointed civil servant	Village Consultative Body (BPD); no equivalent in small urban precincts

Source: Aspinall and Berenschot (2019, p. xi).

Table 4.3 Voter turnout in pilkada (since introduction of simultaneously held elections in 2015)

Election date	Number of elections	Average turnout (percentage)
December 2015	269	68.82
February 2017	101	74
June 2018	171	73.24
December 2020	270	76.13

Sources: Assorted media reports and publications from the Indonesian General Election Commission, available at https://www.kpu.go.id/

them against other contenders. According to estimates by the national police and the Corruption Eradication Commission (Komisi Pemberantasan Korupsi, KPK) quoted by Movanita (2018) and Nugroho (2020), pilkada campaigns in 2018 and 2020 cost up to 100 billion rupiah (US$ 7 Mio). Only entrenched elites can afford such huge expenses, leaving the pool of candidates largely restricted to career politicians, bureaucrats and entrepreneurs with good connections to locally powerful families and elite networks. In some areas, pilkada have facilitated the rise and entrenchment of political dynasties (Savirani 2016).

The commercialisation of electoral politics through political consultants and campaign advisors has also had other detrimental effects on the quality of local democracy. Apart from financial prowess, electability based on public opinion surveys is usually the most important variable for parties to decide whom they will nominate, but this reliance on survey data can actually stifle competition and accountability if the figures show a seemingly unassailable lead for a certain candidate and no contender is willing to take the risk of mounting a challenge. Since

2015, the number of elections that featured only 1 candidate has increased from just 3 in 2015 and 9 in 2017 to 16 in 2018 and 25 in 2020 (Aman 2020). Voters in these elections were presented with a rather peculiar ballot paper featuring only one candidate and a blank box.

Despite the inauspicious structural and institutional environment, in some instances candidates from outside the established elite have managed to challenge the status quo. Over the years, a new crop of charismatic political entrepreneurs with distinctive communication styles and no or few prior links to established elite networks has emerged. Endowed with a combination of populist appeal and techno-cratic expertise, these pragmatic newcomers have proven particularly adept at craft-ing and conveying the kind of campaign messages that resonate with voters who are disillusioned with politics as usual. The rise of Jokowi is the most exceptional example of such an unorthodox political career that took off at the local level, but pilkada have also produced other 'innovative technocrats' (Hatherell 2019) such as Ridwan Kamil in West Java or Tri Rismaharini ('Risma') in East Java. Like Jokowi, these leaders rose to prominence due to their successful terms as mayor (Ridwan Kamil in Bandung, Tri Rismaharini in Surabaya) and then built on their merit-based popularity to become provincial governor or, in the case of Risma, cabinet minister.

Achievements and Shortcomings of Regional Autonomy

The career trajectories of these technocrats may be exceptional, but they do illus-trate that direct local elections have provided new incentives for local leaders to develop programmatic track records that can help improve prospects for re-elec-tion. Since the introduction of the pilkada, many governors, mayors and district heads have taken proactive steps to attract investment and improve economic con-ditions, while others have sought to attract voters by focusing on cleansing local bureaucracies from entrenched practices of corruption and nepotism. Moreover, programmes to improve access to primary education and health facilities are now commonplace in the regions, especially in areas where many voters come from lower socio-economic backgrounds (Aspinall 2014a).

As a result, public service delivery has improved in many regions, even though there is still significant geographic variation across the archipelago. According to Berenschot and Mulder (2019), this variation is directly linked to the charac-ter of local economies and the prevalence of clientelism, whereas Fossati (2016) has demonstrated with regard to healthcare for the poor that local politicians are particularly responsive to low-income constituents in districts where elections are highly competitive. At a broader macro level, however, the economic results of decentralisation have been rather mediocre. Poverty at the provincial level may have declined since the introduction of regional autonomy, but not at extraor-dinary rates (Ilmma & Wai-Poi 2014, p. 116). And despite President Jokowi's emphasis on infrastructure development in the less-developed Eastern half of the country, the large gap in economic productivity between areas on Sumatra, Java, Bali and Kalimantan, on the one hand, and Eastern Indonesia, on the other, remains largely unchanged.

A key problem for almost all local governments has been the ongoing reliance on financial assistance from the central government (Patunru & Rahman 2014, p. 164). When regional autonomy was introduced, the central government had erroneously assumed that the regular provision of financial assistance from Jakarta in the form of a national General Purpose Fund, a Specific Allocation Grant and a Revenue Sharing Grant would be enough to facilitate the acceleration of regional development. But as it turned out, many local governments used these funds primarily for wages and administrative expenditures (Sjahrir, Kis-Katos & Schulze 2014), whilst the remainder of the funds tended to disappear in fictitious projects, markups and other forms of corruption and mismanagement.

In fact, corruption at the local level is now just as deeply engrained as it is at the national level, prompting Aspinall (2019, p. 52) to state flatly that 'corruption is not an exception but the rule in contemporary Indonesia'. Hopes that decentralisation would reduce corruption were not fulfilled. Instead, the abuse of power spread from Jakarta to the regions as the devolution of power opened up a broad range of new opportunities for local politicians to engage in illicit transactions (Davidson 2007). Especially in the forestry and mining sectors, district heads have requested enormous bribes in return for logging and mining permits. Over the years, the KPK has investigated numerous local executive leaders and members of local parliaments. In 2018, the district head of Cirebon, Sunjaya Purwadisastra, had the dubious honour of becoming the 100th local leader to be formally charged by the KPK since the commission was established in 2002 (Husodo 2018).

Interestingly, data from the KPK show that corruption is worst at the margins of the archipelago. In 2019, KPK commissioner Laode Syarif declared North Sumatra the most corrupt province in Indonesia, followed by Aceh, Riau, Papua, West Papua and Banten (Mustholih 2019). The prevalence of corruption in Aceh, Papua and West Papua is particularly striking because these provinces enjoy special privileges due to their status as regions with special autonomy. Clearly, the influx of extra financial resources as part of this autonomy has not reduced the penchant for corruption among local elites in these regions.

Special Autonomy for Aceh and Papua

Out of 34 provinces in Indonesia, five enjoy a special status that sets them apart from the rest. Jakarta and Yogyakarta owe their autonomy to their status as the current and former capital (Yogyakarta was Indonesia's capital between 1946-1948). Aceh, Papua and West Papua, by contrast, were granted special autonomy as part of the central government's efforts to quell long-lasting insurgencies.

In Aceh, two early attempts at introducing special autonomy via legislation in 1999 and 2001 failed to end decades of civil war, but in 2005, just a few months after the devastating 2004 Boxing Day tsunami, the Indonesian government and the rebel movement GAM finally sealed a peace deal which entailed a comprehensive autonomy package for the restive province at the northern tip of Sumatra. The following year, the Law on the Governing of Aceh formalised the autonomy package. Though the law still placed significant limits on Acehnese self-governance, it has become a quasi-constitution for the province, providing important political, economic and socio-religious concessions.

Politically, Aceh became the only Indonesian province where local political parties are allowed. This provision led to the formation of the Partai Aceh and a few other local parties which then contested elections at the provincial, municipal and district level. Thanks to the backing of many former GAM leaders, Partai Aceh has won all three elections for the new provincial parliament (Dewan Perwakilan Rakyat Aceh, DPRA) in 2009, 2014 and 2019. The party's vote share, however, has declined progressively as a result of factional infighting and voter dissatisfaction with Partai Aceh's track record. The internal conflicts also spilt over into the gubernatorial elections, where former GAM members have repeatedly competed against each other in bitterly fought contests. The 2017 election was won by Irwandi Yusuf, a former GAM leader who had already been governor between 2007 and 2012, but subsequently fell out with Partai Aceh and then formed his own party. Irwandi's second term, however, ended prematurely in 2019 when he was jailed for corruption (Jakarta Post 2019).

Economically, Aceh has benefitted from special autonomy because the central government agreed to channel large amounts of cash into the Acehnese economy. Of particular importance has been a provision in the 2006 law which provides for funds worth 2 percent of the national General Purpose Fund to be paid to the provincial government until 2022, with further payments worth 1 percent of the fund guaranteed until 2027. The influx of this money provided important opportunities for the Acehnese government to support social aid programmes and reintegration efforts for former combatants, but as Aspinall (2014b, p. 476) noted, much of this money has been misappropriated for 'predatory capture and patronage purposes'. Thus, while poverty levels in Aceh have declined over the last decade, they remain among the highest in Sumatra, especially in rural areas that have missed out on the reconstruction boom that followed the tsunami and the subsequent end of the conflict.

Finally, from a legal and socio-religious perspective, the main feature of Aceh's special status is its adoption of sharia law. The central government's decision to allow Aceh to become the only Indonesian province to use Islamic law led to the development of a new religious bureaucracy, which soon emerged as a counterweight to the political dominance of former GAM rebels (International Crisis Group 2006). Under the watchful eye of organisations like the Acehnese Ulama Organisation (Majelis Pemusyawaratan Ulama, MPU), the Office for Syariat Islam (Dewan Syariat Islam, DSI) and the sharia police (Wilayatul Hisbah, WH), restrictions on pluralism were increasingly tightened. In 2015, the Islamic Criminal Code was introduced and since then, the province has often made headlines for its harsh punishment regime, which tends to disproportionately target women and sexual minorities for alleged moral offences such as sex outside marriage, being in close proximity to male friends or wearing inappropriate clothing (Afrianty 2018).

Compared to Aceh, special autonomy in Indonesia's easternmost provinces of Papua and West Papua has done very little to address long-standing grievances, not to mention end the insurgency waged by the Free Papua Organisation (Organisasi Papua Merdeka, OPM). As Jakarta has steadfastly refused to accept the kind of third-party mediation that helped resolve the Aceh conflict, the Indonesian military continues to have a strong presence in Papua, especially around the massive Freeport gold and copper mine where violence has long been rife and escalated again in late 2019 and early 2020 (Institute for Policy Analysis of Conflict 2020). In the shadow of the ongoing conflict, Jakarta's special autonomy package for Papua and West Papua has focused primarily on economic and infrastructure development, without paying much attention to socio-political grievances.

Arguably, the most noteworthy acknowledgement of Papua's political and cultural distinctiveness was a passage in the special autonomy law which provided for the establishment of a Papuan People's Council (Majelis Rakyat Papua, MRP) to preserve and uphold Papuan identity. At the time when the autonomy law was first passed in 2001, there was only one province covering the whole Western half of the island of New Guinea, yet this vast province was home to over 200 indigenous ethnic and tribal groups. The MRP was therefore conceived as an institution that could unite these diverse groups from all over Papua. But before it was even created, the central government decided to split Papua into new administrative entities. After some legal wrangling, the new province of West Papua was created in 2003, an act described by Nolan, Jones and Solahuddin (2014, p. 412) as 'perhaps the single act by any post-Suharto government that most convinced Papuans of Jakarta's continued bad faith'. A few years later, the initially well-intended gesture of creating a unifying institution in recognition of Papuan values was further undermined when the new West Papua province set up a separate MRP in 2011.

The special autonomy law for Papua and West Papua was revised and extended for another 20 years in 2021, but no specific programmes or policies that would address the political dimension of the conflict have been implemented since (for a discussion of human rights issues in Papua, see Chapter 10). Instead, the central government seems intent on continuing to focus on pouring money into the region, in the hope that economic development would tame secessionist tendencies. Like in Aceh, special autonomy in Papua and West Papua has channelled funds worth 2 percent of the national General Purpose Fund to the provincial governments. In addition, revenue shares from forestry, fishing and mining increased drastically with special autonomy. But large chunks of this money have disappeared through local corruption so that both Papua and West Papua remain among the poorest provinces in Indonesia. Rural areas in particular have received far too little investment in health and education infrastructure, as is reflected in weak human development indicators (Resosudarmo et al. 2014).

All in all, special autonomy has provided far more tangible outcomes in Aceh than in Papua. As Aceh obtained its special autonomy as a result of tense peace negotiations rather than as a pre-emptive gesture from the central government, the province at the northern tip of Sumatra was able to secure some distinct privileges such as local political parties and its own legal system. Moreover, the Indonesian military has withdrawn from Aceh while it retains a strong and heavily resented presence in Papua. But while these outcomes have helped to maintain the peace in Aceh, the quality of democracy has declined as religious morality politics has squashed pluralism and diversity. In Papua, meanwhile, special autonomy has done very little to alter the widespread belief among Papuans that they are second-class citizens in an overbearing, quasi-colonial Indonesian state. Developments such as the racial abuse of Papuan students in Surabaya in 2019 and the Jokowi government's refusal to let the Papua governor issue a provincial lockdown regulation to contain the spread of the coronavirus in 2020 have only served to reinforce this belief (Institute for Policy Analysis of Conflict 2020). Accordingly, the extension of special autonomy in 2021 was actually rejected rather than welcomed by many Papuans who feared that the revised law will do nothing to address Papuan grievances.

Jakarta and the Regions

One of the ironies of Indonesia's decentralisation has been that the central government has done virtually nothing to address the shortcomings of Papua's unpopular special autonomy framework, while at the same time continuously tinkering with the broader regional autonomy regulations for the rest of the country, even though decentralisation has actually been very popular with people in the regions, both elites and ordinary citizens (Mietzner 2014). Former president Susilo Bambang Yudhoyono, for example, issued a moratorium on *pemekaran* towards the end of his first term. Though the ban on establishing new administrative regions has been heavily contested, no new province has been created since the formation of the North Kalimantan province in 2012. The growth of districts and municipalities also slowed down significantly after Yudhoyono's announcement.

Less successful have been attempts to stop local governments from issuing controversial regional bylaws (peraturan daerah or perda). Many local governments have used such perda to introduce local taxes, issue lucrative permits for mining and logging concessions or to impose religious dress codes for public servants or women in public spaces. According to Butt (2010, p. 178), many of these perda were 'unclear, unnecessary, misdirected, exploitative of citizens and investors, or even unconstitutional'. The central government has repeatedly warned local governments against issuing perda that contravene national legislation and the Ministry of Home Affairs has revoked thousands of perda over the years. But in a blow to the government's ambitions to assert its authority over the districts, the Constitutional Court declared in 2017 that the government had no right to repeal local regulations. Instead, it handed the task of reviewing perda to the Supreme Court which, in contrast to the central government, views regional governments as having 'a broad discretion to pass laws to implement almost any policies' (Butt 2017).

In early 2021, the contestation over local regulations entered a new round when three ministers of the Jokowi cabinet issued a joint decree that targeted perda prescribing religious dress codes in state schools. No longer able to directly repeal such bylaws, Education and Culture Minister Nadiem Makarim, Home Affairs

Minister Tito Karnavian and Religious Affairs Minister Yaqut Cholil Qoumas attempted to circumvent the Constitutional Court ruling by ordering local governments and school principals to abandon all local regulations that require girls in state schools to wear a headscarf (jilbab). At the same time, the ministers called on citizens to challenge discriminatory and oppressive bylaws issued by governors, district heads and mayors by filing for judicial reviews in the Supreme Court (BBC 2021). The initiative was widely seen as a part of the government's agenda to curb alleged Islamisation in the education sector, but it also revealed another layer in the contested relationship between the central and local governments.

Perhaps the most controversial attempt at weakening regional autonomy, however, was the ultimately short-lived abolition of direct local elections in 2014 (Tomsa 2015). Citing the high costs of electoral administration, the parties' corrupt candidate recruitment systems, the rise of dynasties and the frequent tensions between local executive leaders and their deputies, the central government under the then president Susilo Bambang Yudhoyono was keen to undermine the popular support base of local executive leaders in order to make it easier for Jakarta to exert its influence on local governments. Civil society organisations, local elites and the general public had long resisted attempts by the central government to push through revisions to the regional election law, but in September 2014, conservative elites finally seemed to have achieved their goal when parliament passed a new law which mandated a return to indirect elections through local parliaments. However, another public outcry prompted outgoing President Yudhoyono to repeal the legislation at the last minute by issuing a Government Regulation in Lieu of Law (Perppu).

While the Perppu ensured that the pilkada were retained, other aspects of regional autonomy received an overhaul in 2014. Together with the controversial regional election law, the DPR also passed a revised regional government law, which restructured the responsibilities between different tiers of government. The aim was to take away some powers from the district level, especially in regard to natural resource management, and shift these to the provincial level where the status of governors was strengthened in an attempt to 'redress the problem of the "missing middle"' (Ostwald et al 2016, p. 146). Arguably, the central government was hoping that governors may be easier to control than district heads, many of whom had fallen foul of the central government due to the excessive use of controversial regional bylaws.

But rather than become docile extended arms of the central government, provincial governors have increasingly used their elevated status to assert themselves as powerful new actors in Indonesia's decentralised political landscape. This became particularly evident in the early stages of the Covid-19 health emergency in 2020, when governors like Anies Baswedan (Jakarta), Ridwan Kamil (West Java) or Lukas Enembe (Papua) openly defied the central government's policies and challenged President Jokowi to allow provincial governments to issue regional lockdowns. The governor of Central Java, Ganjar Pranowo, has also become a high-profile personality who is expected to use his position as springboard for higher office at the national level.

Conclusion

Twenty years after the end of the highly centralised New Order regime, Indonesia remains a unitary state on paper, but comprehensive decentralisation measures have turned it into a quasi-federal republic where sub-national regions enjoy far-reaching autonomy. Initially, this autonomy was deliberately devolved to the third administrative tier. Later on, some of the new powers were shifted to provincial governments while the central government has also sought to reassert itself over the regions by halting the extreme administrative fragmentation that had occurred in the early years of the decentralisation process.

As a consequence of the contested nature of decentralisation, relations between the central government and its counterparts in the regions have not always been smooth. Buoyed by the strong public support bases they have built in their constituencies thanks to the introduction of direct elections, local leaders have grown increasingly confident in their communication with the central government. This has resulted in some serious resistance against central government policies, illustrated for example by the successful Constitutional Court challenge against Jakarta's continued revocations of local bylaws, which was led by more than 40 district governments and the Indonesian Association of District Governments.

Resistance and resentment against Jakarta's overbearing dominance of course were the key triggers that prompted the central government to introduce regional autonomy in the first place. However, compared to the situation in 1999, when Indonesia had just emerged out of more than 30 years of centralised authoritarian rule, the grievances we see today are rather different. More importantly perhaps, there are different institutional mechanisms available to solve them. Even with the new trend towards recentralisation, Indonesia is unlikely to return to the kind of centralised state it was before 1998.

Arguably, the only places in the country where anti-Jakarta sentiment has changed very little are Papua and West Papua. The ineffectiveness of the special autonomy package for these two provinces demonstrates that special autonomy is by no means a panacea for addressing regional grievances. As long as Jakarta's understanding of special autonomy remains limited to funnelling extra cash into an already corrupt local state apparatus, tensions are likely to remain high in Indonesia's far east.

References

Afrianty, D 2018, 'Women's responses to the implementation of Islamic law in Aceh', in RW Hefner (ed.), *Routledge handbook of contemporary Indonesia*, Routledge, London and New York, pp. 346–353.

Aman, A 2020, *Indonesia's big-size COVID-19 elections – what to watch for*, viewed 11 February 2021, <https://www.idea.int/news-media/news/indonesia%E2%80%99s-big-size-covid-19-elections-%E2%80%93-what-watch>.

Aspinall, E 2009, *Islam and nation: separatist rebellion in Aceh, Indonesia*, NUS Press, Singapore.

Aspinall, E 2014a, 'Health care and democratization in Indonesia', *Democratization*, vol. 21, no. 5, pp. 803–823.

Aspinall, E 2014b, 'Special autonomy, predatory peace and the resolution of the Aceh conflict', in H Hill (ed.), *Regional dynamics in a decentralised Indonesia*, Institute of Southeast Asian Studies, Singapore, pp. 460–481.

Aspinall, E 2019, 'Fighting corruption when corruption is pervasive: the case of Indonesia', in C Chen & ML Weiss (eds), *The political logics of anti-corruption efforts in Asia*, State University of New York Press, Albany, pp. 49–76.

Aspinall, E & Berenschot, W 2019, *Democracy for sale: elections, clientelism, and the state in Indonesia*, Cornell University Press, Ithaca.

Azanella, LA & Dewi, RK 2018, '64 kepala daerah petahana terpilih pada pilkada serentak 2018', *Kompas*, 26 July, viewed 11 February 2021, <https://nasional.kompas.com/read/2018/07/26/18520301/64-kepala-daerah-petahana-terpilih-pada-pilkada-serentak-2018>.

BBC 2021, 'SKB tiga menteri soal seragam sekolah, apakah efektif dan mengapa tidak menyasar perda?', *BBC.com*, 5 February, viewed 11 February 2021, <https://www.bbc.com/indonesia/indonesia-55762516>.

Berenschot, W & Mulder, P 2019, 'Explaining regional variation in local governance: clientelism and state-dependency in Indonesia', *World Development*, vol. 122, pp. 233–244.

Bertrand, J 2004, *Nationalism and ethnic conflict in Indonesia*, Cambridge University Press, Cambridge.

Booth, A 2011, 'Splitting, splitting and splitting again: a brief history of the development of regional government in Indonesia since independence', *Bijdragen tot de Taal-. Land- en Volkenkunde*, vol. 167, no. 1, pp. 31–59.

Buehler, M 2010, 'Decentralisation and local democracy in Indonesia: the marginalisation of the public sphere', in E Aspinall & M Mietzner (eds), *Problems of democratisation in Indonesia: elections, institutions and society*, Institute of Southeast Asian Studies, Singapore, pp. 267–287.

Bünte, M 2008, 'Indonesia's protracted decentralization: contested reforms and their unintended consequences', in M Bünte & A Ufen (eds), *Democratization in post-Suharto Indonesia*, Routledge, London and New York, pp. 102–124.

Butt, S 2010, 'Regional autonomy and legal disorder: the proliferation of local laws in Indonesia', *Sydney Law Review*, vol. 32, no. 2, pp. 177–191.

Butt, S 2017, 'Constitutional Court lets local governments off the leash', *Indonesia at Melbourne*, 4 July, viewed 11 February 2021, <https://indonesiaatmelbourne.unimelb.edu.au/constitutional-court-lets-local-governments-off-the-leash/>.

Crouch, H 1988, *The army and politics in Indonesia*, Cornell University Press, Ithaca.

Davidson, JS 2007, 'Politics-as-usual on trial: regional anti-corruption campaigns in Indonesia', *The Pacific Review*, vol. 20, no. 1, pp. 75–99.

Davidson, JS 2009, *From rebellion to riots: collective violence on Indonesian Borneo*, NUS Press, Singapore.

Fossati, D 2016, 'Is Indonesian local government accountable to the poor? Evidence from health policy implementation', *Journal of East Asian Studies*, vol. 16, no. 3, pp. 307–330.

Hatherell, M 2019, *Political representation in Indonesia: the emergence of the innovative technocrats*, Routledge, London and New York.

Husodo, AT 2018, 'Dirty money, rotten politicians: KPK targets local leaders', *Indonesia at Melbourne*, 6 December, viewed 11 February 2021, <https://indonesiaatmelbourne

.unimelb.edu.au/dirty-money-rotten-politicians-kpk-arrests-record-number-of-local -leaders/>.

Ilmma, A & Wai-Poi, M 2014, 'Patterns of regional poverty in the new Indonesia', in H Hill (ed.), *Regional dynamics in a decentralised Indonesia*, Institute of Southeast Asian Studies, Singapore, pp. 98–131.

Institute for Policy Analysis of Conflict 2020, *Covid-19 and conflict in Papua*, IPAC Short Briefing No. 2, IPAC, Jakarta.

International Crisis Group 2006, *Islamic law and criminal justice in Aceh*, Asia Report No. 117, ICG, Jakarta/Brussels.

Jakarta Post 2019, 'Appellate court extends Irwandi Yusuf's prison term, political participation ban', 15 August, viewed 11 February 2021, <https://www.thejakartapost .com/news/2019/08/15/appellate-court-extends-irwandi-yusufs-prison-term-political -participation-ban.html>.

Kristiansen, S & Ramli, M 2006, 'Buying an income: the market for civil service positions in Indonesia', *Contemporary Southeast Asia*, vol. 28, no. 2, pp. 207–233.

McRae, D & Zhang, D 2015, 'Local elections: the power of incumbency', *Indonesia at Melbourne*, 8 December, viewed 11 February 2021, <https://indonesiaatmelbourne .unimelb.edu.au/local-elections-the-power-of-incumbency/>.

Menteri Dalam Negeri Republik Indonesia 2019, *Peraturan Menteri Dalam Negeri Republik Indonesia Nomor 72 Tahun 2019 Tentang Perubahan Atas Peraturan Menteri Dalam Negeri Republik Indonesia Nomor 137 Tahun 2017 tentang Kode dan Data Wilayah Administrasi Pemerintahan*, Menteri Dalam Negeri Republik Indonesia, Jakarta.

Mietzner, M 2010, 'Indonesia's direct elections: empowering the electorate or entrenching the New Order oligarchy?' in E Aspinall & G Fealy (eds), *Soeharto's new order and its legacy*, ANU E Press, Canberra, pp. 173–190.

Mietzner, M 2014, 'Indonesia's decentralisation: the rise of local identities and the survival of the nation-state', in H Hill (ed.), *Regional Dynamics in a Decentralised Indonesia*, Institute of Southeast Asian Studies, Singapore, pp. 45–67.

Movanita, ANK 2018, Kapolri sebut biaya kampanye pilkada sampai Rp 100 miliar ciptakan budaya korup', *Kompas*, 6 March, viewed 11 February 2021, <https://nasional .kompas.com/read/2018/03/06/17375041/kapolri-sebut-biaya-kampanye-pilkada -sampai-rp-100-miliar-ciptakan-budaya>.

Mustholih 2019, 'KPK sebut Sumut provinsi terkorup di Indonesia', *Media Indonesia*, 12 April, viewed 11 February 2021, <https://mediaindonesia.com/read/detail/229265 -kpk-sebut-sumut-provinsi-terkorup-di-indonesia>.

Nolan, C, Jones, S & Solahuddin 2014, 'The political impact of carving up Papua', in H Hill (ed.), *Regional dynamics in a decentralised Indonesia*, Institute of Southeast Asian Studies, Singapore, pp. 409–432.

Nugroho, J 2020, 'Indonesia's Omnibus Law won't kill corruption', *Lowy Interpreter*, 4 December, viewed 11 February 2021, <https://www.lowyinstitute.org/the-interpreter /indonesia-s-omnibus-law-won-t-kill-corruption>.

Ostwald, K, Tajima, Y & Samphantharak, K 2016, 'Indonesia's decentralisation experiment: motivations, successes, and unintended consequences', *Journal of Southeast Asian Economies*, vol. 33, no. 2, pp. 139–156.

Patunru, AA & Rahman, EA 2014, 'Local governance and development outcomes', in H Hill (ed.) *Regional dynamics in a decentralised Indonesia*, Institute of Southeast Asian Studies, Singapore, pp. 156–185.

Ramage, DE 1997, *Politics in Indonesia: democracy, Islam and the ideology of tolerance*, Routledge, London and New York.

Resosudarmo, BP, Mollet, JA, Raya, UR & Kaiwai, H 2014, 'Development in Papua after special autonomy', in H Hill (ed.), *Regional dynamics in a decentralised Indonesia*, Institute of Southeast Asian Studies, Singapore, pp. 433–459.

Savirani, A 2016, 'Survival against the odds: the Djunaid family of Pekalongan, Central Java', *South East Asia Research*, vol. 24, no. 3, pp. 407–419.

Schulze, KE 2001, 'The East Timor referendum crisis and its impact on Indonesian politics', *Studies in Conflict and Terrorism*, vol. 24, no. 1, pp. 77–82.

Schulze, KE 2004, *The Free Aceh Movement (GAM): anatomy of a separatist organization*, Policy Studies no. 2, East-West Center, Washington DC.

Sjahrir, BS, Kis-Katos, K & Schulze, GG 2014, 'Administrative overspending in Indonesian districts: the role of local politics', *World Development*, vol. 59, pp. 166–183.

Tomsa, D 2015, 'Toning down the big bang: the politics of decentralisation during the Yudhoyono years', E Aspinall, M Mietzner & D Tomsa (eds), *The Yudhoyono presidency: Indonesia's decade of stability and stagnation*, Institute of Southeast Asian Studies, Singapore, pp. 155–174.

Trihartono, A 2014, 'Beyond measuring the voice of the people: the evolving role of political polling in Indonesia's local leader elections', *Southeast Asian Studies*, vol. 3, no. 1, pp. 151–182.

Van Klinken, G 2007, *Communal violence and democratization in Indonesia: small town wars*, Routledge, London and New York.

Ward, K 1974, *The 1971 election in Indonesia: an East Java case study*, Monash Papers on Southeast Asia No. 2, Monash University, Centre of Southeast Asian Studies, Clayton.

World Bank 2003, *Decentralizing Indonesia: a regional public expenditure review overview report*, World Bank – East Asia Poverty Reduction and Economic Management Unit, Jakarta.

5 The Judiciary

Introduction

In 2014 – and again in 2019 – presidential candidate Prabowo Subianto appealed to Indonesia's Constitutional Court (Mahkamah Konstitusi, MK) to challenge the election results. In both instances, the Prabowo team based their appeal on a number of alleged issues, including errors in vote counting by the General Election Commission (Komisi Pemilihan Umum, KPU), fraud in voter lists and money politics. In both instances, the Court rejected the entire claim and stated that the case put forward by Prabowo's team did not provide strong evidence. The Prabowo camp's claims were by no means unique in that election disputes – whether national, provincial, or at the city and district level – have been regularly heard by the Constitutional Court. Though the Court dismissed most electoral disputes for lack of evidence, in some cases, it has actually ordered recounts or even a re-election. By hearing and deciding on electoral disputes, the Court has ensured that electoral processes are free and fair and occasional errors do not negate the results or credibility of elections (Butt 2015). This also illustrates that the Constitutional Court is at the centre of major political events.

The Constitutional Court is a relative newcomer in Indonesia's judicial landscape. Established in 2003, the Court responded to lacunae in Indonesia's legal system where there was no institution that was mandated to review the constitutionality of laws and have the power to declare them unconstitutional. In addition, the Court's establishment was a response to an absence of the courts in presiding over political matters (Mietzner 2010). That until then courts were largely unable to adjudicate in political conflicts was the result of decades in which the power of the judiciary – and in particular the Supreme Court, the highest institution in Indonesia's judicial system – was eroded through political interference, corruption and mismanagement (Pompe 2005). The democratisation process in 1998 opened up new opportunities for the judiciary to provide checks and balances on executive power. But while the Constitutional Court, along with the Corruption Eradication Commission (Komisi Pemberantasan Korupsi, KPK) and its associated anti-corruption courts, has seized these opportunities and become

DOI: 10.4324/9780429459511-5

an important pillar of Indonesian democracy, other sections of the judiciary have remained remarkably resistant to reform.

This chapter will discuss some of the reforms that were introduced after 1998 and analyse why efforts to enhance the independence of the judiciary and to bolster institutions that can provide checks and balances remain strongly contested and sometimes actively resisted. In doing so, it will pay particular attention to what many observers regard as one of the biggest challenges of this sector: corruption. Overall, the chapter will argue that despite some achievements in combatting corruption and advancing judicial reform, the courts remain one of the weakest links in Indonesia's institutional set-up due to inadequate budgets and facilities, the uneven implementation of court decisions, ongoing political interference in legal processes and embedded practices of nepotism and bribery.

The chapter will begin with a brief historical background of the legal system, focusing on the main challenges that came to the forefront under the New Order: corruption and executive control over the judiciary. The chapter will then give an overview of the general reforms that took place after 1998, focusing particularly on the Supreme Court. To highlight the diverse range of courts that operate in Indonesia, the chapter will then consider how Islam influences the judiciary, by considering the Religious Courts and the Sharia Courts in Aceh. In the last two sections, the chapter discusses the establishment and development of the Constitutional Court and the KPK.

The Judiciary under the New Order

Following the events of 1965, the new government that rose to power went to great lengths to differentiate itself from the Sukarno government. One example of this was a new emphasis on constitutionalism and legality (Lev 2011, Pompe 2005), including an emphasis on human rights in political discourses while legal instruments were also used to portray the New Order government and its policies as legitimate (Lubis 1993). Initial pledges to reinstate parliamentary democracy and the rule of law (Pompe 2005, p. 77), however, were soon exposed to be mere lip service to improve Indonesia's international standing and attract investors and aid (Lev 2011). It is therefore unsurprising that the shifts in power that took place following 1965 did not strengthen the independence of the judiciary.

Indeed, as soon as Suharto's position became more secure, the political standing and influence of the judiciary declined. This became particularly evident in 1970 when the Law on the Basic Principles of the Judiciary was passed. This law, which formed the foundation of the place and role of the judiciary in the New Order period (Pompe 2005, p. 79), had a number of provisions which significantly reduced the authority of the judiciary, even though it also contained a commitment to the independence of the judiciary (Bourchier 1999, p. 202). Amongst others, this law determined that court administration came under the control of the Ministry of Justice, and that constitutional review of laws passed by parliament would not be allowed (Pompe 2005, pp. 100–101). While the law established that the Supreme Court would act as the court of final appeal for all other courts, it also determined that court administration, including budgeting, would be the task of relevant government departments. This meant that the general courts, and later the administrative courts (established in 1991), fell under the Ministry of Justice, the religious courts under the Ministry of Religious Affairs, and the military courts under the Ministry of Defence (Pompe 2005, pp. 109–110). This administrative structure also meant that judges had a strong incentive to comply with their superiors in the bureaucracy to advance their career (Bourchier 1999, p. 203). As such, the law enabled the New Order regime to exert control over the judiciary.

In addition to the limitations placed on the judiciary through regulations, the regime also controlled the legal system through the appointment of military figures or other political loyalists to important positions in the judicial system, including the posts of Attorney General and chief of the Supreme Court. Although the power of the Supreme Court was limited through the 1970 law, it was given wide powers to correct 'judicial errors' of lower courts. This created a legal apparatus that was aligned with the interests of the executive, and where corruption was rife (Bourchier 1999, p. 203–204).

It was therefore evident that during the New Order, the role and power of the judiciary was heavily restricted, and that the government was also often hostile to its goals and interests. As a result,

> judges grew up and made their careers in an environment that accorded neither respect nor relevance to their function. It deeply demoralised the judiciary, contributed to the dramatic weakening of its professional capabilities and boosted corruption in a service that until 1970 had still been relatively clean.
> (Pompe 2005, p. 111)

Needless to say, when the New Order fell, there was not only a pressing need to reform the judiciary but also profound challenges to enable these changes to succeed.

Reforming the Judiciary

Following the end of the New Order, many reforms were targeted at strengthening the judiciary. The Supreme Court was central to many of these reforms, as strengthening of this Court in particular was believed to benefit the judiciary as a whole. Among other changes, the constitutional amendments between 1999 and 2002 restored the separation of powers needed for judicial independence. Other regulatory changes, as well as internal reforms, sought to improve the functioning and standing of the courts.

A major structural change was the introduction of the so-called one roof (*satu atap*) reforms which gave the Supreme Court jurisdiction of all matters of court administration, including the Religious Courts (Crouch 2019). The purpose of these changes was to bring control over the lower courts from the government to the Supreme Court to improve judicial independence. Supervision of the judiciary, meanwhile, was addressed by the 2001 establishment of the Judicial Commission (Komisi Yudisial, KY). This Commission is charged with supervising judges' compliance with codes of conduct, advises parliament on judicial appointments and reviews complaints about the behaviour of judges (Lindsey & Butt 2018). In addition, the budget of the Court has gradually increased, including the salary of judges to address entrenched corruption. Other changes have touched upon transparency, for instance, through the publication of court decisions, new opportunities for professional development and more training, while access to the court has been improved by waiving fees for the poor (Assegaf 2019).

Overall, these reforms have made a positive impact on the functioning of the Supreme Court. In sharp contrast to practices under the New Order, the Court has not shied away from cases involving the government, political parties and big businesses, and has occasionally ruled against their interest. For example, the Court has revoked government licences in cases such as the construction of cement companies in Central Java's Kendeng mountain region. In its ruling (2016), the Supreme Court held that the construction of cement factories in this region violated Kendeng's status as an area of geological importance, thereby deciding in favour of farmers who had long protested the mining activities (Walton 2018). The Supreme Court also adjudicated in politically sensitive cases such as internal leadership conflict within the Golkar Party, in which the Court ruled against the government decision to support Agung Laksono as Golkar chairperson (Mietzner 2016). The Court has also convicted members of parliament and other high-ranking officials in corruption cases, including by overturning acquittal decisions by lower courts (Assegaf 2019, p. 41). This illustrates a growing confidence within the judiciary, and particularly the Supreme Court, to tackle politically sensitive cases.

At the same time, concerns remain. For instance, the implementation of decisions is uneven, and the Court remains subject to political interference: in the Kendeng case, for instance, the Governor of Central Java Ganjar Pranowo refused to accept the ruling and instead issued a new law permitting factories to continue mining (Walton 2018). In another notable example from 2007, a Suharto loyalist judge was appointed in a case against *Time* magazine, which had published critical reports about the Suharto family, even if the decision that ruled in favour of Suharto was later overturned (Wiratraman 2014). Members of parliament have also used their influence over judicial appointments and budgeting to secure cases involving their political parties and allies. In addition, in the broader judiciary, inadequate budgets and facilities continue to challenge the functioning of the courts, resulting in their dependency on local governments, and even businesses. Examples of this include district judges receiving free housing and cars from businesses such as Freeport in Papua, and the local government in Surabaya. Similarly, the courts are dependent on good relationships with the security apparatus to ensure they are willing to safeguard trials (Assegaf 2019, pp. 41–42). These relationships and dependencies may impact negatively on judicial independence when courts hear cases involving these parties.

Embedded practices of nepotism and bribery are also difficult to shake off. The Supreme Court remains reluctant towards oversight from other institutions such as the Judicial Commission (Assegaf 2019; Lindsey & Butt 2018). In fact, the Supreme Court has ignored most of the Commission's recommendations (Tehusijarana 2019) and has gone to great lengths to minimise oversight, including through a 2006 appeal to the Constitutional Court. The Constitutional Court decided in the Supreme Court's favour, stating that the Commission's reviews might place 'unjustifiable' pressure on judges (Lindsey & Butt 2018). These developments have weakened public confidence in the Court (Assegaf 2019, p. 43). Taken together, there has been some noteworthy progress in judicial reform since 1998; however, the extent of that progress has been limited as a result of resistance from power holders, entrenched corruption and limited success of reforms in other political and legal institutions.

Islam and the Courts

The position of Islam in Indonesia's political and legal structures has been the subject of recurring debate. To the dismay of many pious Muslims, the words 'Islam', 'Islamic law' and 'sharia' do not feature in the Constitution (Elson 2009). In fact, although Indonesia is widely known as the world's largest Muslim nation, it is not an Islamic state, and Islam is not the official state religion (Otto 2010). At the same time, however, Indonesia cannot be considered a fully secular state either: the first principle of Pancasila is 'the belief in One Almighty God'. To translate this principle into state policy and practice, the Indonesian state structure has since the earliest years of independence, included the Ministry of Religious Affairs, which was established in 1946. One important aspect where the presence of Islamic – or sharia – law in Indonesia's judiciary is evident are the Religious Courts.

Under the New Order, the Religious Courts were formally designated as one of the four pillars of the Indonesian judicial system (Van Huis 2019). A law passed in 1989 on the Religious Courts allowed for the establishment of these courts at the district level, with jurisdiction for marriage (including polygamous marriages) and divorce, inheritance, and religious endowments. Furthermore, the law stipulated that Religious Appellate Courts were provided at the provincial level, while oversight was to be in the hands of the executive – in this case, the Ministry of Religious Affairs (Otto 2010) – in line with the organisation of the administration of other courts.

Throughout Indonesian political history, the Religious Courts have been a site of contestation between secular and religious authority. In 1973, for instance, the New Order government was convinced it would be able to pass a Marriage Bill that included significant legal reforms and a transfer of jurisdiction on certain Islamic family law matters from the Religious Courts to the civil courts. Islamic opposition to these plans was fierce, however, and as a consequence the government gave in to the demands of Muslim organisations. The more controversial articles were removed, and the Religious Courts retained their jurisdiction in marriage, divorce and polygamy (Van Huis 2019).

Following the end of the New Order, judicial reform also affected the Religious Courts. This included the recognition of the Religious Courts in the constitution and the designation of the Supreme Court, rather than the Ministry of Religious Affairs, as administrator of all court branches. In 2006, the 1989 law was amended, expanding the Courts' jurisdiction to include matters of Islamic finance. This amendment also acknowledged the special status of Religious Courts in autonomous regions, most notably the Sharia Courts in Aceh, which are discussed below. While in practice the majority of the work of the Religious Courts is related to marriage and divorce (Lindsey & Butt 2018), the changes surrounding the courts illustrate that they are both increasingly incorporated into Indonesia's civil legal system and a reflection of the mainstreaming of Islam in Indonesian politics.

The establishment of Sharia Courts in Aceh cannot be separated from the devolution of power that characterised Indonesia after 1998 (see Chapter 4), and efforts to resolve the long-running conflict in the region. As President Habibie called for the violence in Aceh to cease, there were increasing calls for a referendum on independence for Aceh – not dissimilar to developments in East Timor. Instead, a Law on Special Autonomy was passed that included provisions for the implementation of Islamic law. Subsequent Indonesian presidents Abdurrahman Wahid and Megawati Sukarnoputri promoted a religious approach in order to secure stability in Aceh. This played into the hands of conservative Muslims and in particular Aceh's branch of the Indonesian Council of Islamic Scholars (Majelis Ulama Indonesia, MUI), which had already issued several Islamising *fatwa*, such as the obligation for women to wear veils. More *qanun* or regional regulations soon followed (Ichwan 2007), and in 2001, the Nanggroe Aceh Darusalam Autonomy Law was passed. Following the enactment of the law, the Aceh government set up a 27-member all-male council of *ulama*, which positioned itself as a fourth branch of government in Aceh, alongside the judiciary, legislature and executive (Harsono 2019, p. 14). The Special Autonomy Law was also the basis on which the Sharia Courts were established the following year. The jurisdiction of the Sharia Courts in Aceh is more expansive than the Religious Courts, including criminal offences related to alcohol, gambling and *khalwat*, or unmarried and unrelated individuals of different sexes being together in isolated spaces (Feener 2014).

In 2006, the Law on Special Autonomy of Aceh further regulated the mandate of the provincial government to issue *qanun* and the jurisdiction of the Sharia Courts. The 2006 law confirmed the validity of regulations that had emerged since 2002, most notably the *qanun* that criminalised gambling and drinking, and prescribed the corporal punishment of caning. It also broadened the jurisdiction of the Sharia Courts by adding elements of criminal and commercial law. Finally, the 2006 law also determined that every adherent of Islam must obey and carry out Islamic law, and everybody who lives or is present in Aceh is obliged to respect the implementation of Islamic law, irrespective of their religion (Otto 2010).

Box 5.1: Human Rights and Sharia Law in Aceh

Aceh is the only province in Indonesia that is authorised to implement sharia law. Supporters of sharia law claim that this is a complete system that provides guidance on all matters in life, and ultimately promotes values such as charity, social welfare and communal harmony. However, human rights advocates have claimed that its application in Aceh has negative effects on many groups in society, particularly the poor, women and young people, denying them the right to make personal decisions that are central to their lives and the expression of their identity. These sharia-based ordinances (*qanun*) apply to all of Aceh's population, including non-Muslims (Harsono 2019). One ordinance that has been criticised particularly strongly by human rights organisations prohibits 'seclusion' between unmarried individuals from different sexes and who are not related by blood to be together in isolated places (*khalwat*). Violations of this law are punishable by caning, a six-month jail term and/or monetary fines. While passed to prevent adultery, the wording of the law is so broad that it can be applied to a much wider range of behaviours, including merely sitting and talking to a member of the opposite sex, irrespective of any evidence of intimacy. Abuses that have taken place in the course of investigations under this law include the forced submission of women and girls to virginity exams, rape and forced marriage to secure release. Another law that impinges on human rights standards are those pertaining to Islamic dress. Acehnese law requires that all Muslims wear Islamic attire; however, far more strict requirements are placed on women. Implementation of this law is often arbitrary and is disproportionally targeted at women as well as the poor. Transgender women too are susceptible for being targeted by the Sharia Police. Other regulations have imposed curfews on women, supposedly to reduce sexual violence, while in some parts of the province men and women are forbidden to have meals together unless they are married or related. Exercise has also been limited with a ban on football for women. Despite these limitations, many Acehnese, including younger people, support sharia law, stating that it is in line with Acehnese traditions. Sharia law in Aceh has also influenced the development of other regional regulations in Indonesia with local governments looking at Aceh to implement dress codes and other regulations based on Islam, restricting women's rights. While there have been some attempts to change the way that sharia law is applied, Islamic groups continue to argue that the strict penal code and the public nature of punishments have a deterrent effect.

While the implementation of Aceh's *qanun* was initially considered by most Acehnese as symbolic, the 2004 tsunami and its aftermath saw a strong religious revival in the region, including an appeal to strengthen Islamic law and the role of the state in implementing this (Feener 2013). This has been reflected in an increasing willingness of Islamic courts to exercise their jurisdiction (Lindsey & Hooker 2007). Human rights organisations have recorded that since the enactment of Aceh's *qanun* in 2001, there has been an increase in human rights abuses (see Box 5.1), which is disproportionally felt by women and sexual minorities (Harsono 2019, p. 16). In 2015, Aceh's Sharia Criminal Code was enacted, and according to Human Rights Watch (2017) more than 300 people were punished by caning in the first year. Nevertheless, many Acehnese support the regulations, stating that they are in line with Acehnese traditions (Salvá 2019).

The Constitutional Court

As discussed above, key concerns pertaining to the Indonesian judiciary – and in particular the Supreme Court – included that there was no judicial review of the constitutionality of laws and that the courts were unable to respond to political conflict. The latter in particular came to the fore in the early years of *reformasi*, when three major events posed a profound threat to political stability: first, the 1998 special session of the People's Consultative Assembly (Majelis Permusyawaratan Rakyat, MPR), where a standoff between the security apparatus and demonstrating students led to the killing of 17 people; second, electoral disputes in 1999 for which no recourse was available, and third, the 2001 impeachment of President Abdurrahman Wahid, a process that was not adequately provided for in the Constitution. The absence of clear judicial processes and arbitrators thus not only resulted in unrest, but also allowed for a greater role for the military in politics (Mietzner 2010, pp. 401–403).

Rather than opting for reforming the Supreme Court, legislators voted in favour of the establishment of a new court during the last round of constitutional amendments in 2002, and the Constitutional Court was established the following year. The decision to establish a new court reflected broader trends in transitional democracies where constitutional courts are believed to support transition to and consolidation of stable democratic regimes (Horowitz 2006, p. 128). The Indonesian Constitutional Court has five main functions, including constitutional review, investigating allegations of electoral impropriety or error, settling conflicts between state institutions, dissolving political parties that have violated certain regulations and providing a decision if parliament suspects that either the president or the vice-president has committed treason or corruption or any other serious crimes (Butt 2015). This mandate thus placed the court at the forefront of Indonesian politics, as well as legal and democratic progress.

The Constitutional Court sits independent from Indonesia's other courts. It is the court of first and final instance in matters over which it has jurisdiction. Following its establishment, it quickly developed a reputation as Indonesia's most respected and independent court (Lindsey & Butt 2018). A key factor contributing to this reputation has been the introduction of a multitrack recruitment system, whereby nine judges serve five-year, renewable terms, appointed by the president, parliament and the Supreme Court, with each of these filling three positions. This has created a diverse composition and has reduced dependency of judges on their nominating institution. In addition, the provision of budgetary autonomy has enabled the Court to offer judges better salary packages, which have proven sufficiently attractive to help reduce incentives for corruption (Mietzner 2010). Furthermore, leadership also played an important role. The first chief justice of the Court, Jimly Asshiddiqie, spent considerable time to ensure that the Court was taken seriously. This included not only his insistence on the building of an elaborate neoclassical courthouse, but also his strong support for the professional development of judges (Butt 2012, Roux 2019).

Since its establishment, the Court has been frequently lauded for its progressive stance, thereby contributing to democratic practices (Dressel & Bünte 2014, p. 15). Between 2005 and 2008, for example, the Court determined that the national budget for education was unconstitutional, as less than the 20 percent stated in the Constitution had been allocated. The Court urged the government and legislature to meet the 20 percent requirement, but legislators were slow to respond; so in 2008, the Court invalidated the budget and thus effectively imposed a 20 percent allocation from the state budget starting in 2009 (Butt 2015, pp. 128–129). The Court has also taken on issues of civil and political rights. In late 2018, it held that the marriage age of 16 for girls as provided for in Indonesia's Marriage Law was unconstitutional. In its ruling, the Court stated that marrying at such a young age violates children's rights to education and a healthy life as guaranteed by the constitution. Referring to Indonesia's obligations to international human rights treaties, the Court reversed a decision on the same issue it had made three years prior (Afrianty 2019). These decisions illustrate that the Constitutional Court represents an effective pathway through which Indonesian citizens and rights groups can challenge government policies and even earlier decisions made by the Court (Rosser 2015, p. 199).

At the same time, there have been concerns about the politicisation of the court and its attempts to make its decisions more politically acceptable (Butt 2012). This was, for instance, reflected in some decisions that seemed to focus on maintaining social order, including the appeasement of conservative Islamic groups. The most conspicuous example of this was a ruling about the controversial Blasphemy Law in 2009. A coalition of legal aid and human rights groups challenged the law in the court, arguing that it was against a number of constitutional provisions, including the right to freedom of religion. In response to this challenge, a wide range of submissions in favour of the law were submitted, including from high-ranking government representatives and influential Islamic organisations. Court proceedings were often disrupted by the vocal presence of radical Islamic groups. Given the strong public interest, the Constitutional Court approached this case very carefully. In the end, it decided that the Blasphemy Law was constitutional, but it also acknowledged the need to reform this law and tasked the legislature to do so. A consequence of this decision was that the state retained broad powers to place limitations on religious freedom, while some authority was given to religious leaders to determine the 'correct' interpretations of religions (Crouch 2012).

Over time, it has also become apparent that despite the multitrack appointment system and greater remuneration of judges, the Court is not immune from corruption (Dressel & Bünte 2014). In 2013, the Constitutional Court's chief justice Akil Mochtar was caught red-handed receiving bribes in an election dispute. In 2017, another judge, Patrialis Akbar, was also prosecuted for receiving money in a review case. Akbar was sentenced to eight years imprisonment by the Jakarta Anti-Corruption Court, while Mochtar was sentenced to life imprisonment (Lindsey & Butt 2018). Both cases caused serious damage to the reputation of the Court and resulted in calls from civil society groups for greater transparency and better regulation of the appointment procedure for judges (Aziezi 2016).

Corruption

The corruption cases involving Akil Mochtar and Patrialis Akbar showed just how pervasive corruption is in contemporary Indonesia. The two Constitutional Court judges joined hundreds of legislators, local government heads, bureaucrats and businesspeople who have been convicted for corruption in Indonesia since the beginning of the reformasi era. According to Transparency International's Corruption Perception Index, a commonly cited global corruption survey by experts and businesspeople that considers perceived levels of public sector corruption, Indonesia made some noticeable progress in its fight against corruption over the years (for example through the aforementioned high-profile arrests), but the positive trend was reversed in 2020 when the country's score in the CPI fell for the first time in many years (see Figure 5.1). Accordingly, Indonesia's ranking dropped from 85th to 102nd out of 180 countries in the 2020 index (Transparency International 2021).

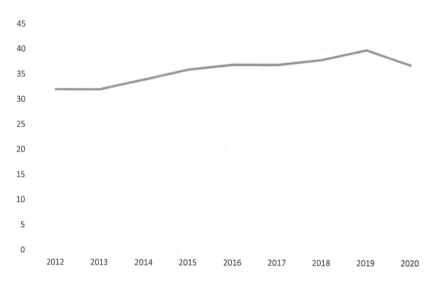

Figure 5.1 Indonesia in the Corruption Perception Index, 2012–2020

Corruption can take a wide variety of forms, ranging from so-called petty corruption, where individuals pay a small bribe to speed up the delivery of services, to the payment of large sums to individuals or organisations to achieve certain outcomes, including the granting of business licences and favourable judicial decisions. Back in the New Order, the courts had played a key role in institutionalised corruption as they evolved into a branch of the executive that ensured that the military and the bureaucracy could do whatever they wanted, even if corruption was officially illegal. Today, the institutionalised corruption inherited from the Suharto era remains deeply entrenched, not only but also especially in the judiciary. Despite some achievements in making courts operate more independently, decisions can still be 'bought' at virtually all levels of the judicial system. As such, more than two decades after the fall of authoritarianism, courts do not provide an effective forum for the resolution of cases (Lindsey & Butt 2018).

The main bulwark against corruption in Indonesia is the Corruption Eradication Commission (Komisi Pemberantasan Korupsi, KPK). Established in 2003, the KPK has the legal mandate to investigate and prosecute corruption cases, monitor government agencies and coordinate and supervise anti-corruption institutions. At the time of its establishment, the KPK was granted investigative powers that the police lack, including wiretapping, the freezing of bank accounts and the ability to issue travel bans. In order to prevent prosecutions from being dropped in return for bribes, the KPK was not allowed to abandon any cases once they had progressed beyond an initial investigation. The commission also had the authority to take control of a case handled by the police or prosecutors, a response to the general perception that these bodies were usually ineffective in pursuing corruption cases. The quality and integrity of KPK commissioners was supported through a rigorous and transparent, as well as competitive, appointment process. Overall, appointments to the KPK have been well-regarded (Butt 2011, p. 382).

The Anti-Corruption Courts associated with the KPK were established within the Central Jakarta district court, and their only function is to hear cases that the KPK prosecutes. Appeals are available within the jurisdiction of the Jakarta High Court and subsequently the Supreme Court. While initially only established in Jakarta, from 2009 Anti-Corruption Courts were also established in all of Indonesia's provinces (Crouch 2019, p. 5). These courts have been lauded for their success, which has been attributed to the use of three so-called ad hoc judges on a five-judge panel. These judges are usually drawn from academics, retired judges and lawyers. As non-career judges, they have a reputation for being more professional because they do not work in the existing judiciary. Anti-Corruption Courts have not held back in prosecuting high-profile figures, with defendants ranging from senior officials of major political parties and legislators to governors and mayors as well as bureaucrats and businesspeople. The KPK's indiscriminate pursuit of justice, coupled with its near 100 percent conviction rate, greatly enhanced the commission's popular legitimacy (Butt 2011, p. 383), even though at the provincial levels some judges became entangled in corruption scandals, with some even being caught red-handed (Butt 2019a).

However, the popularity of the KPK and its willingness to examine high-profile figures have also resulted in pushback from political elites and the police against the commission. In 2009, two KPK commissioners were arrested by the police and accused of bribery. Earlier, the National Chief of Police had found that the Commission had been tapping his phone in the course of an investigation. The Chief then compared the Commission to a common house gecko that was fighting a crocodile – the police. The case led to the suspension of the KPK commissioners, who were arrested on charges of extortion and bribery. The commissioners denied the charges and said they were framed to weaken the Commission.

The so-called Gecko vs. Crocodile case captured the imagination of the Indonesian public, and many used social media to rally support for the embattled commission. Most Indonesians thought of the charges as fabricated and as the case against the KPK commissioners evolved, a Facebook group of more than 1 million members emerged. Facebook supporters took their activism to the streets in a show of support of the gecko (or the Commission), and by doing so successfully forced the government to act in accordance with public demands and drop the anti-corruption charges (Lim 2013).

The 'Gecko vs. Crocodile' affair was not an isolated event. In 2014, newly elected President Joko Widodo announced his plan to appoint Budi Gunawan as national police chief. The KPK then revealed that Gunawan was under investigation, and asked for him not to be appointed. Once again, the police retaliated by charging all KPK commissioners with various offences, without providing evidence, similar to what had happened in 2009. In 2017, Novel Baswedan, a leading KPK investigator tasked with investigating police corruption, was attacked with acid in Jakarta, nearly blinding him. It took three years before two members of the police force were eventually charged and sentenced to minor jail sentences for the attack, but Baswedan and human rights activists expressed doubt that the jailed men were the actual perpetrators (ABC 2020).

It is not only the police though that has tried to weaken the KPK. Similarly, national legislators have consistently threatened to reduce the commission's powers, cut its budget or disband it altogether (Butt 2019a). In 2019, these efforts came to a climax when parliament passed amendments to the establishing law of the commission, which are likely to have far-reaching implications as they affect fundamental features of the KPK. They include a removal of the prohibition to ban investigations and prosecutions, as well as a limitation of the commission's investigative powers. Wiretapping, for instance, which in the past was crucial for obtaining evidence, is now subject to approval from a Supervisory Board, which in turn is appointed by the president. This is expected to slow down the investigative process, and no criteria have been formulated for the Board to consider in approving a wiretapping application. This makes the operation of the KPK highly dependent on the Board and its presidential appointees (Butt 2019b).

The amendments were passed through parliament extremely fast, behind closed doors, and without input from the commission or external experts, despite mass protests around the country against the amendments. Moreover, only 107 legislators were present to vote on the amendments – well below the

281 required, although the speaker of parliament claimed that 289 cast their vote, some via messaging applications. Official justifications for the amendments argue that reform of the organisation was needed to enhance the effectiveness of the KPK. Lawmakers have maintained that the amendments were necessary because of alleged weak coordination between the KPK and other law enforcement bodies, violations of regulations by the staff and overlapping powers between the KPK and other institutions. In addition, some legislators also suggested that corruption had actually increased since the body was established (Butt 2019b).

However, there is little evidence to support these allegations. Civil society organisations in Indonesia have widely refuted these arguments and have said that the amendments were pushed through as legislators and their powerful allies fear investigation by the KPK. They have also long advocated for the budget for the KPK to be increased, so that the commission can handle more cases. If anything, the pressures that the KPK and the Anti-Corruption Courts are confronted with illustrate that the process of tackling corruption in an environment where corruption is endemic, is highly complex and is likely to fall victim to political interests (Aspinall 2019, Schütte 2011).

Conclusion

This chapter has sketched the evolution and key features of the Indonesian judiciary. It showed that at the end of the New Order, the judicial system was in disarray. Decades of authoritarian rule had left the judiciary institutionally weak, and with corruption rampant at all levels of the system, there was little public confidence in the legal system. To overcome this after the end of the New Order, the justice sector in Indonesia has witnessed significant reforms. These reforms have sought to address key issues, including judicial independence, a lack of oversight mechanisms, the judiciary's inability to arbitrate in political disputes and entrenched corruption. Reforms have included bringing all courts under the jurisdiction of the Supreme Court, thereby removing executive control. Much attention has been paid to the professional development and appointment of judges, as well as their remuneration. The need to have an institution that could arbitrate in political conflicts was addressed through the establishment of the Constitutional Court. Moreover, in a bid to tackle entrenched corruption, the Corruption Eradication Commission was established and for a significant period of time this commission, along with its associated Anti-Corruption Courts, enjoyed high levels of public legitimacy.

While many positive steps have been taken towards the creation of a stronger and more effective legal system, many challenges remain. Although the executive no longer has direct control over the judiciary, court decisions are not always implemented, and on various occasions the courts have fallen victim to political interference. Similarly, the decentralisation of power and special autonomy have created a myriad of regional regulations, many of which in contradiction with human rights norms guaranteed in the Constitution and particularly impacting on women and minorities. Moreover, the rising influence of political Islam and social conservatism has influenced the courts while corruption remains a key impediment to the functioning of the judiciary, continuously damaging public trust in the court system. Finally, the development of the KPK from an island of integrity to an emasculated institution shows the strong resistance of political elites towards reformist institutions and policies. This underlines that although significant inroads towards a stronger legal system have been made after 1998, there is still a long way to go.

References

ABC 2020, 'Indonesian policemen jailed for acid attack on graft investigator Novel Baswedan', 17 July, viewed 25 March 2021, <https://www.abc.net.au/news/2020-07-17/indonesian-policemen-jailed-for-acid-attack-graft-investigator/12465144>.

Afrianty, D 2019, 'Child marriage: Constitutional Court finally ditches religious arguments', viewed 20 March 2021, <https://indonesiaatmelbourne.unimelb.edu.au/child-marriage-constitutional-court-finally-ditches-religious-arguments/>.

Assegaf, RS 2019, 'The Supreme Court: *reformasi*, independence and the failure to ensure legal certainty', in M Crouch (ed.), *The politics of court reform: judicial change and legal culture in Indonesia*, Cambridge University Press, Cambridge, pp. 31–58.

Aspinall, E 2019, 'Fighting corruption when corruption Is pervasive: the case of Indonesia', in ML Weiss and C Chen (eds), *The political logics of anticorruption efforts in Asia*, SUNY Press, Albany, pp. 49–68.

Aziezi, MT 2016, 'Is anyone watching the Constitutional Court judges?', viewed 23 March 2021, <https://indonesiaatmelbourne.unimelb.edu.au/is-anyone-watching-the-constitutional-court-judges/>.

Bourchier, D 1999, 'Magic memos, collusion and judges with attitude: notes on the politics of law in contemporary Indonesia', in K Jayasuriya (ed.), *Law, capitalism and power in Asia: the rule of law and legal institutions*, Routledge, London, pp. 199–215.

Butt, S 2011, 'Anti-corruption reform in Indonesia: an obituary?', *Bulletin of Indonesian Economic Studies*, vol. 47, no. 3, pp. 381–384.

Butt, S 2012, 'Indonesia's Constitutional Court: conservative activist or strategic operator?', in B Dressel (ed.), *The judicialisation of politics in Asia*, Routlegde, London, pp. 98–116.

Butt, S 2015, *The Constitutional Court and democracy in Indonesia*, Brill Nijhoff, Leiden & Boston.

Butt, S 2019a, 'Indonesia's Anti-Corruption Courts and the persistence of judicial culture', in M Crouch (ed.), *The politics of court reform. Judicial change and legal culture in Indonesia*, Cambridge University Press, Cambridge, pp. 151–173.

Butt, S 2019b, 'Amendments spell disaster for the KPK', viewed 20 February 2021, <https://indonesiaatmelbourne.unimelb.edu.au/amendments-spell-disaster-for-the-kpk/>.

Crouch, MA 2012, 'Law and religion in Indonesia: the Constitutional Court and the Blasphemy Law', *Asian Journal of Comparative Law*, vol. 7, no. 1, pp. 1–46.

Crouch, M 2019, 'The judicial reform landscape in Indonesia: innovation, specialisation and the legacy of Dan S. Lev', in M Crouch (ed.), *The politics of court reform: judicial change and legal culture in Indonesia*, Cambridge University Press, Cambridge, pp. 1–28.

Dressel, B & Bünte, M 2014, 'Constitutional politics in Southeast Asia: from contestation to constitutionalism?', *Contemporary Southeast Asia: A Journal of International and Strategic Affairs*, vol. 36, no. 1, pp. 1–22.

Elson, RE 2009, 'Another look at the Jakarta Charter controversy of 1945', *Indonesia*, no. 88, pp. 105–130.

Feener, RM 2013, *Shari'a and social engineering: the implementation of Islamic law in contemporary Aceh*, Indonesia, Oxford University Press, Oxford.

Feener, RM 2014, 'Muslim religious authority in modern Asia: established patterns and evolving profiles', *Asian Journal of Social Science*, vol. 42, no. 5, pp. 501–516.

Harsono, A 2019, *Race, islam and power: ethnic and religious violence in post-Suharto Indonesia*, Monash University Publishing, Melbourne.

Horowitz, DL 2006, 'Constitutional courts: a primer for decisionmakers', *Journal of Democracy*, vol. 17, no. 4, pp. 125–137.

Human Rights Watch 2017, 'Indonesia's Aceh authorities lash hundreds under sharia statutes', viewed 10 March 2021, <https://www.hrw.org/news/2017/02/08/indonesias-aceh-authorities-lash-hundreds-under-sharia-statutes>.

Ichwan, MN 2007, 'The politics of shari'atization: central governmental and regional discourses of shari'a implementation in Aceh', in RM Feener & M Cammack (eds), *Islamic law in contemporary Indonesia: ideas and institutions*, Harvard University Press, Boston, pp. 193–215.

Lev, DS 2011, *No concessions: the life of Yap Thiam Hien, Indonesian human rights lawyer*, University of Washington Press, Seattle.

Lim, M 2013, 'Many clicks but little sticks: social media activism in Indonesia', *Journal of Contemporary Asia*, vol. 13, no. 4, pp. 636–657.

Lindsey, T & Butt, S 2018, *Indonesian law*, Oxford University Press, Oxford.

Lindsey, T & Hooker, MB 2007, 'Shari'a revival in Aceh', in RM Feener & M Cammack (eds), *Islamic law in contemporary Indonesia: ideas and institutions*, Harvard University Press, Boston, pp. 216–254.

Lubis, TM 1993, *In search of human Rights: legal-political dilemmas of Indonesia's New Order 1966–1990*, PT Gramedia Pustaka Utama, Jakarta.

Mietzner, M 2010, 'Political conflict resolution and democratic consolidation in Indonesia: the role of the Constitutional Court', *Journal of East Asian Studies*, vol. 10, no. 3, pp. 397–424.

Mietzner, M 2016, 'Coercing loyalty: coalitional presidentialism and party politics in Jokowi's Indonesia', *Contemporary Southeast Asia*, vol. 38, no. 2, pp. 209–232.

Otto, JM 2010, 'Sharia and national law in Indonesia', in JM Otto (ed.), *Sharia incorporated: a comparative overview of the legal systems of twelve muslim countries in past and present*, Leiden University Press, Leiden, pp. 433–490.

Pompe, S 2005, *The Indonesian Supreme Court: a study of institutional collapse*, Cornell University Press, Ithaca.

Rosser, A 2015, 'Law and the realisation of human rights: insights from Indonesia's education sector', *Asian Studies Review*, vol. 39, no. 2, pp. 194–212.

Roux, T 2019, 'The Constitutional Court: a Levian take on its place in the *Reformasi*', in M Crouch (ed.), *The politics of court reform. Judicial change and legal culture in Indonesia*, Cambridge University Press, Cambridge, pp. 245–264.

Salvá, A 2019, 'Aceh, Indonesia: when dating meets sharia law', viewed 18 March 2021, <https://thediplomat.com/2019/07/aceh-indonesia-when-dating-meets-sharia-law/>.

Schütte, SA 2011, 'Appointing top officials in a democratic Indonesia: the Corruption Eradication Commission', *Bulletin of Indonesian Economic Studies*, vol. 47, no. 3, pp. 355–379.

Tehusijarana, KM 2019, 'Supreme Court snubs most judicial commission recommendations', viewed 15 January 2021, <https://www.thejakartapost.com/news/2019/01/04/supreme-court-snubs-most-judicial-commissions-recommendations.html>.

Transparency International 2021, 'Corruption Perceptions Index', viewed 26 March 2021, <https://www.transparency.org/en/cpi/2020/index/>.

Van Huis, SC 2019, 'The Religious Courts: does Lev's analysis still hold?', in M Crouch (ed), *The politics of court reform: judicial change and legal culture in Indonesia*, Cambridge University Press, Cambridge, pp. 109–132.

Walton, K 2018, 'Indonesia: a concrete block and a hard case', viewed 10 March 2021, <https://www.lowyinstitute.org/the-interpreter/indonesia-concrete-block>.

Wiratraman, HP 2014, *Press freedom, law and politics in Indonesia: a socio-legal study*, Leiden University Press, Leiden.

6 Islam and Politics

Introduction

In late February 2020, as the Covid-19 pandemic was beginning to spread around the world, Indonesia's vice-president Ma'ruf Amin and the then health minister Terawan Agus Putranto attended an Islamic congress in Bangka Belitung. Asked why Indonesia was yet to report its first Covid case, the two government officials claimed that Indonesians would be fine as long as they prayed regularly. A few weeks later, when Indonesia had finally confirmed its first cases but still maintained that its numbers were very low, thousands of Islamic pilgrims gathered in Gowa in South Sulawesi for a mass rally of the global Tablighi Jama'at movement of evangelical Muslims. For several days, local government officials tried in vain to stop the arrival of pilgrims until at last the organisers agreed to close the event on 18 March. At that time, an estimated 8,500 people were already in Gowa for the rally and more than 1,000 of them were later confirmed to have contracted the virus. Yet another month later, millions of Indonesians were getting ready for the annual *mudik*, the mass movement of Indonesians from urban centres back to their home villages to celebrate Idul Fitri, one of the most important days in the Islamic calendar. Well aware of the cultural and religious significance of *mudik*, the government was initially reluctant to acknowledge the health risks associated with mass travel, but eventually decided on 21 April to ban the exodus of city dwellers to their home villages. Many Indonesians, however, were already on the road by then, with many more still following after the ban was announced.

These three vignettes from the early months of the Covid-19 pandemic illustrate the central importance of Islam in Indonesian public life. At the very beginning, piety was seen as a way to stave off the pandemic, while later on, as case numbers began to rise, governments at both the national and local levels found it difficult to enforce strict containment measures if these measures hurt religious sensitivities. As the virus continued to spread, the central government therefore sought support from religious leaders in distributing their health message. In 2020, the three most prominent Islamic organisations in Indonesia, the Indonesian Council of Ulama (Majelis Ulama Indonesia, MUI), Nahdlatul Ulama (NU) and Muhammadiyah, all came out in support of stricter measures, issuing religious rulings (*fatwas*) that ordered their followers 'to avoid mass gatherings at mosques'

DOI: 10.4324/9780429459511-6

(Hosen 2020). Similarly, when Indonesia rolled out its vaccination programme in early 2021, these three organisations again supported the government by issuing *fatwas*, which declared that the vaccine was *halal* and that 'it is an obligation for every Muslim to get vaccinated' (Rochmyaningsih 2021).

The MUI is the highest Islamic authority in Indonesia, while NU and Muhammadiyah are mass organisations with millions of followers, so the *fatwas* of these organisations matter. Significantly, the latter two have a reputation as moderate representatives of what Hefner (2000) once called 'civil Islam', and Indonesia owes much of its image as a tolerant Islamic society to the prominence of these two mass organisations. But Indonesian Islam is diverse, and the country also has a long history of more radical, ideological interpretations of the faith, sometimes described as Islamism. Broadly defined as a 'self-defined Islamic religious agenda [that is pursued] through engagement with the state' (Mecham 2017, p. 12), Islamism usually denotes an ambition to make Islam the main foundation of politics and the law, even though there is much disagreement between Islamists over how this should be achieved. The MUI, for instance, may be regarded as an Islamist organisation, but its bureaucratic-legal approach to Islamising Indonesia differs from the street-based mobilisation of other groups. Significantly, during the Covid-19 pandemic, some Islamist groups initially joined the more moderate Islamic mass organisations in their support for social restrictions, but later in 2020 repeatedly defied bans on mass gatherings, sometimes for religious reasons, sometimes for political purposes.

In fact, tensions between Islamists and moderate pluralists have steadily increased during the Jokowi presidency, raising concerns among observers that polarisation could cause serious damage to the social fabric of Indonesian democracy (Davidson 2018, Warburton 2020). In light of these concerns, this chapter will assess the state of Indonesian Islam as a political force since the end of the Suharto era. It discusses the rise of Islamism, but also highlights that pluralism continues to resonate with many Indonesians, including key members of the political elite. Indeed, under President Jokowi pluralists have made a concerted effort to reclaim seemingly lost ground from the Islamists. In doing so, however, they have not sought to revitalise the fading narrative of democratic reform and tolerance, but rather resorted to a mix of repression and patronage-fuelled co-optation which threatens to further erode the democratic foundations of the Indonesian state.

The chapter will begin with a brief recap of the early evolution of Islam in Indonesia before independence. It then traces the origins of Islamism during the independence struggle and the marginalisation of political Islam during the New Order, before concentrating on the various facets of the relationship between Islam and the state since 1998. After an examination of the role of Islamic parties, the chapter zooms in on the main drivers of Indonesia's conservative turn. A concluding outlook about the prospects for political Islam in Indonesia wraps up the chapter.

Origins of Islam in Indonesia

Muslims are believed to have visited the islands that make up Indonesia today as early as the 8th or 9th century. But the history of Islam in Indonesia begins in earnest in the 13th and 14th centuries when the growing influx of Muslim traders and mystical Islamic teachers from India, China and the Arab and Malay peninsulas set in motion an incremental cultural transition in which several local rulers across the archipelago adopted Islam. The first conversions took place in the northern parts of Sumatra, and from there the new faith gradually spread to Java and other islands further east. Some of the early Islamic states imposed the new religion on rival kingdoms after defeating them in small-scale wars (Ricklefs 2001, p. 16), but the more prominent dynamic in the expansion of Islam was that it was driven by traders and religious saints rather than warriors. Especially in coastal areas located along important trade routes, local rulers often converted to Islam in the hope of gaining better access to the thriving spice trade that passed through the region (Means 2009, p. 21). Further inland, charismatic Muslim saints associated with Sufism, a brand of Islam that focuses on the spiritual and mystical dimensions of the religion rather than the obligations of sharia law (Howell 2001, p. 702), were instrumental in spreading the faith through proselytisation that even reached some aristocrats in the mighty Hindu-Buddhist kingdom of Majapahit.

Indeed, Sufism's influence was particularly strong on the island of Java, where pre-Islamic traditions rooted in animism and Hindu-Buddhism combined with the new religion to forge a 'mystic synthesis' (Ricklefs 2006). Adherents of this mysticism followed the five pillars of Islam – the declaration of faith, the five daily prayers, fasting during Ramadhan, paying alms and performing the pilgrimage to Mecca if one can afford to do so – but at the same time continued to uphold their belief in multiple spiritual forces. Javanese Islam thus became known to be tolerant and accommodating of other belief systems, even though this mystic synthesis manifested itself somewhat differently among the various social classes in Java's hierarchical society. While many rural peasant communities continued to prioritise pre-Islamic rituals, urban and coastal communities tended to be drawn more strongly to Islamic doctrine, resulting in greater concentrations of orthodox Muslims in urban centres and along the coastlines. The differences between these communities were most prominently described by American anthropologist Clifford Geertz (1976), who distinguished between the less pious *abangan* and the more orthodox *santri*.

Over the course of the prolonged Dutch colonial period, Islam gradually developed into a defining feature of personal identity across the archipelago. Although Hinduism survived as the dominant religion on the island of Bali and some Christian communities emerged in the wake of missionary activities in Sumatra and the Eastern parts of the colony (Aritonang & Steenbrink 2008), Islam became widely established by the 18th and 19th centuries. In response, the Dutch sought to accommodate religious leaders into the colonial power structures wherever possible as they were concerned about the potential for religion to morph into a source of anti-colonial resistance. By and large, this strategy was successful, but in some areas Islam did become a focal point for rebellion against the Dutch. Foremost examples include the Padri movement in West Sumatra (1803-1837) and the war in Aceh (1873-1904), the last great war of the colonial era in which local Islamic leaders and their followers fought against the Dutch under the banner of a 'holy war' (Reid 1969).

Emerging Religious Cleavages

By the time the Aceh War ended, a major schism was emerging in the *santri* community that has continued to shape religious dynamics in Indonesia until today. Driven by a group of religious scholars who had just returned to Indonesia after studying in the Middle East, a wave of modernist Islamic thought swept the archipelago, challenging the foundations of the hitherto dominant strand of traditionalist Islam whose religious identity had long been characterised by the 'acceptance and even preservation of beliefs and practices that have evolved in local cultural contexts over the centuries' (Bush 2009, p. 30). The modernists rejected these syncretic influences and the central role granted to Islamic leaders (*ulama* or *kiai*) in interpreting religious doctrine and jurisprudence. Instead, they promoted stricter adherence to the Qur'an itself and to independent judgment (*ijtihad*) of the scriptures. Moreover, modernists sought to align religious piety with the need to increase access to modern science and technology in order to improve socioeconomic living conditions for the *ummah*, or community of believers (Mietzner 2009, p. 72).

The rift between traditionalists and modernists was institutionalised in the formation of two rival mass organisations. In 1912, the modernists established Muhammadiyah, an organisation focused on education and social activities which soon developed a large support base among urban upper- and middle-class Muslims, including many on the outer islands of the archipelago. In 1926, traditionalists followed suit, mustering their own long-running network of Islamic boarding schools (*pesantren*) in East and Central Java to set up NU. Both Muhammadiyah and NU quickly grew into highly influential socio-political organisations with millions of members and significant political clout. In the early years, for example, both groups played important roles in supporting the nationalist movement that mobilised against the Dutch. During the Japanese occupation, they joined the Islamic umbrella organisation Masyumi, which accommodated a broad range of Muslim groups and figures, including not only moderate clerics and intellectuals, but also radical Islamists intent on turning Indonesia into a sharia-based Islamic state after independence (Madinier 2015).

Within the nationalist movement, the idea of an Islamic state had substantial support, but as explained in Chapter 2, the Islamists eventually lost this battle as secular leaders around Mohammad Hatta succeeded in removing a crucial reference to sharia law from Indonesia's Constitution. After this so-called Jakarta Charter was removed from the constitutional text, Indonesia adopted the Pancasila, a new state ideology that merely acknowledged 'belief in one God' as one of the five key principles that were written into the preamble of the constitution. The controversial circumstances of that last-minute change, perceived by some Muslims as an 'act of treason' (Elson 2009, p. 105), not only entrenched a deep socio-political cleavage in Indonesia, but it also ensured that the struggle for an Islamic state would continue to shape Indonesian politics long after the declaration of independence.

In the postcolonial era, this struggle was taken up by a broad array of parties, movements and insurgencies, but no matter what form the struggle took, the Indonesian state always pushed back successfully. Masyumi, for example, which had transformed itself into a political party in 1945 and fought for sharia law in the Constitutional Assembly that convened between 1956 and 1959, was banned in 1960, while an armed rebellion by Islamists in West Java, the so-called Darul Islam movement, was defeated in 1962. During the decades of authoritarian rule under President Suharto (1966–1998), political Islam was systematically marginalised, with only one tame Islamic party, the United Development Party (Partai Persatuan Pembangunan, PPP), allowed to compete in the regime's stage-managed elections. The influential mass organisations Muhammadiyah and NU retreated from politics to focus on social activities, which was particularly significant in the case of NU as it had briefly operated as a political party between 1952 and 1973 (Effendy 2003).

In the twilight years of Suharto's New Order regime, however, Islamic activism awakened again, on a range of different fronts. For example, a number of modernist intellectuals inspired by a global surge in Islamic revivalism in the wake of the Iranian revolution sought to infiltrate the regime from within by joining the state-sponsored Indonesian Association of Muslim Intellectuals (Ikatan Cendekiawan Muslim Indonesia, ICMI), which was led by one of Suharto's closest allies, Research and Technology Minister B.J. Habibie. Other modernists, however, sensed the risk of co-optation and rejected this approach. Instead, they somewhat reluctantly joined forces with prominent NU leaders like Abdurrahman Wahid in expressing subtle opposition to the Suharto regime. As advocates of 'civil Islam' (Hefner 2000), these reformers pushed for democratic change, grounded in religious reasoning. Meanwhile, at the most conservative and radical end of the Islamic spectrum, young student activists started mobilising around the so-called *tarbiyah* movement, whose ultimate aim was to replace the authoritarian New Order with a sharia-based Islamic state, but through peaceful means.

Electoral Politics and Islamic Parties since 1998

When Suharto resigned in 1998, the fragmentation of political Islam found its organisational expression in the formation of numerous Islamic parties keen to contest the first free and fair elections since 1955. Most prominently, the leaders of NU and Muhammadiyah both established their own parties and quickly built loyal support bases in the stronghold areas of the respective mass organisations. Thus, the traditionalist National Awakening Party (Partai Kebangkitan Bangsa, PKB) became deeply rooted in the rural heartlands of East and, to a lesser extent, Central Java, while the modernist National Mandate Party (Partai Amanat Nasional, PAN) drew most of its support from urban Muslims and those living in areas outside Java, especially Sumatra. At the conservative end of the spectrum, the young and well-educated among Indonesia's most pious Muslims gravitated towards the Justice Party (later renamed Partai Keadilan Sejahtera - Prosperous

Justice Party, PKS), which had been founded by leaders of the campus-based *tar-biyah* movement. Older and less well-educated conservatives, meanwhile, largely stuck with the PPP, which sought to build on its high levels of name recognition as the only Islamic party from the New Order period.

The close links with relatively clearly delineated constituencies and the ability to utilise pre-existing institutional networks from affiliated organisations, movements and parties helped these four parties become established as key pillars of the Indonesian party system. They have contested all parliamentary elections since 1999 and after staving off competition from smaller Islamic fringe parties in the early post-Suharto years have now become the only Islamic parties to be represented in the legislature. However, as Table 6.1 also shows, the broader appeal of these Islamic parties is remarkably limited, with none of them being able to win double digit vote shares in the last three elections and their combined vote share consistently struggling to climb over the 30 percent mark.

To explain why Islamic parties have been a solid but ultimately underwhelming electoral force in Indonesia, analysts have pointed to a range of constraining factors. First, even though the various streams of Indonesian Islam provide a strong sense of identity for these parties, reliance on religion as the only source of value infusion also limits these parties' ability to reach out to voters who are more concerned with concrete policy challenges such as economic development and corruption, rather than the role of religion in public life. Second, Islamic parties have struggled to match the enormous financial resources that oligarchic party patrons have invested in more secular personalistic parties such as Gerindra, Nasdem or the Democratic Party (Mietzner 2013). Third, all Islamic parties have been plagued by recurring episodes of factional infighting, which in some instances led to defections and loss of support. In the early years of party formation, some of these internal divisions occurred over programmatic differences, but far more common have been squabbles over access to patronage fought between clientelistic networks within the parties (Fionna & Tomsa 2020).

Table 6.1 Electoral results of Islamic parties, 1999-2019

Party	1999	2004	2009	2014	2019
Partai Kebangkitan Bangsa (PKB)	12.61	10.57	4.94	9.04	9.69
Partai Persatuan Pembangunan (PPP)	10.71	8.15	5.32	6.53	4.52
Partai Amanat Nasional (PAN)	7.12	6.44	6.01	7.59	6.84
Partai Keadilan Sejahtera (PKS)	1.36*	7.34	7.88	6.79	8.21
Combined Vote Share	**31.8**	**32.5**	**24.15**	**29.95**	**29.26**

* In 1999, PKS competed under the name PK (Partai Keadilan, Justice Party).
Sources: Ananta, Arifin & Suryadinata (2005, p. 14/22) plus assorted publications from the Indonesian General Election Commission, available at https://www.kpu.go.id/

Despite the fragmentation of political Islam, there is one important commonality between all of Indonesia's contemporary Islamic parties, namely their commitment to Pancasila as the main ideological foundation of the state. Unlike many other Muslim majority countries, Indonesia today has no radical Islamist parties that strive to establish a strict Islamic state based on sharia law. Back in the 1950s, Masyumi had pursued that goal and in the early years of the post-Suharto era, parties like PPP and PKS initially pledged to revive that struggle. But after a PPP-backed proposal to insert sharia law into the constitution was rejected during the constitutional reform process between 1999 and 2002 (Hosen 2005, p. 427), no further attempt to turn Indonesia into a formal Islamic state has been made.

Instead, both PPP and PKS have transformed into conservative mainstream Islamic parties which essentially accept the procedural elements of Indonesian democracy, even if they still seem reluctant to accept the principle of religious freedom (Tomsa 2019). The transformation of PKS has been particularly remarkable. Initially formed as the Justice Party (Partai Keadilan, PK) in the immediate aftermath of the fall of Suharto, PKS was designed as a hierarchical cadre party based on small cells with *dakwah* (literally, call, preaching; Islamic outreach) as the party's main goal (Shihab & Nugroho 2009). Committed to using their *dakwah* activities for the promotion of sharia law in Indonesia, PKS distinguished itself from other Islamic parties because it drew its inspiration not from domestic predecessors such as Masyumi but from Islamists in the Middle East. During the first two post-Suharto elections in 1999 and 2004, PKS promoted an Islamist vision called the Medina Charter, which was modelled upon the constitution of Medina during the time the city-state was ruled by the Prophet Muhammad.

Following the 2004 election, however, the party became increasingly moderate in its ideological outlook. In line with key assumptions of the so-called inclusion-moderation thesis, which posits that radical anti-system parties that become immersed in democratic procedures and institutions will adjust their behaviour and ideology in response to democracy's institutional incentives to moderate, the party began to woo centrist voters, recruit non-Muslims as candidates and build coalitions with parties that do not share its conservative religious values (Tomsa 2012). Thanks to its hierarchical organisational structure, PKS was able to impose the centrally devised moderation strategy onto the entire party apparatus despite resistance from ideological diehards and weaker institutional incentives at the local level (Buehler 2012). Today, the PKS is still morally and politically conservative, but it is no longer a radical Islamist party.

Box 6.1: Islamist Terrorism in Indonesia

On Christmas Eve 2000, a series of coordinated bomb attacks on churches across Indonesia marked the beginning of a deadly decade of Islamist terrorism in Indonesia. Between 2000 and 2009, militant extremists inspired by the global terror network Al Qaeda carried out a series of high-profile bomb attacks in Bali and Jakarta as well as smaller attacks on churches and Christians on other islands. The perpetrators were members of Jemaah Islamiyah (JI), an extremist group that had emerged out of the remnants of the Darul Islam movement which had fought for the establishment of an Islamic state in Indonesia between 1948 and 1962. Founded by two radical Islamic clerics, Abdullah Sungkar and Abu Bakar Ba'asyir, JI grew into a formidable terror network with a territorial command structure centred around small religious study circles.

The Indonesian government was initially slow to respond to the new security threat, but in April 2003 the DPR passed an anti-terrorism law. Two months later, the police set up a new special counterterrorism unit called Detachment 88 (Densus 88), which was given wide-ranging surveillance and operational capabilities. With funding, equipment and training from Australia and the United States, Densus 88 soon transformed into what Barton (2018) called 'one of the world's best counterterrorism units', responsible for more than 1,200 arrests of terror suspects (as of 2018). Many other alleged terrorists were killed during Densus 88 operations, leading to allegations from mainstream Muslim groups that the special unit was at times abusing its mandate (Jakarta Post 2013). The operations of Densus 88 are complemented by deradicalisation programmes run by Indonesia's National Counter Terrorism Agency (Badan Nasional Penanggulan Terorisme, BNPT) and selected non-governmental organisations with the aim of rehabilitating convicted terrorists.

This double-pronged strategy was quite successful in addressing the threat posed by JI. By 2011, the organisation had largely abandoned its armed struggle. But neither JI as an organisation nor Islamic extremism as an ideology disappeared. While JI shifted its focus from bombings to radical proselytisation, other militant networks emerged ready to take the fight to the Indonesian state. Initially scattered around a small number of extremists, the advent of the Islamic State of Iraq and Sham (ISIS) eventually prompted the formation of Jamaah Ansharut Daulah (JAD), a new umbrella organisation for a broad range of Indonesian groups that pledged allegiance to ISIS and its leader Abu Bakar Al Baghdadi.

Since its establishment in 2014, JAD has been responsible for a range of terror attacks in Indonesia, including bombings and gun attacks in Jakarta, a bombing in Samarinda and armed assaults on police officers in Bima and Pekanbaru. The deadliest attack occurred in Surabaya in 2018, when six members of one family, including four young children, carried out coordinated suicide bombings on three churches. Following the Surabaya attacks, the Indonesian government moved swiftly to revise its anti-terror legislation in an attempt to signal its determination to fight extremism. Among the more controversial measures enshrined in the new law was an affirmation that the Indonesian Armed Forces would now be more directly involved in counterterrorism measures (Nabbs-Keller 2018).

By and large, Indonesia has been reasonably successful in its fight against Islamic extremism. Although militant groups like JAD and JI remain active, their capacity to mount large-scale attacks has been severely curtailed due to the combined effort of Densus 88, the BNPT and moderate Islamic organisations engaged in deradicalisation programmes and the development of ideological counternarratives. Nevertheless, challenges remain. Among the most pressing are a reform of the prison system, which is widely believed to facilitate rather than hinder the radicalisation and recruitment of new sympathisers into existing terror networks (IPAC 2016), and the difficult reintegration of Indonesians who had joined ISIS in Syria but later returned to Indonesia (Laksmi 2020). The magnitude of these challenges is certainly not lost on the government. In early 2020, President Jokowi announced that close to 700 Indonesian ISIS sympathisers still locked up in prisons in Syria, Iraq and Turkey would not be allowed to return home. It seems that the task of monitoring those who had managed to return earlier is already challenging enough.

Beyond Electoral Politics: Indonesia's Conservative Religious Turn

The moderation of the PKS does not mean that Islamism has become irrelevant in Indonesia. On the contrary, since at least the mid-2000s, the country has gone through a gradual but persistent Islamisation process as political actors responded to the initial rise of the PKS by promoting an increasingly conservative religious agenda. During the presidency of Susilo Bambang Yudhoyono, this trend was evident in controversial legislation such as the 2008 Anti-Pornography Law, a growing number of blasphemy cases brought to court, recurring discrimination against religious minorities and a large number of sharia-inspired by-laws at the provincial and district level (Bush 2015).

An influential driver of this creeping Islamisation has been the Indonesian Council of Ulama (MUI). Founded in 1975 as an organisational tool to help the Suharto regime control Islamic elites, the MUI reinvented itself after 1998 to become the highest Islamic authority in Indonesia. Though it maintains close relations with the government and receives funding from the Ministry of Religious Affairs, it has grown increasingly independent in recent years. Unlike NU and Muhammadiyah, it has no mass membership but instead comprises representatives of ten Islamic organisations, including the two moderate giants, but also several smaller and more conservative groups such as Persatuan Islam, Syarikat Islam or Persatuan Tarbiyah Islamiyah, among others. In the early post-Suharto period, MUI leaders adroitly utilised this diverse membership to stake a claim on being the only legitimate organisation to represent the entire Indonesian *ummah* (Schäfer 2019).

To underpin this claim while simultaneously furthering its autonomy from the state, the MUI has sought and gained an important role in the management of the Islamic pilgrimage (*hajj*), immersed itself in the regulation of the burgeoning Islamic banking and insurance sectors and, for a while at least, established a quasi-monopoly on the certification of *halal* products in Indonesia (Lindsey 2012). Through these manoeuvres, the council was able to strengthen its financial clout and tighten its grip over a socio-legal process some observers have described as the 'bureaucratization of religion' (Künkler 2018). Especially its role in halal certification was widely believed to be highly lucrative. Quoting figures from 2014, Fenwick (2018) estimated that the MUI generated annual funds of up to US\$ 600,000 from issuing halal certificates, which is substantially more than what most observers believed the organisation received in direct state funding. More recently, the MUI has lost some of its control over halal certification after it got caught up in corruption allegations, but despite the establishment of a new Halal Products Certification Agency under the control of the Ministry of Religious Affairs, the MUI has managed to retain a foothold in the new certification system.

If *hajj* management, Islamic banking and halal certification provided the MUI with financial independence, the council's main instrument to assert its religious and legal authority have been *fatwas*, a type of legal opinion relating to Islamic law issued by religious scholars in response to a question from an individual, a judge, government body or corporate entity (Hosen 2008, p. 159). Over the years, MUI has issued numerous controversial fatwas condemning liberalism, secularism and pluralism in general and targeting specific religious and sexual minorities like the Ahmadiyah sect or the LGBT community. Significantly, the council has not only proven adept at finding new ways to disseminate these *fatwas* through digital media, but also built strategic alliances with both state and non-state actors to enforce them on the ground. In evaluating the MUI's agenda, Hasyim (2020, p. 34) has argued that 'the organisation's increased independence from the state and the conservative turn of its *fatwas* have led it to promote shariatisation – the implementation of sharia in the legal and public sphere of Indonesia – rather than democracy'.

Beyond the MUI, this shariatisation has also been driven by a broad range of other groups and actors. First, charismatic preachers started to amass huge followings through savvy social media campaigns where they spread messages about pious Islamic lifestyle choices and political preferences (Hew 2018). Second, conservative civil society groups intensified lobbying for legal changes aimed at enshrining traditional family values in law while at the same time criminalising consensual sexual relationships outside marriage and blocking efforts to penalise sexual violence against women (Davies 2019). Third, Islamist vigilante groups like the Islamic Defenders Front (Front Pembela Islam, FPI) became increasingly brazen in their attacks on religious and sexual minorities. Fourth, at the local level numerous executive leaders, including many with ostensibly secular backgrounds, introduced sharia-inspired by-laws in a bid to enhance their popularity with conservative religious voters (Buehler 2016). Significantly, these governors, mayors and district heads often worked closely together with some of the aforementioned groups and actors in order to maximise their capacity to reach their target constituencies. In 2016, this pattern of collaboration between opportunistic political elites and Islamist actors culminated in the largest mass mobilisation in Indonesia since the anti-Suharto protests in 1998.

Mobilising Islamist Sentiment, Deepening Polarisation: From the Anti-Ahok Demonstrations to the 2019 Elections

In November and December 2016, hundreds of thousands of Muslims converged on the national monument in Jakarta in two consecutive mass demonstrations, demanding that the then incumbent governor of the Indonesian capital, Basuki Tjahaja Purnama, an ethnic Chinese Christian then better known as Ahok, be jailed over remarks he made about the Qur'an while campaigning for his re-election. Known for his abrasive rhetoric, Ahok had told an audience at a campaign event that he did not expect them to vote for him because, so he maintained, they had been deceived or lied to by people who referred to the Qu'ran's verse 51 of the Al-Maidah chapter when advising Muslim voters not to support non-Muslim leaders (Lim 2017, p. 416). When an edited video of the speech appeared on social media soon after the event, conservative Muslims denounced Ahok's remarks as blasphemous, asserting 'that Ahok had claimed that the Qur'an "lied" to Muslims' (Osman & Waikar 2018, p. 98).

On 11 October 2016, the MUI issued a 'religious stance and opinion' on the Ahok case, which Islamists subsequently referred to as a *fatwa*. In the statement, the MUI confirmed that in their view Ahok's remarks constituted blasphemy. Before long, Islamist hardliners from organisations such as FPI and Hizbut Tahrir Indonesia joined forces with Ahok's political opponents in the election to mobilise protests against the incumbent governor. After mass demonstrations on 4 November and 2 December, the pressure to prosecute Ahok became so intense that the Indonesian state eventually buckled and put Ahok on trial. Despite a public apology and evidence that the video of his speech had been edited, Ahok was convicted to two years imprisonment.

The events surrounding the downfall of Jakarta's first ethnic Chinese governor marked a turning point in the relationship between Islam and politics in Indonesia. Up until the mobilisation against Ahok, the Islamisation agenda had largely focused on social and moral issues, targeting primarily deviant behaviour and groups that do not fall within the parameters of established Islamic orthodoxy as promulgated by organisations like the MUI, but also NU and Muhammadiyah (Menchik 2014). Accordingly, incidents of intolerance, discrimination and violence were often related to these so-called deviant minorities such as the Ahmadiyah or Shia, as well as atheists and sexual minorities like the LGBT community. Civil society groups and human rights activists have meticulously documented these incidents over the years, warning that intolerance had become the norm (Hamid 2018) and that Indonesia was 'no model for Muslim democracy' (Harsono 2012).

The Ahok case, however, differed from earlier incidents of religious intolerance because it moved beyond issues of morality and deviant interpretations of faith to target the political aspirations of non-Muslims from a mainstream religious minority. Backed by powerful political figures like Prabowo Subianto and for-mer president Susilo Bambang Yudhoyono, the Islamist groups that organised the anti-Ahok protests deliberately crafted a mobilisation narrative which emphasised that 'political positions should be reserved for Muslims, and that Muslims had an obligation to vote for Muslim candidates' (Mietzner, Muhtadi & Halida 2018, p. 167). An important implication of this narrative was that the impact of the mass demonstrations on both the wider community as well as the government differed significantly from earlier incidents of religious intolerance or even violence.

First, in contrast to intolerant attitudes toward Ahmadiyah or LGBT groups, which are widespread among large majorities of Indonesians (Pinandita 2020), the mobilisa-tion against Ahok divided Indonesians, resulting in sharp religious polarisation that pitched radicals and conservatives against moderates and pluralists. The effects of this religious polarisation on social cohesion were immense as communities, neighbour-hoods and families became deeply divided over Ahok's fate. Second, this religious polarisation now overlapped with the political polarisation that had swept Indonesia since the 2014 presidential election when the eventual winner Jokowi had framed his run for the presidency as a pro-reform campaign while his opponent Prabowo Subianto promoted a populist variant of neo-authoritarianism (Davidson 2018). In the 2017 Jakarta election, the two resumed their rivalry as Ahok was widely seen as a Jokowi ally, whereas Prabowo Subianto backed the eventual winner of the election, Anies Baswedan, and the Islamists who mobilised against Ahok.

This broader context ensured that President Jokowi would not allow the Islamists to enjoy their triumph for too long. Spooked by the prospect of a similar Islamist mobilisation against his own 2019 re-election campaign, Jokowi moved swiftly after Ahok was jailed in early May 2017. Within just a few months, his government had manufactured pornography charges against FPI leader Habib Rizieq Shihab and banned Hizbut Tahrir Indonesia, another organisation that was involved in the mobilisation against Ahok. Habib Rizieq went into exile in Saudi Arabia in response to the charges against him, but other repressive government measures still followed, prompting observers like Mietzner (2018) to describe Jokowi's approach as 'fighting illiberalism with illiberalism'.

At the same time, however, the president also began courting the less radi-cal elements of the mobilisation, especially NU, whose supporters had initially been divided over the Ahok case (Nuraniyah 2020, p. 90). In the run-up to the 2019 elections, NU became the main focus of Jokowi's pro-Islam offensive as he showered the organisation with patronage and eventually accepted senior NU figure Ma'ruf Amin as his vice-presidential running mate in 2019. In the end, the double-pronged strategy of repression and accommodation served its purpose as Jokowi once again defeated Prabowo Subianto, whose support from hardline Islamists was insufficient to mount a serious challenge against the incumbent.

After the 2019 election, Indonesia's Islamists quickly lost their momentum, for at least three main reasons. First, the movement was left effectively without leadership after its most powerful political patron, Prabowo Subianto, defected to the Jokowi camp and became Defence Minister. Without Prabowo's resources and the cha-risma of Habib Rizieq, who was still in exile at this time, the movement struggled to maintain its mobilisation potential. Second, even if they wanted to continue mobilising protests and demonstrations, the Covid-19 outbreak and the associated restrictions on mass gatherings that came into force in early 2020 deprived them of these opportunities. Third, the Jokowi government not only continued, but arguably intensified its campaign against Islamist groups and the creeping Islamisation of politics and society. Of particular concern to Jokowi and other pluralists has been the perceived infiltration of Islamists into the civil service and higher education institutions. In response, the government not only introduced the vetting of civil servants and the certification of preachers, but it also instructed managers in higher education institutions, state-owned enterprises and even private industries to monitor pious students and employees (Fealy 2020, p. 312).

As a result of these factors, the Islamist movement that shook Indonesian politics in 2016 and 2017 'has not become the political force that many feared' (IPAC 2020, p. 1). Even the return of Habib Rizieq from exile in late 2020 could not swing the pendulum back in the Islamists' favour as the FPI leader was quickly arrested and charged with violating Covid-19 regulations. Yet, even though the government may have been successful in weakening the organisations that represent Islamism in Indonesia, the ideas that underpin them continue to resonate with sizeable segments of the Indonesian population.

Indeed, while organisations and charismatic leaders may have been instrumental in driving the Islamisation agenda in recent years, it is also important to note that they found fertile ground in a society that was already in the midst of a socio-cultural transformation towards greater piety since at least the 1990s. Long before Islamists began infiltrating state institutions and mobilising against non-Muslim politicians, scholars had already documented noticeable growth in Islamic education (Jackson & Parker 2008), Islamic banking and tourism (Juoro 2008) as well as Islamic publishing, entertainment and fashion industries (Hoesterey & Clark 2012, Jones 2007).

Taken together, these multifaceted processes of social change, sometimes dubbed 'the commodification of Islam' (Fealy 2008, p. 16), not only helped facilitate the mainstreaming of religious piety in political discourse, but it also affected how Indonesians perceive the role of religion in public life. In the 2018 Global Attitudes Survey conducted by the Pew Research Center, 83 percent of Indonesian respondents expressed the belief that 'religion has a bigger impact on their nation today than it did 20 years ago' (Pew Research Center 2019, p. 23). Even more remarkably, the same survey also found that 85 percent of those polled in Indonesia favoured an even greater role for religion in their nation. For both questions, Indonesia scored a much higher percentage than all other 26 countries included in the survey. While the political implications of these figures are not necessarily straightforward – 'a greater role for religion' can mean many things – it seems clear that the religious turn in Indonesia is both a top-down and a bottom-up process.

Conclusion

Islam has shaped Indonesian politics since the struggle for independence when a deep cleavage about the relationship between religion and the state first emerged.

This basic cleavage has waxed and waned in significance over time, but it never completely disappeared. In today's party system, four parties have a distinct Islamic identity, while the other five have a more pluralist outlook. In the five elections since 1998, support for the four Islamic parties has been relatively stable with a combined vote share of around 30 percent, but the more meaningful developments in religious politics have taken place outside the electoral arena. Extraparliamentary groups like the MUI or the FPI have proven much more influential in shaping the Islamist agenda than Islamic parties in parliament as even the most conservative of these parties such as the PKS and PPP have moderated to an extent that many Islamists no longer feel adequately represented in the country's formal political institutions.

Thus, despite moderate electoral and parliamentary politics, the cleavage between Islamists and pluralists today is arguably at its most profound since the 1950s. From the 'populist morality movement' (Davies 2019) that seeks to ban all extramarital sex to the Islamists who seek to limit the political rights of non-Muslims, the combined influence of political Islam has gradually changed the face of Indonesian Islam. Significantly, survey data shows that the drive towards increased piety is spearheaded by Muslims from higher, not lower socio-economic and educational backgrounds (Mietzner & Muhtadi 2018, p. 484). This has provided the new Islamisation agenda with enormous resources, as was evident for example in the extremely well-organised mass protests against Ahok.

But the contest over the place of religion in Indonesian politics and society is fought with equal determination by the defenders of the country's pluralist legacy. So much so, in fact, that almost any measure, democratic or not, seems justifiable as long as it helps to rein in the advance of the Islamists. President Jokowi's repressive measures against his Islamist opponents since 2017 have set a dangerous precedent that may have implications not only for the future of Islam's place in Indonesia, but also for the future of democratic governance in the country. That Indonesia's democracy ratings have declined in recent years is not only due to the illiberal attacks of Islamists on non-Muslims, but also the illiberal response to these attacks by the Indonesian government.

References

Ananta, A, Arifin, EN & Suryadinata, L 2005, *Emerging Democracy in Indonesia*, Institute of Southeast Asian Affairs, Singapore.

Aritonang, JS & Steenbrink, K (eds) 2008, *A history of Christianity in Indonesia*, Brill, Leiden.

Barton, G 2018, 'How Indonesia's counter-terrorism force has become a model for the region', *The Conversation*, 2 July, viewed 13 March 2021, <https://theconversation.com/how-indonesias-counter-terrorism-force-has-become-a-model-for-the-region-97368>.

Buehler, M 2012, 'Revisiting the inclusion-moderation thesis in the context of decentralised institutions: the behavior of Indonesia's Prosperous Justice Party in national and local politics', *Party Politics*, vol. 19, no. 2, pp. 210–229.

Buehler, M 2016, *The politics of Shari'a law: Islamist activists and the state in democratizing Indonesia*, Cambridge University Press, Cambridge, UK.

Bush, R 2009, *Nahdlatul Ulama and the struggle for power within Islam and politics in Indonesia*, Institute of Southeast Asian Studies, Singapore.

Bush, R 2015, 'Religious politics and minority rights during the Yudhoyono presidency', in E Aspinall, M Mietzner & D Tomsa (eds), *The Yudhoyono presidency: Indonesia's decade of stability and stagnation*, Institute of Southeast Asian Studies, Singapore, pp. 239–257.

Davidson, JS 2018, *Indonesia: twenty years of democracy*, Cambridge University Press, Cambridge.

Davies, SG 2019, 'How a populist morality movement is blocking a law against sexual violence in Indonesia', *The Conversation*, 19 September, viewed 13 March 2021, <https://theconversation.com/how-a-populist-morality-movement-is-blocking-a-law-against-sexual-violence-in-indonesia-analysis-123448>.

Effendy, B 2003, *Islam and the state in Indonesia*, Institute of Southeast Asian Studies, Singapore.

Elson, RE 2009, 'Another look at the Jakarta Charter controversy of 1945', *Indonesia*, vol. 88, pp. 105–130.

Fealy, G 2008, 'Consuming Islam: commodified religion and aspirational pietism in contemporary Indonesia', in G Fealy & S White (eds), *Expressing Islam: religious life and politics in Indonesia*, Institute of Southeast Asian Studies, Singapore, pp. 15–39.

Fealy, G 2020, 'Jokowi in the Covid-19 era: repressive pluralism, dynasticism and the overbearing state, *Bulletin of Indonesian Economic Studies*, vol. 56, no. 3, pp. 301–323.

Fenwick, S 2018, 'Eat, pray, regulate: the Indonesian Ulama Council and the management of Islamic affairs', *Journal of Law and Religion*, vol. 33, no. 2, pp. 271–290.

Fionna, U & Tomsa, D 2020, 'Changing patterns of factionalism in Indonesia: from principle to patronage', *Journal of Current Southeast Asian Affairs*, vol. 39, no. 1, pp. 39–58.

Geertz, C 1976, *The religion of Java*, University of Chicago Press, Chicago and London.

Hamid, S 2018, *Normalising intolerance: elections, religion and everyday life in Indonesia*, CILIS Policy Paper 17, Centre for Indonesian Law, Islam and Society, Melbourne.

Harsono, A 2012, 'Indonesia is no model for Muslim democracy', *New York Times*, 22 May.

Hasyim, S 2020, 'Fatwas and democracy: Majelis Ulama Indonesia (MUI, Indonesian Ulema Council) and rising conservatism in Indonesian Islam', *TRaNS: Trans -Regional and -National Studies of Southeast Asia*, vol. 8, no. 1, pp. 21–35.

Hefner, RW 2000, *Civil Islam: Muslims and democratisation in Indonesia*, Princeton University Press, Princeton.

Hew, WW 2018, 'The art of *dakwah*: social media, visual persuasion and the Islamist propagation of Felix Siauw', *Indonesia and the Malay World*, vol. 46, no. 134, pp. 61–79.

Hoesterey, JB & Clark, M 2012, 'Film Islami: gender, piety and pop culture in post-authoritarian Indonesia', *Asian Studies Review*, vol. 36, no. 2, pp. 207–226.

Hosen, N 2005, 'Religion and the Indonesian constitution: A recent debate', *Journal of Southeast Asian Studies*, vol. 36, no. 3, pp. 419–440.

Hosen, N 2008, 'Online fatwa in Indonesia: from fatwa shopping to googling a kiai', in G Fealy & S White (eds), *Expressing Islam: religious life and politics in Indonesia*, Institute of Southeast Asian Affairs, Singapore, pp. 159–173.

Hosen, N 2020, 'When religion meets Covid-19 in Indonesia: more than a matter of conservatives and moderates', *Indonesia at Melbourne*, 29 April, viewed 13 March 2021, <https://indonesiaatmelbourne.unimelb.edu.au/when-religion-meets-covid-19-in -indonesia-more-than-a-matter-of-conservatives-and-moderates/>.

Howell, JD 2001, 'Sufism and the Indonesian Islamic revival', *The Journal of Asian Studies*, vol. 60, no. 3, pp. 701–729.

IPAC 2016, *Update on Indonesian pro-ISIS prisoners and deradicalisation efforts*, IPAC Report No. 34, IPAC, Jakarta.

IPAC 2020, *Indonesian Islamists: activists in search of an issue*, IPAC Report No. 65, IPAC, Jakarta.

Jackson, E & Parker, L 2008, 'Enriched with knowledge: modernisation, Islamisation and the future of Islamic education in Indonesia', *Review of Indonesian and Malaysian Affairs*, vol. 42, no. 1, pp. 21–53.

Jakarta Post 2013, 'Muslim groups want Densus 88 dissolved over rights abuses', 1 March.

Jones, C 2007, 'Fashion and faith in urban Indonesia', *Fashion Theory*, vol. 11, no. 2–3, pp. 211–231.

Juoro, U 2008, 'The development of Islamic banking in the post-crisis Indonesian economy', in G Fealy & S White (eds), *Expressing Islam: religious life and politics in Indonesia*, Institute of Southeast Asian Studies, Singapore, pp. 229–250.

Künkler, M 2018, 'The bureaucratisation of religion in Southeast Asia: expanding or restricting religious freedom?', *Journal of Law and Religion*, vol. 33, no. 2, pp. 192–197.

Laksmi, S 2020, 'Handling returning terrorist fighters is a big problem, monitoring their funds is another', *The Conversation*, 9 March, viewed 13 March 2021, <https://theconversation.com/handling-returning-terrorist-fighters-is-a-big-problem -monitoring-their-funds-is-another-132107>.

Lim, M 2017, 'Freedom to hate: social media, algorithmic enclaves, and the rise of tribal nationalism in Indonesia, *Critical Asian Studies*, vol. 49, no. 3, pp. 411–427.

Lindsey, T 2012, 'Monopolising Islam: the Indonesian Ulama Council and state regulation of the 'Islamic economy', *Bulletin of Indonesian Economic Studies*, vol. 48, no. 2, pp. 253–274.

Madinier, R 2015, *Islam and politics in Indonesia: the Masyumi Party between democracy and integralism*, NUS Press, Singapore.

Means, GP 2009, *Political Islam in Southeast Asia*, Lynne Rienner, Boulder and London.

Mecham, Q 2017, *Institutional origins of Islamist political mobilisation*, Cambridge University Press, Cambridge.

Menchik, J 2014, 'Productive intolerance: godly nationalism in Indonesia', *Comparative Studies in Society and History*, vol. 56, no. 3, pp. 591–621.

Mietzner, M 2009, *Military politics, Islam, and the state in Indonesia: from turbulent transition to democratic consolidation*, Institute of Southeast Asian Studies, Singapore.

Mietzner, M 2013, *Money, power and ideology: political parties in post-authoritarian Indonesia*, NUS Press, Singapore.

Mietzner, M 2018, 'Fighting illiberalism with illiberalism: Islamist populism and democratic deconsolidation in Indonesia', *Pacific Affairs*, vol. 91, no. 2, pp. 261–282.

Mietzner, M & Muhtadi, B 2018, 'Explaining the 2016 Islamist mobilisation in Indonesia: religious intolerance, militant groups and the politics of accommodation', *Asian Studies Review*, vol. 42, no. 3, pp. 479–497.

Mietzner, M, Muhtadi, B & Halida, R 2018, 'Entrepreneurs of grievance: drivers and effects of Indonesia's Islamist mobilisation', *Bijdragen tot de Taal-, Land- en Volkenkunde*, vol. 174, pp. 159–187.

Nabbs-Keller, G 2018, 'Indonesia's revised anti-terrorism law', *Australian Outlook*, 26 August, viewed 13 March 2021, <https://www.internationalaffairs.org.au/australianoutlook/indonesias-revised-anti-terrorism-law/>.

Nuraniyah, N 2020, 'Divided Muslims: militant pluralism, polarisation, and democratic backsliding', in T Power & E Warburton (eds), *Democracy in Indonesia: from stagnation to regression*, ISEAS-Yusof Ishak Institute, Singapore, pp. 81–100.

Osman, MNM & Waikar, P 2018, 'Fear and loathing: uncivil Islamism and Indonesia's anti-Ahok movement', *Indonesia*, vol. 106, pp. 89–109.

Pew Research Center 2019, *A changing world: global views on diversity, gender equality, family life and the importance of religion*, Pew Research Center, Washington DC.

Pinandita, A 2020, 'More Indonesians tolerant of homosexuality, though vast majority still says no: Pew Survey', *Jakarta Post*, 26 June.

Reid, A 1969, *The contest for North Sumatra: Acheh, the Netherlands and Britain, 1858–1898*, Oxford University Press, Kuala Lumpur.

Ricklefs, MC 2001, *A history of modern Indonesia since c. 1200*, 4th edn, Palgrave, Houndmills, Basingstoke.

Ricklefs, MC 2006, *Mystic synthesis in Java: a history of Islamisation from the fourteenth to the early nineteenth centuries*, EastBridge, Norwalk.

Rochmyaningsih, D 2021, 'COVID-19 cases are soaring in Indonesia. Can a new health minister turn things around?', *Science*, 15 January, viewed 13 March 2021, <https://www.sciencemag.org/news/2021/01/covid-19-cases-are-soaring-indonesia-can-new-health-minister-turn-things-around>.

Schäfer, S 2019, 'Democratic decline in Indonesia: the role of religious authorities', *Pacific Affairs*, vol. 92, no. 2, pp. 235–255.

Shihab, N & Nugroho, Y 2009, 'The ties that bind: law, Islamisation and Indonesia's Prosperous Justice Party (PKS)', *Australian Journal of Asian Law*, vol. 10, no. 2, pp. 233–267.

Tomsa, D 2012, 'Moderating Islamism in Indonesia: tracing patterns of party change in the Prosperous Justice Party', *Political Research Quarterly*, vol. 65, no. 3, pp. 486–498.

Tomsa, D 2019, 'Islamism and party politics in Indonesia' in *Oxford research encyclopedia of politics*, Oxford University Press, https://oxfordre.com/politics/view/10.1093/acrefore/9780190228637.001.0001/acrefore-9780190228637-e-1157, viewed 13 March 2021.

Warburton, E 2020, 'How polarised is Indonesia and why does it matter?', in T Power & E Warburton (eds), *Democracy in Indonesia: from stagnation to regression*, ISEAS-Yusof Ishak Institute, Singapore, pp. 63–80.

7 Civil Society and the Media

Introduction

In September 2019, thousands of students mobilised in cities across Indonesia. In Jakarta, the security forces blocked streets leading to the parliament and used teargas and water cannons to disperse the crowd. Dramatic scenes unfolded as clashes between students and riot police broke out, leaving three protestors dead. Similar clashes also occurred in other Indonesian cities, and two more students died in Southeast Sulawesi. The protests were ignited by a range of issues, including amendments proposed by parliament to weaken the popular Corruption Eradication Commission (Komisi Pemberantasan Korupsi, KPK), and proposed changes to the Criminal Code that would see the criminalisation of extramarital sex and defamation of the president. In addition, the protestors criticised the government's failure to stop peatland fires in Sumatra and Kalimantan, ongoing military aggression in Papua and the criminalisation of activists while also demanding for human rights violators to be held to account in a court of law. As one of the slogans of the protests made clear, to the students, reform had been corrupted (*reformasi dikorupsi*).

Indonesia had not witnessed student protests at such a large scale since 1998, when students brought an end to the Suharto regime. Like the student protests in 1998, which had paved the way for democratisation, these protests more than 20 years later underlined the critical role civil society can play in establishing and defending democracy (Diamond 1994), particularly in the direction of more open, participatory and accountable politics (Alagappa 2004). At the same time, however, the emergence of mass student protests two decades after the fall of authoritarianism should not merely be seen as a reaction to the specific issues the protests addressed. Serious as these issues are, the 2019 student protests need to be seen in the broader political context where many Indonesians have felt increasingly frustrated about their lack of influence on political decision-making processes. As such, the forceful re-emergence of student protests on Indonesia's political stage was both a sign of Indonesia's democratic regression (Aspinall 2020) as well as the anger this regression has caused amongst progressive activists.

In contrast to the 1998 protests, however, the 2019 protests were short-lived and failed to achieve their goals. This raises the question why, despite significant

DOI: 10.4324/9780429459511-7

legal and political reforms since the fall of Suharto, student activists and other parts of civil society have only had limited success in strengthening democracy. Similarly, it also raises the question why the Indonesian media, despite often being described as one of the liveliest in Southeast Asia, has not done more to support the students' cause and not provided more critical reporting on Indonesia's multiple democratic deficits. As this chapter will argue, reasons for this can be found in the legacies of authoritarianism, oligarchic control of media organisations, social and political conservatism as well as outright state repression.

This chapter will start by providing some brief background of the context in which civil society and the media operated during the New Order. The chapter will then turn to the post-1998 media reforms, particularly those related to the print and broadcast media. It will then discuss the emergence of digital technologies and social media, before addressing the challenges posed by media ownership and content. The chapter continues by shifting the focus to civil society, addressing both the rapid growth of civil society organisations as well as the key challenges civil society is facing. These include weak institutionalisation and fragmentation, the influence of 'uncivil' groups and polarisation as well as the increased willingness of the government to use coercion against civil society groups of all stripes, including progressive movements.

Civil Society and the Media under Authoritarianism

Civil society is a contested concept, but a commonly used definition describes it as 'organised collective activities that are not part of the household, the market (or more general economic production) and the state' (Kopecký & Mudde 2003, p. 11). Often idealised in normative terms as a liberal democratic bulwark against an almighty state, civil society tends to be associated with functions like accountability, the protection of civil liberties and the promotion of tolerance and social trust. In reality though, many organisations that operate within that public sphere between the state, the market and the family do not struggle for democratic values. Rather, they promote social exclusion, discrimination and intolerance. Some openly reject democracy as a system of government and some use violence to achieve their non-democratic goals. To distinguish these groups from those that fit into the more conventional understanding of civil society, scholars have used the term 'uncivil society' (Diamond 1994, Keane 1998). Despite limitations to these distinctions – some groups may move in and out of civil and uncivil society, depending on external circumstances – this chapter adopts this distinction and regards uncivil society as a subset of civil society. As will be outlined below, Indonesia's public sphere is a fiercely contested space where both civil and uncivil society groups operate in a constant struggle for public support. The origins of this struggle date back to the immediate post-independence period.

Indeed, Indonesians have long engaged in political organisations and activism. During the 1950s and 1960s, Indonesia was characterised by a diverse civil society where people were actively taking part in many different associations, including labour unions, women's groups and peasant associations, as well as organisations for artists, students and other groups. However, people's political engagement did not translate into progressive democratic politics. Instead, Indonesian society and politics became increasingly polarised, and in the late 1950s the country slid into authoritarianism (see Chapter 2). The tensions between rivalling groups came to a peak in 1965, when the persecution of members of the Indonesian Communist Party (Partai Komunis Indonesia, PKI) marked not only the end of leftist political thought in Indonesia but also saw fundamental changes to associational life.

In order to maintain political order, Suharto's New Order depoliticised and demobilised society. This was achieved through outright repression, strict limitations on political parties as well as through legal and ideological frameworks. The so-called floating mass doctrine, introduced in 1971, reserved politics for a small urban elite, while the majority of Indonesians were expected to refrain from political activities and concentrate on economic development (Hadiz 2000). In 1978, the Normalisation of Campus Life policy was introduced, targeting students who had historically been at the forefront of political change (see Box 7.1). The policy banned political expression from university campuses and placed student activities under the supervision of university rectors, which stifled student protest (Aspinall 2012).

Depoliticisation was further entrenched by the promulgation of a Law on Societal Organisations in 1985, which determined that all social organisations should comply with the state ideology Pancasila, which negated 'the very notion of legitimate oppositional politics' (Hadiz 2000, p. 15). This had far-reaching effects on the development of civil society. To ensure organisational survival under the New Order regime, most civil society groups generally developed in the form of government-established institutions, parties and organisations that collaborated or compromised with the state. These so-called proto-oppositional civil society organisations (Aspinall 2004, p. 72) were sometimes critical of state policies and actions, and also promoted democratic reforms, but overall refrained from demanding systemic change.

Box 7.1: Students in Political History

The protests of students, and more broadly young people, have often taken a central position in Indonesian political history and represent a distinctive political force, namely that of a moral force or movement. In emphasising moral principles and ethics (i.e. transparent governance), youth are supposedly removed from the less desirable elements of the political world, such as corruption, and align themselves with the interests of the nation rather than personal gains (Aspinall 2012). Throughout Indonesian history, students have been at the centre of major political events. During the struggle for independence, for instance, students were the driving force behind the 1928 Youth Pledge, whereby young nationalists proclaimed one motherland, one nation and one language, which gave birth to the idea of a unified Indonesia for the first time in history. In 1945, as Indonesia found itself in a power vacuum following the surrender of Japan to the Allied forces, young Indonesians grew impatient for a declaration of independence. On 16 August, a group of youth (*pemuda*) kidnapped Sukarno and Hatta, forcing them to proclaim independence the following day. In 1965 and 1966, anti-communist student groups played a key role in influencing public opinion towards Sukarno, eventually ousting him from power while also publicly calling for the elimination of all leftist elements in government. These protests were important in legitimising the role of the army and groups supported by them. However, while many student groups had been actively involved in removing Sukarno from power, many also quickly became disenchanted with the new government. Even under the constraints imposed on civil society under the New Order, students several times spoke out against the regime, most notably during the 1974 Malari protests, where students protested corruption, high prices and inequality in foreign investments. While the regime responded to protests violently, this did not prevent students from criticising the government. This culminated in 1998, this time demanding for Suharto to step down and for the government to initiate reforms. While violent clashes between students and the security apparatus continued during the early *reformasi* years, over time student protests appeared to fade into the background. In more recent years, however, they have resurfaced on the political and social stage. In 2019, students across the country protested a wide range of issues considered a threat to democracy, ranging from proposed changes to legislation to ongoing military aggression. In response, the government postponed the amendments to a number of bills. Although many of the changes that were put on hold in 2019 were eventually included in the 2020 Omnibus Law, it is clear that student mobilisations in Indonesia have not only been prominent, but also politically consequential.

Pancasila was not only placed at the centre of associational life, but was also made integral to the country's media system. For the New Order regime, the media's role was to safeguard the state ideology through 'free but responsible' coverage, in contrast to the 'libertine' and 'irresponsible' Western press. This meant that media outlets were expected to avoid reporting that could ignite ethnic, religious, racial and inter-group tensions. In this vein, the media was also not to represent any party politics. Instead, it was expected to be a partner of the government, either by supporting government policies or avoiding political debates (Sen & Hill 2000). This resulted in a state-led media system with only a single television and radio channel. Through the two outlets TVRI (Televisi Republik Indonesia, Television of the Republic of Indonesia) and RRI (Radio Republik Indonesia, Radio of the Republic of Indonesia), the state effectively monopolised news production in Indonesian broadcasting. The prime focus of TVRI and RRI news coverage was on the president and other high-ranking officials, confirming their authority and existing power hierarchies (Kitley 2000).

Meanwhile, the printed presses were kept on a tight leash through an extensive system of press permits and controls. The newspaper and magazine industries had to obtain a Permit to Publish from the Department of Information, as well as a Permit to Print from the military authorities. Without these, publications could not be legally produced. The permit system gave the executive and the military much control over the printed press, enabling them to ban any publications it considered a threat to public order. This led to regular bans of publications and the blacklisting of journalists, which barred them from further employment in the industry (Sen & Hill 2000, p. 53). Moreover, media workers' vulnerability to retaliation from the military and other authorities also led to widespread self-censorship (Tapsell 2012).

Despite these significant constraints imposed by the state, the New Order regime could never fully stifle the development of civil society and the media. Student activism, for instance, moved off campuses and went underground, where students started exploring more radical forms of political action (Aspinall 2012). Similarly, artists, intellectuals and activists used creative and literary means to counter the New Order's control over the broader cultural climate (Jurriëns 2004). In the late New Order, new technologies such as the internet brought more opportunities for Indonesians to access and share news not censored by the authorities, while these also enabled foreign news services to receive timely and accurate information that was not mediated by the government (Sen & Hill 2000).

The crucial importance of civil society and the media was readily apparent in the final year of the New Order. The economic crisis that hit Indonesia in 1997 triggered protests against the regime across Indonesian cities. These protests were led by students who for all their differences, especially along the traditional Islamist-pluralist divide, were united in demanding Suharto's resignation (Mietzner 2021). The broad support for the student movement was in part the result of unprecedented independent media reporting on the protests which emerged despite the government's monopoly on media production. Even private channels, which had only been established in the 1990s but focused on entertainment rather than news, reported on the political events that unfolded. While broadcasters largely refrained from criticising the government, the images that entered people's households had a power of their own and laid bare the brutality of the security forces. Moreover, the advance of digital technologies, such as the internet and mobile phones, connected educated middle classes to demonstrations. For all their limitations, civil society and the media thus had a direct hand in the fall of Suharto in May 1998.

Media in Indonesia after 1998

The end of authoritarianism heralded significant changes for print and broadcast media. For print media the enactment of the 1999 Press Law was particularly significant. Promulgated during the presidency of B.J. Habibie, this law was one of his first, and possibly most notable achievements. The law includes guarantees for the freedom of the press, eliminated licencing as a way of control and removed the government's ability to ban publications. The law also removed limitations on who could practice journalism, and guaranteed journalists' to be free from censorship. Journalists' rights to refuse disclosure of their sources and to join professional associations of their own choice were also included in the law. This legitimised independent media organisations, such as the Alliance of Independent Journalists (Aliansi Jurnalis Independen, AJI), which in fact had been established during the New Order in response to government censorship. Importantly, the law also provided penalties for those who sought to restrict press freedom. As such, the Press Law fundamentally altered the relationship between the press and the government (Steele 2012).

Broadcast media also changed significantly. Under Habibie, permits were issued for new commercial television stations, while TVRI and RRI's monopoly on news production was also lifted. Only days after Abdurrahman Wahid assumed the presidency in October 1999, the Department of Information was abolished, a decision that was widely supported by civil society groups that considered the department the embodiment of an authoritarian media system. As TVRI and RRI transformed from state-controlled broadcasters to public broadcasters, civil society organisations actively lobbied for a new Broadcasting Law, which was eventually passed in 2002. This law altered the former broadcasting system in which the government was the sole regulator to one that was pluralist, distinguishing between public, private and community broadcasters. This law also established an independent non-governmental regulator, the Indonesian Broadcasting Commission (Komisi Penyiaran Indonesia, KPI), to monitor the media (Masduki 2020). As a result, Indonesia now has a vibrant media industry, characterised by hundreds of national and regional radio and television stations, and many more print publications (Jurriëns 2004).

In addition, in the past decade the Indonesian media landscape has also been altered dramatically through the surge of digital technology, which is quickly becoming the centre of Indonesians' daily lives. Jakarta was once called the most active city on Twitter, and in 2016 Indonesia had the fourth highest number of Facebook users worldwide (Jurriëns & Tapsell 2017). In 2020, the Indonesian Internet Service Provider Association (Asosiasi Penyelenggara Jasa Internet Indonesia, APJII) estimated that the country's internet penetration rate is nearly at 75 percent. While connectivity is highly concentrated in urban centres, the overwhelming majority (95 percent) of Indonesians access the online world through smartphones. APJII's data also showed that most Indonesians use the internet for more than eight hours per day to access social media, chat applications as well as various services (Herman 2020). Given the high use of smartphones, it is unsurprising that Indonesia is a thriving e-commerce industry, including ride-hail and on-demand services. Politically, digital platforms are used for online activism and campaigning, as well as organising mass rallies and election monitoring. The popularity of social media in particular has led some observers to point at its ability to act as a tool of change, with its low cost, broad availability and reasonable resistance to control and censorship supposedly contributing to its democratising potential (Lim 2013).

However, the relaxation of press controls, a free broadcast sector and the increasing centrality of digital technologies in the everyday life of Indonesians have not necessarily contributed to the strengthening of liberal democracy. In the past few years, Freedom House has consistently evaluated Indonesia as a 'partly free' country in its annual *Freedom in the World* and *Freedom on the Net* reports (Freedom House 2020a, 2020b). Various challenges to press freedom can be identified, including legal and regulatory restrictions, including the increased use of the Electronic Information and Transactions (ITE) Law, physical attacks on journalists, including from vigilante and hard-line groups, and the use of internet blackouts (see Chapter 10).

Increased social conservatism has also impacted the media, leading at best to self-censorship and at worst to the reproduction of intolerant discourses and attitudes. In recent years, the broadcasting watchdog KPI has come under increasing criticism from pluralist groups for censoring content for what the KPI says is 'inconsistency with Indonesian standards'. Examples of this are the blurring of athletes' bodies and even the censoring of cartoon characters wearing bikinis. The KPI's decision to do so has meant that many broadcasters in Indonesia, in an attempt to avoid fines, have been erring on the side of caution in their broadcasting (Parlina 2016). Another manifestation of social conservatism's mark on media reporting is that derogatory terms have become increasingly commonplace in political discourse about political and ethnic minorities (Hamid 2018). Such reporting, which ironically is far less often sanctioned by the KPI, contributes to the marginalisation of and violence towards these groups (Harsono 2019) and poses challenges for the freedoms of those who do not, or are not seen to, identify with the status quo.

Similarly, while social media has at times facilitated progressive social movements, their success remains highly dependent on the ability of the activists to craft issue-specific narratives that resonate with broader dominant narratives. This means that issues associated with high-risk actions or ideologies are unlikely to gain traction through social media activism (Lim 2013). Moreover, it would be naïve to think that the digital world only offers opportunities for liberal ideas. Indeed, conservative and radical groups are also very adept at using these channels to spread their ideas and, at the extreme end of the spectrum, to recruit and train terrorists (Nuraniyah 2017). Social media is also often employed in political smear campaigns, with Jokowi's opponents in 2014 using these platforms to question his piousness and descent, while a manipulated video of a speech by Jakarta governor Basuki Tjahaja Purnama ('Ahok') was at the base of the blasphemy charges against him (see Chapter 10). During the 2019 presidential race, both Jokowi and Prabowo supporters utilised social media platforms for negative campaigning and hoaxes (Purdey, Missbach & McRae 2020, pp. 189-190). These uses of social media platforms have done little to strengthen democracy, instead only further exacerbating political, ethnic and religious differences and deepening social and political polarisation.

Media Ownership and Content

One of the defining features of the post-1998 media landscape has been the exponential growth of media outlets. This diversity – especially compared to the New Order period – is often regarded as a strength. At the same time, however, media ownership has been a key concern for scholars and activists concerned with media freedom because the Indonesian media is controlled by less than a dozen powerful figures and more than half of the ten national, free-to-air channels are owned by entrepreneurs with political interests (Souisa 2019). The emergence of politically entrenched elites in the media landscape first became apparent during the 2004 elections when political candidates became increasingly aware of how central media was in reaching voters (Tapsell 2015). Close ties between politicians and media owners quickly materialised, with some media bosses increasingly fulfilling political roles. Surya Paloh, the owner of the newspaper Media Indonesia and the 24-hour television news channel Metro TV, for example, is also the founder and chairperson of the Nasdem Party (Partai NasDem, National Democratic Party).

The influence of media ownership and content on political processes came into sharp view during the 2014 elections. Media tycoons like Surya Paloh or Hary Tanoesoedibjo, who owns the MNC (Media Nusantara Citra) Group, openly used their media outlets to promote the interests of their own political parties and the presidential candidates they supported. The problems of this partisan media environment became evident on the night of the elections when media siding with Joko Widodo and Jusuf Kalla (including Paloh's Media Group) offered quick counts that were favourable to this pair, while those that supported Jokowi's rival Prabowo Subianto reported that Prabowo was leading in their counts. So strong was this partisanship that one channel (Metro TV) declared Jokowi the winner, with another (tvOne, owned by former Golkar chief Aburizal Bakrie) announcing that Prabowo had won. While media partisanship remained evident during the 2019 elections as well, most media companies by then supported the incumbent Jokowi. This led to less polarised reporting in the mainstream media (it continued on social media though), but also to less lively debates on political ideas and policies, and more biased coverage that was supportive of the government (Souisa 2019).

In addition, the problem of media ownership has intensified as a result of increased conglomeration and platform convergence with many owners now controlling not one but multiple platforms. Tanoesoedibjo's MNC group is an excellent example of a multi-platform media group as it includes four television stations, a radio station, a newspaper and an online publication. Other media tycoons like Surya Paloh, Chairul Tanjung or Aburizal Bakrie also own several outlets across different platforms. The political alignment of media bosses has impacted on journalists, who often refrain from critically reporting on issues involving their superiors or the political candidates backed by them. In an extreme case, Aburizal Bakrie purchased the newspaper *Surabaya Post* in 2008, two years after a massive mud volcano had erupted in the town of Sidoarjo after gas drilling by a company owned by Bakrie. Following Bakrie's purchase of the newspaper, its journalists were no longer able to report on the role of Bakrie's company in the mudflow disaster and the lack of compensation given to victims (Tapsell 2015, p. 33). The reforms of the post-authoritarian era have thus created a media environment with multiple outlets across different platforms but whose diversity is nevertheless superficial as many outlets are controlled by a small number of media oligarchs. As a consequence, media content is often adjusted to owners' economic and political agendas, with little consideration for the public good or responsible reporting. This severely compromises the media's ability to act as a vehicle for holding the government accountable.

Civil Society after 1998

Where the media is heavily commercialised and politicised, progressive civil society organisations have an even more important role to play in enhancing accountability. In Indonesia, the political reforms passed in the early *reformasi* years provided a fertile environment for a lively civil society as political freedoms were significantly expanded with the incorporation of civil and political rights in the legal framework (see Chapter 10).

Moreover, foreign donors were now directly able to provide Indonesian organisations with funds, and this support provided many NGOs with the infrastructure necessary for their functioning, although funding alone was by no means a guarantee for their success (Dibley & Ford 2019). Still, it has been estimated that in the first two years alone (1998-2000), the number of non-governmental organisations (NGOs) reached about 70,000. In the context of the economic crisis, many of these new organisations were focused on poverty alleviation, often supporting the government in these endeavours. In addition, many new labour unions and journalist associations were established, as well as legal advocacy groups, women's associations, environmental organisations and a broad-based anti-corruption movement (Beittinger-Lee 2009).

Among those that benefited profoundly from democratisation was the labour movement. Severely repressed under the New Order (Hadiz 1997), unions were barely present in the 1998 protests against the Suharto regime. However, new recognitions of freedom of association and workers' rights translated into the rapid establishment of new unions, both at the national and local levels. A lack of institutionalised links to political parties, however, made it difficult for the labour movement to identify a natural ally or have a political force representing workers' interests. Instead, the movement relied on a range of other strategies such as policy advocacy, collective mobilisation as well as litigation to generate attention for the plight of workers. While this had overall mixed results, in some cases political elites have accommodated the interests of the movement, including in key issues such as minimum wages (Caraway & Ford 2019).

Another prominent pillar of Indonesian civil society is the anti-corruption movement. In fact, even during the New Order, student activists and other regime critics had already repeatedly pointed to corruption as a major problem in Indonesian politics (Setiyono & McLeod 2010). During the 1998 student protests, ending KKN (corruption, collusion and nepotism) was one of the main demands of the demonstrators. Once Suharto had resigned, however, it soon became clear that corruption was not going away. Thus, a growing number of new civil society organisations emerged, dedicated to exposing and documenting the corrupt practices of Indonesia's elite. Among the most prominent groups to lead the struggle against corruption are Indonesia Corruption Watch (ICW), Transparency International Indonesia (TII) and the Pusat Studi Hukum dan Kebijakan Indonesia (PSHK, Indonesian Centre for Law and Policy Studies), with smaller groups emerging in the regions away from the urban centres (Tomsa 2015). Since 2004, they have received institutional support from Indonesia's most popular institution, the Corruption Eradication Commission (Komisi Pemberantasan Korupsi, KPK). Over the years, galvanising public support for the KPK has become one of the main activities for Indonesian civil society as the commission became a frequent target for politically motivated attacks. Through campaigns such as 'Gecko vs Crocodile' in 2009 and 'Coins for the KPK' in 2012 (Schütte 2013), civil society was able to mobilise massive public support for the commission in its battles against elite attempts to curb its powers. In addition, students organised numerous demonstrations in support of the KPK, culminating in the 2019 mass protests mentioned in the introduction of this chapter.

The rapid growth of civil society and some of their successes in supporting the development of democracy contributed to positive evaluations on the state of Indonesian democracy in the early 2000s. As regressive elites started first initiatives to roll back some of the early reforms of the post-Suharto era, civil society was widely seen as an effective bulwark against the interests of the entrenched elite (Mietzner 2012). International leaders, too, sung Indonesia's praises, for example former US President Barack Obama, who during his 2010 visit stated that 'Indonesian democracy is sustained and fortified by its checks and balances: a dynamic civil society; political parties and unions; a vibrant media and engaged citizens who have ensured that - in Indonesia - there will be no turning back from democracy' (Obama 2010).

However, a closer look at some of the civil society groups that were already prominent during the late 1990s and early 2000s – for instance, students and progressive Islamic groups - reveal a more complex picture. While the student movement was at the forefront of democratisation, it dissipated quickly, not least because prominent members of the student movement moved into government or political parties. At the same time, the increased privatisation of the higher education sector also significantly weakened the movement (Sastramidjaja 2019).

Similarly, progressive Islamic scholars who during the late New Order had used religious teachings to push for political reforms and who established progressive networks and organisations after the fall of Suharto soon came under pressure from conservative Islamic groups that also emerged as a result of political liberalisation (Fealy 2019). Within just a few years, progressive groups like the Liberal Islam Network (Jaringan Islam Liberal, JIL) became increasingly vilified for promoting values that were deemed 'contrary to the teachings of Islam' by the Indonesian Council of Ulama (Majelis Ulama Indonesia, MUI), Indonesia's highest Islamic authority. When the MUI issued a fatwa condemning religious pluralism, secularism and liberalism in 2005, physical threats against JIL members increased and shortly the network's foreign donors withdrew their funding after they, too, received threats from radical Islamists.

Institutional Weakness and Fragmentation

The examples of the student movement and liberal Islamic groups highlight some of the political forces that have weakened progressive civil society over time. In addition, another key challenge for civil society in Indonesia has been its institutional weakness. To an extent this can be explained by the legacy of authoritarianism, in which society as a whole was depoliticised and demobilised, and which continues to influence the development of civil society. This was apparent in the immediate years after *reformasi*, with Aspinall (2004, p. 86) noting that civil society groups generally have modest goals and do not seek to transform the state or the larger social order. Instead, they mostly focus on 'restraining, seeking redress from, or gaining other desirable policy outcomes from the state'. As a result of systematic repression under the New Order, pro-democracy groups that might be regarded as more radical remain poorly organised. More established organisations may have fewer problems in terms of organisation but these groups have been so deeply influenced by a history of compromise during the New Order regime that they are ill-equipped to lead radical reform processes (Aspinall 2004).

Closely related to institutional weakness is the fragmentation of civil society. This does not only refer to the sheer number of organisations, but more to the internal tensions and differences. To some extent, fragmentation has historically been part of Indonesian civil society: political parties, for instance, continue to be divided along socio-religious lines. However, beyond the political sphere, fragmentation is also part of activist groups. One example is the Indonesian human rights movement, which has long lacked cohesiveness and is internally divided (McGregor & Setiawan 2019). However, even organisations that claim larger followings – such as those representing peasants and workers – lack coherent umbrella bodies. This prevents such groups from forming effective coalitions, in turn limiting their ability to be a catalyst for progressive change.

A source of fragmentation is competition for funding. Civil society groups remain highly dependent on foreign donors or governments in order to survive. NGOs and community organisations are therefore constantly focused on finding projects that secure income while they are also in increasing competition with one another (Aspinall 2013). This has not only prevented organisations to work together on similar goals, but it has also created dependencies between organisations in Jakarta and their local branches, as well as organisations affiliated with them. Similarly, activists who have had repeated success in accessing funding sources also tend to have elevated influence within pro-democracy circles, which sometimes leads to internal tensions between activists (Aspinall 2019, p. 192).

'Uncivil' Society and Polarisation

In addition to institutional weakness and fragmentation, the ability of progressive civil society groups to strengthen democracy is also undermined by 'uncivil' society organisations. 'Uncivil' society organisations can be defined as those elements of civil society that 'have a negative influence on human development, peace, security and democracy' (Beittinger-Lee 2009, p. 20). Arguably, the most prominent representatives of uncivil society are vigilante (*preman*) groups that have a long history of attacking or intimidating liberal civil society activists, religious and sexual minorities as well as leftist groups, often at the direction of the security apparatus (Jaffrey 2019). Some of these *preman* like the Pancasila Youth (Pemuda Pancasila) have their origins in the New Order period, whilst others were formed afterwards.

With the rise of religious conservatism in recent years, Islamist vigilante groups like the Islamic Defenders Front (Front Pembela Islam, FPI) have grown into significant pressure groups that can mobilise large numbers of followers for political purposes. Long known primarily for its violent raids on entertainment venues and its fight against vice and 'immoral acts' (Wilson 2006, p. 285), the FPI developed close ties with influential power brokers at the highest level who often turned a blind eye on the organisation's violent attacks against political opponents. The impact of 'uncivil' society groups on liberal civil society actors has been evident in a wide array of issues. The mobilisation of Islamist groups in the mass protests against Ahok is perhaps the most compelling example (see Chapters 6 and 10), but vigilante groups have also perpetrated violence and intimidation against artists and intellectuals as well as LGBT Indonesians (see Chapter 9). Another example of growing illiberal or uncivil Islam can be observed in the rise of anti-feminist activists whose political engagement stems from their unease with progressive women's rights activism (Rinaldo 2019).

Over the last two electoral cycles, the divisions between Islamists and pluralists have become so deep that many pluralists have become increasingly intolerant themselves, approving the government's heavy-handed crackdown on Islamist groups without consideration for due legal process. To justify their views and actions, pluralist actors have used a hyper-nationalist defence of the Pancasila. This became especially evident following the Islamist mobilisation against Ahok in 2017, when President Jokowi initiated a new national holiday, Pancasila Day. As Jokowi referred increasingly often to the sanctity of the Unitary State of Indonesia, and boldly stated that he would ban any organisation considered to contravene the Pancasila, his rhetoric sounded eerily similar to the kind of state propaganda heard under authoritarianism (Hadiz 2017).

Jokowi made good on his threats in July 2017 when a new government regulation allowed the ban of organisations considered to be at odds with the Pancasila. While directed primarily at the transnational Islamist organisation Hizbut Tahrir Indonesia, the decree has the potential for the unilateral ban of any organisation deemed undesirable by the government (see Chapter 10). Worryingly, the decree was supported by many liberal civil society actors, who argued that the ban was necessary for the survival of the Indonesian nation (Mietzner 2021). As such, actors who openly presented themselves as supporters of a pluralist Indonesia increasingly resorted to illiberal measures and appeared comfortable to sacrifice democratic freedoms so long as it served the goal of curbing the growing influence of Islamist groups. The polarisation between conservatives and pluralists also came to the fore during the 2019 elections, when pluralist groups and actors sided with the Jokowi camp, while Islamist groups supported the Prabowo campaign. Within this climate, the shrinking group of principled pro-democracy activists advocated for abstention (*golput*), only to attract criticism from all sides. The government even went so far as to threaten those choosing to abstain with criminal sanctions, even though the legal basis for that is questionable (Mudhoffir & A'yun 2019).

Coercion

The government's threats to deploy punitive measures towards those who expressed frustration illustrates an increased willingness of political elites to restrict the capacity of civil society groups to protest. This was evident in the government's response to the 2019 student protests mentioned at the beginning of this chapter. In many ways, these protests against weakening the KPK and amending the Criminal Code were remarkable, not only for their scale and geographical spread, but also for their ability to move beyond the deep divisions that had come to define civil society in the years prior. Indeed, the protests saw both pluralist and Islamist student groups come together, putting forward a strong reformist agenda in opposition to corruption and power abuse by the ruling elite (Mietzner 2021). The government initially seemed to be caught off guard by the protests and put the proposed amendments on hold, but eventually passed the changes to the KPK law, severely weakening the anti-graft body (Butt 2019).

Not only did the government ignore the demands of the students, but it also deployed the security apparatus against them, in what was the most heavy-handed response to student protests since 1998. The police used water cannons and tear gas to disperse the crowd, and in Kendari, the capital of Southeast Sulawesi, two students died as a result of gunshot wounds (The Straits Times 2019). In addition, protestors were also subjected to intimidation by state agencies, with the Minister for Higher Education warning university rectors to prevent students from joining the protests and asking them to 'engage nicely in a dialogue' instead. He added that if students chose to protest, they would 'face the police and military' (Swaragita 2019). This was so effective that in some cases, students reported being threatened with being expelled or the suspension of their scholarship (CNN Indonesia 2019).

Despite the harsh response from the state, student activists have continued to mobilise against the ongoing rollback of democratic achievements. In 2020, widespread protests erupted once again, this time in response to the so-called omnibus bill, which sought to amend 79 laws and, according to the government, would facilitate investment and support job creation. Critics pointed at the implications the bill would have on social protections, including worker's rights, allowing employers to slash severance pay from 32 monthly wages to only 19 times, and making it easier for them to hire staff as contract and part-time workers. Concerns were also raised with regard to environmental protection, with environmental risk assessments only required for 'high-risk' investments in what could further damage Indonesia's ecosystems (Hosen, Kingsley & Lindsey 2020). Despite the protests, the bill was passed into law by parliament in October 2020.

Once again, students and workers took to the streets, mobilising thousands of people all across Indonesia. But the government responded to these protests in a similar fashion to those in 2019. Once again, the police used violence against demonstrators and this time detained more than 5,000 people (Lane 2020). Again, the Ministry for Higher Education called upon universities to prevent students from engaging in protests, stating that 'it's better and more elegant to do academic research than rally' (Nurbaiti & Syakriah 2020). It does not require much imagination to see the parallels with the depoliticisation of students, and indeed society as a whole, under authoritarianism several decades prior.

Conclusion

Civil society and the media can play a key oversight role towards more accountable governance. They can counterbalance the power of the state, oppose authoritarianism and prevent the state from being controlled by vested interests. However, the democratising potential of civil society and the media is not a given. This chapter has brought some of Indonesia's democratic deficits into sharp view. While the respective contexts of civil society and the media differ, they are also closely related to one another. In general, four factors can be identified that have negatively influenced the democratising potential of civil society and the media: the legacies of authoritarianism, oligarchic control, social and political conservatism and outright repression.

The legacies of authoritarianism are manifested in civil society by the long-term impact that the New Order's policies of demobilisation and depoliticisation have had. Despite its rapid growth, civil society in Indonesia remains overall institutionally weak and fragmented, which is further exacerbated by a dependency on foreign funding, which has increased competition among civil society actors. Parallel to the growth of civil society, Indonesia also witnessed the expansion of print and broadcast media, while social media platforms have also become increasingly influential. However, much of the Indonesian media is in the hands of powerful oligarchs who have not held back in using their platforms to their own political advantage.

Rising social and political conservatism have also made their mark on civil society and the media. Illiberal civil society groups are as much part of the political and social fabric as liberal ones. A freer media landscape and the rise of social media have also provided new platforms for these groups to disseminate their ideas and gain popular support. Indeed, illiberal groups have gained such traction that deep divisions have emerged within civil society.

Finally, what perhaps constitutes the greatest threat is the repression that is used against civil society actors. In the early years of the *reformasi* era, this repression was particularly directed at liberal civil society actors and media workers, often perpetrated by Islamist groups or those backed by them. However, in recent years, the government has also actively engaged in the repression of civil society actors. Initially, these repressions were targeted at Islamist groups, but more progressive actors who criticise the government have also come under attack. Overall, the space for civil society in Indonesia is shrinking rapidly, with devastating consequences for human rights, political trust and social cohesion.

References

Alagappa, M 2004, 'Civil society and political change: an analytical framework', in M Alagappa (ed), *Civil society and political change in Asia. Expanding and Contradicting Democratic Space*, Stanford University Press, Stanford, pp. 25–57.

Aspinall, E 2004, 'Indonesia: transformation of civil society and democratic breakthrough', in M Alagappa (ed), *Civil society and political change in Asia. Expanding and Contradicting Democratic Space*, Stanford University Press, Stanford, pp. 61–86.

Aspinall, E 2012, 'Indonesia: moral force politics and the struggle against authoritarianism', in ML Weiss & E Aspinall (eds), *Student activism in Asia: between protest and powerlessness*, University of Minnesota Press, Minneapolis & London, pp. 153–179.

Aspinall, E 2013, 'A nation in fragments. Patronage and neoliberalism in contemporary Indonesia', *Critical Asian Studies*, vol. 45, no. 1, pp. 27–54.

Aspinall, E 2019, 'Conclusion: social movements, patronage democracy, and populist backlash in Indonesia', in T Dibley & M Ford (eds), *Activists in transition. Progressive politics in democratic Indonesia*, Cornell University Press, Ithaca, pp. 187–201.

Aspinall, E 2020, 'Indonesian protests point to old patterns', *New Mandala*, viewed 11 April 2021, <https://www.newmandala.org/indonesian-protests-point-to-old-patterns/>.

Beittinger-Lee, V 2009, (*Un*)*civil society and political change in Indonesia: a contested arena*, Routledge, London & New York.

Butt, S 2019, 'Amendments Spell Disaster for the KPK', viewed 20 February 2021, <https://indonesiaatmelbourne.unimelb.edu.au/amendments-spell-disaster-for-the-kpk/>.

Caraway, T & Ford, M 2019, 'Indonesia's labor movement and democratization', in T Dibley & M Ford (eds), *Activists in transition. Progressive politics in democratic Indonesia*, Cornell University Press, Ithaca, pp. 61–78.

CNN Indonesia 2019, 'Puluhan mahasiswa pedemo melapor diancam DO oleh kampus', viewed 11 April 2021, <https://www.cnnindonesia.com/nasional/20191003200116-20-436577/puluhan-mahasiswa-pedemo-melapor-diancam-do-oleh-kampus>.

Diamond, L 1994, 'Rethinking civil society: towards democratic consolidation', *Journal of Democracy*, vol. 5, no. 3, pp. 4–17.

Dibley, T & Ford, M 2019, 'Introduction: social movements and democratization in Indonesia', in T Dibley & M Ford (eds), *Activists in transition. Progressive politics in democratic Indonesia*, Cornell University Press, Ithaca, pp. 1–21.

Fealy, G 2019, 'Reformasi and the decline of liberal Islam', in T Dibley & M Ford (eds), *Activists in transition. Progressive politics in democratic Indonesia*, Cornell University Press, Ithaca, pp. 117–134.

Freedom House 2020a, 'Freedom in the world 2020: Indonesia', viewed 9 April 2021, <https://freedomhouse.org/country/indonesia/freedom-world/2020>.

Freedom House 2020b, 'Freedom on the net 2020: Indonesia', viewed 9 April 2021, <https://freedomhouse.org/country/indonesia/freedom-net/2020>.

Hadiz, VR 1997, *Workers and the state in new order Indonesia*, Routledge, London and New York.

Hadiz, VR 2000, 'Retrieving the past for the future? Indonesia and the New Order legacy', *Southeast Asian Journal of Social Science*, vol. 28, no. 2, pp. 11–33.

Hadiz, VR 2017, 'Indonesia's year of democratic setbacks: towards a new phase of deepening illiberalism?', *Bulletin of Indonesian Economic Studies*, vol. 53, no. 3, pp. 261–278.

Hamid, S 2018, 'Normalising intolerance: elections, religions and everyday life in Indonesia', viewed 10 April 2021, <https://law.unimelb.edu.au/centres/cilis/research /publications/cilis-policy-papers/normalising-intolerance-elections,-religion-and -everyday-life-in-indonesia>.

Harsono, A 2019, 'Indonesia's journalists grapple with Islamism', viewed 11 April 2021, < https://fpif.org/indonesias-journalists-grapple-with-islamism/>.

Herman 2020, 'Indonesia has 197 million internet users in 2020, APJII survey shows', viewed 10 April 2021, <https://jakartaglobe.id/tech/indonesia-has-197-million-internet -users-in-2020-apjii-survey-shows>.

Hosen, N, Kingsley, JJ & Lindsey, T 2020, 'Indonesia's omnibus bill: typo or 'mistaken instruction?', viewed 11 April 2021, <https://indonesiaatmelbourne.unimelb.edu.au/ indonesias-omnibus-bill-typo-or-mistaken-instruction/>.

Jaffrey, S 2019, 'In the state's stead? Vigilantism and policing of religious offence in Indonesia', in T Power & E Warburton (eds), *Democracy in Indonesia: from stagnation to regression?*, ISEAS Yusof Ishak Institute, Singapore, pp. 303–325.

Jurriëns, E 2004, *From monologue to dialogue: radio and reform in Indonesia*, KITLV Press, Leiden.

Jurriëns, E & Tapsell, R 2017, 'Challenges and opportunities of the digital 'revolution' in Indonesia', in E Jurriëns & R Tapsell, *Digital Indonesia: connectivity and divergence*, ISEAS Yusof Ishak Institute, Singapore, pp. 1–18.

Keane, J 1998, *Civil society: old images, new visions*, Polity Press, Cambridge and Malden.

Kitley, P 2000, *Television, nation and culture in Indonesia*, Ohio University Press, Athens.

Kopecký, P & Mudde, C 2003, 'Rethinking civil society', *Democratization*, vol. 10, no. 3, pp. 1–14.

Lane, M 2020, 'Protests against the Omnibus law and the evolution of Indonesia's social opposition', viewed 11 April 2021, <https://www.iseas.edu.sg/wp-content/uploads /2020/11/ISEAS_Perspective_2020_128.pdf>.

Lim, M 2013, 'Many clicks but little sticks: social media activism in Indonesia', *Journal of Contemporary Asia*, vol. 43, no. 4, pp. 636–657.

Masduki 2020, *Public service broadcasting and post-authoritarian Indonesia*, Palgrave Macmillan, Singapore.

McGregor, K & Setiawan, K 2019, 'Shifting from international to 'Indonesian' justice measures: two decades of addressing past human rights violations', *Journal of Contemporary Asia*, vol. 49, no. 5, pp. 837–861.

Mietzner, M 2012, 'Indonesia's democratic stagnation: anti-reformist elites and resilient civil society', *Democratization*, vol. 19, no. 2, pp. 209–229.

Mietzner, M 2021, 'Sources of resistance to democratic decline: Indonesian civil society and its trials', *Democratization*, vol. 28, no. 1, pp. 161–178.

Mudhoffir, AM & A'yun, RQ 2019, 'Can golput save Indonesian democracy?', viewed 8 April 2021, <https://indonesiaatmelbourne.unimelb.edu.au/can-golput-save -indonesian-democracy/>.

Nuraniyah, N 2017, 'Online extremism: the advent of encrypted private chat groups', in E Jurriëns & R Tapsell, *Digital Indonesia: connectivity and divergence*, ISEAS Yusof Ishak Institute, Singapore, pp. 163–185.

Nurbaiti, A & Syakriah, A 2020, 'Don't join protests, education ministry says', viewed 11 April 2021,<https://www.thejakartapost.com/news/2020/10/10/dont-join-protests-education-ministry-says.html>.

Obama, B 2010, 'Remarks by the President at the University of Indonesia in Jakarta, Indonesia', viewed 8 April 2010, <https://obamawhitehouse.archives.gov/the-press-office/2010/11/10/remarks-president-university-indonesia-jakarta-indonesia>.

Parlina, I 2016, 'Self-censorship runs amok on local television', viewed 7 April 2021, <https://www.thejakartapost.com/news/2016/02/27/self-censorship-runs-amok-local-television.html>.

Purdey, J, Missbach, A & McRae, M 2020, *Indonesia: state and society in transition*, Lynne Rienner Publishers, Boulder & London.

Rinaldo, R 2019, 'The women's movement and Indonesia's transition to democracy', in T Dibley & M Ford (eds), *Activists in transition. Progressive politics in democratic Indonesia*, Cornell University Press, Ithaca, pp. 135–152.

Sastramidjaja, Y 2019, 'Student movements and Indonesia's democratic transition', in T Dibley & M Ford (eds), *Activists in transition. Progressive politics in democratic Indonesia*, Cornell University Press, Ithaca, pp. 23–40.

Schütte, SA 2013, 'Coins for the KPK', *Inside Indonesia*, no. 111, viewed 1 April 2021, <https://www.insideindonesia.org/coins-for-the-kpk>.

Sen, K & Hill, DT 2000, *Media, culture and politics in Indonesia*, Oxford University Press, Oxford.

Setiyono, B & McLeod, RH 2010, 'Civil society organisations' contribution to the anti-corruption movement in Indonesia', *Bulletin of Indonesian Economic Studies*, vol. 46, no. 3, pp. 347–370.

Steele, J 2012, 'The making of the 1999 Indonesian press law', *Indonesia*, no. 94, pp. 1–22.

Souisa, H 2019, 'Partisan players: television and the elections', viewed 10 April 2021, <https://indonesiaatmelbourne.unimelb.edu.au/partisan-players-television-and-the-elections/>.

Swaragita, G 2019, 'Rectors encouraging students to protest will be sanctioned: minister', viewed 11 April 2021, <https://www.thejakartapost.com/news/2019/09/26/rectors-encouraging-students-to-protest-will-be-sanctioned-minister.html>.

Tapsell, R 2012, 'Old tricks in a new era: self-censorship in Indonesian journalism', *Asian Studies Review*, vol. 36, no. 2, pp. 227–245.

Tapsell, R 2015, 'Indonesia's media oligarchy and the 'Jokowi phenomenon'', *Indonesia*, no. 99, pp. 29–50.

The Straits Times 2019, 'Second student dies after Indonesian protestors clash with police', viewed 11 April 2021, <https://www.straitstimes.com/asia/se-asia/second-student-dies-after-indonesian-protesters-clash-with-police>.

Tomsa, D 2015, 'Local politics and corruption in Indonesia's outer islands', *Bijdragen tot de Taal-, Land- en Volkenkunde*, vol. 171, no. 2/3, pp. 196–219.

Wilson, ID 2006, 'Continuity and change: the changing contours of organized violence in post–New Order Indonesia', *Critical Asian Studies*, vol. 38, no. 2, pp. 265–297.

8   Human Development
and Public Health

Introduction

In 2020, the Indonesian Central Bureau of Statistics conducted its first official census in ten years. The results showed that since 2010 Indonesia's population had grown by more than 30 million to over 270 million people (Badan Pusat Statistik 2020). With a birth rate of around 2.3 in 2018, current trends indicate that by 2045 the country will have a population of 311–318 million. Such demographic scenarios raise challenging questions about the Indonesian government's ability to fulfil the basic needs of its citizens in terms of health, education and standards of living. Arguably, these questions have become even more pertinent after the Covid-19 pandemic exposed serious weaknesses in Indonesia's health system and plunged the country's economy into its first recession since the onset of democratisation.

As the pandemic spread through Indonesia in 2020 and 2021, the unprecedented combination of public health and economic policy challenges was threatening to reverse decades of progress made by Indonesia on the Human Development Index (HDI), a statistic composite index that is annually published by the United Nations Development Programme (UNDP). Based on the human development approach pioneered by economist and international development theorist Mahbub ul Haq, the HDI aims at measuring whether people are able to 'be' and 'do' desirable things in life, such as being well nourished, sheltered and healthy, being able to work, having access to education and participating in community life. The index is used to rank countries in four tiers of human development: very high, high, medium and low.

While the HDI is a simplified evaluation of human development, it does provide a good starting point to measure well-being worldwide. The HDI has three main dimensions, namely health, education and standard of living. These are assessed respectively by life expectancy at birth, mean and expected years of schooling and gross national income per capita. Since the 2019 edition, the index also pays greater attention to a country's carbon footprint and the relationship between human development and environmental protection. To that

DOI: 10.4324/9780429459511-8

end, a new Planetary pressures-adjusted HDI (PHDI) was introduced, which takes into account a country's carbon dioxide emissions and material footprint per capita.

This chapter will primarily discuss Indonesia's track record in the original three dimensions, while environmental issues are examined in detail in Chapter 11. By focusing on Indonesia's achievements and challenges in relation to health, education and economic development, the chapter will first highlight the interconnectedness of the three dimensions and the political dynamics that shape social and economic policymaking and its outcomes. The second part of the chapter then zooms in specifically on Indonesia's handling of the Covid-19 pandemic. This section not only discusses some of the major flaws in Indonesia's public health system, but also highlights how the Covid-19 crisis has exposed some of the most pressing threats to Indonesian democracy (Mietzner 2020), including populism, religious conservatism, polarisation and corruption. All in all, this chapter argues that these political factors have not only hampered a more effective response to one of the largest global health crises of our time, but they have also influenced socio-economic development more generally.

Human Development in Indonesia

In the mid-1960s, shortly after the traumatic events of 1965 heralded the regime change from Sukarno's Guided Democracy to Suharto's New Order, the celebrated Swedish economist and sociologist Gunnar Myrdal analysed the state of the Indonesian economy. Given Sukarno's legacy of hyper-inflation, widespread hunger and poverty, Myrdal (1968, p. 489) wrote in his famous book *Asian Drama* that 'there seems to be little prospect of rapid economic growth in Indonesia'. Yet, within

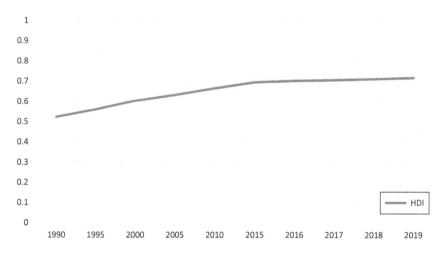

Figure 8.1 Indonesia's Human Development Index, 1990–2019

just a few years, Suharto and his team of technocratic economists achieved exactly that. As they transformed the country's economic fortunes, millions of Indonesians were lifted out of poverty and living standards improved noticeably (Hill 1996). By the time the first Human Development Report was published in 1990, Indonesia was a newly industrialising economy and an important part of what World Bank economists called the 'East Asian economic miracle' (Birdsall et al 1993).

Since then, Indonesia has steadily improved its score on the HDI (Figure 8.1). In the 2018 edition, which was published in 2019, the country reached 'high' human development for the first time, a status it retained the following year. The UNDP called Indonesia's improvements a 'historic achievement' (Arbi 2019) and praised the country's dedicated efforts to reach better health and education outcomes and economic growth. At the same time, however, challenges remain. The introduction of the new PHDI in particular illustrates some of Indonesia's main problems as the difference between its HDI value and the new PHDI was among the largest in East Asia and the Pacific (Sutrisno 2020). But even in the three original dimensions of health, education and economic growth, Indonesia continues to face some significant challenges, as the following sections will outline.

Health

The health dimension of the HDI is captured by life expectancy at birth. Today, Indonesians live longer than ever before. Since the introduction of the HDI in 1990, life expectancy in Indonesia has grown from 62.3 years to 71.7 years in 2020. Women live nearly five years longer than men (74 years for women, compared to 69.6 years for men). This increase is largely a result of the expansion of Indonesia's healthcare system and successful interventions against communicable, maternal, neonatal and nutritional diseases that began during the New Order (Mboi et al 2018).

In 2014, Indonesia achieved an important public health milestone when it launched its first universal health coverage (UHC) scheme. It had been a long time coming. The beginnings of basic healthcare in Indonesia date back as far as the New Order when the Suharto regime expanded the network of low-cost healthcare posts (*puskesmas*) at the local level from about 1,000 in 1969 to more than 6,000 in 1991 (Fossati 2017, p. 184). For more expensive hospital treatment, however, the regime provided little support, neither through subsidies nor health insurance.

It was only after the fall of authoritarianism, and partly in response to the challenges faced by many Indonesians during the economic crisis, that a programme for health insurance for the poor was rolled out. This basic program was implemented through national and regional policies. In 2004, the Law on National Social Security was enacted, followed in 2011 by the Law on the Social Security Agency (BPJS). These laws expanded the coverage and eligibility of state-funded health insurance programmes by including, for example, provision of healthcare in case of old age. In 2014, the government finally launched its National Health Insurance Scheme (Jaminan Kesehatan Nasional or JKN), which aims to provide health coverage for all Indonesians. Premiums for the poor and near poor are covered by the government. By 2017, JKN had contracts with 26,000 health facilities and providers, serving 68 percent of the total population (Mboi et al 2018).

Even before the JKN was launched, many local governments had already experimented with localised healthcare programmes (Fossati 2017). These programmes differed in terms of their coverage, with some providing almost universal and free healthcare, while others pursued a more targeted approach for the poor. Regardless of the details, these local healthcare schemes proved enormously popular and directly contributed to politicians' electoral appeal. Perhaps the most famous example of this is the Jakarta Health Card (Kartu Jakarta Sehat, KJS) programme, which played a significant role in the appeal and election of Jokowi as governor of Jakarta and, subsequently, president of Indonesia (Berenschot, Hanani & Sambodho 2018). All in all, local healthcare schemes helped pave the way for the JKN as they 'put the issue of equity in access to healthcare on the national political agenda' (Fossati 2017, p. 187).

Along with the expansion of the healthcare system, total health expenditure in Indonesia per person rose from 1.9 percent of GDP in 2000 to 2.9 percent of GDP in 2018. Yet, while the increase is notable, Indonesia's overall spending on health is still low in comparison to other countries. For example, Thailand and Malaysia both spent 3.8 percent of GDP on health in 2018, whereas this figure was 5.9 percent in Vietnam (World Bank 2021a). Regionwide, Brunei and Laos were the only Southeast Asian countries to spend smaller percentages of GDP on health than Indonesia in 2018, while figures for comparable economies elsewhere like Brazil (9.5 percent) or South Africa (8.3 percent) were up to three times higher than Indonesia.

Apart from inadequate budget allocations, other healthcare challenges for Indonesia relate to the sheer scope of implementing a nationwide system in an archipelagic state that consists of more than 17,000 islands and stretches 5,200 kilometres from east to west. More than half of Indonesia's population of 270 million live on Java, with the rest of the population unevenly distributed across the nation, which means that there are substantial challenges for the equitable delivery of health services. In fact, Indonesia's national health statistics often disguise substantial regional and socio-economic inequalities, with wealthier provinces providing far better health services and recording better health outcomes than poorer provinces, especially in Eastern Indonesia. For example, Pisani, Kok & Nugroho (2017, p. 268) report that

in Maluku, with a provincial GDP of US$170 per person per year, fully 52% of children under 5 were stunted in 2013, twice the fraction that suffered from stunting in Riau Islands province, where per capita GDP was US$870 a year.

It is clear therefore that healthcare in Indonesia is a matter of both access and quality of service. Reports of misdiagnosis and mistreatment abound, and patients are often turned away from health facilities or have to be transferred elsewhere. Many of the best treatments are not available in Indonesia, while many basic treatments are also missing in the public health system (Aspinall 2014). In the last two decades, while Indonesia has overall seen increased ratios in health workers to the population, the number is still lower than the recommendations of the WHO and there are stark geographical discrepancies (Mahendradhata et al 2017). Ultimately, significant increases in expenditure on health are needed to improve both access and quality, although this may place a burden on taxpayers, which may then also erode elite support for universal coverage (Aspinall 2014).

Indeed, political elites and their role in the broader political economy within which the health system operates are another factor that inhibits better healthcare in Indonesia. One way in which this is apparent is the application of illegal fees on poor patients, for instance by denying them access unless they pay a fee or providing them with poor quality if they are served without fee. This can be attributed to a coalition of interests of state officials and their corporate allies, which exercise authority over the allocation of resources and access. This coalition has had a substantial interest in maintaining illegal fees. In turn, the persistence of these fees means that programmes aimed at providing free healthcare to the poor remain underfunded (Rosser 2012).

Finally, yet more challenges for Indonesia's healthcare system are arising from its very success in advancing human development. Increased life expectancy is a laudable achievement, but it also brings new demographic challenges as the proportion of the population aged over 60 years is growing. In 2017, only 8.6 percent of Indonesians were over 60, but according to UN estimates, this number will increase to nearly 20 percent by 2050 (United Nations 2017). Given the paucity of government facilities specifically designed for the elderly, one of the major challenges for Indonesia will be to maintain the quality of life for this age group. Other challenges are the rise in cardiovascular diseases as well as diseases related to high blood pressure, high blood sugar and tobacco use, all of which have increased dramatically in the past 25 years as a result of poor diets and lifestyle. In fact, Indonesia's rates of high blood pressure and smoking are among the highest in the world (see Box 8.1).

Box 8.1: Indonesia's Tobacco Industry

Indonesia has one of the highest smoking rates in the world. According to the official data, nearly 70 percent of all men and one in five children aged between 13 and 15 smoke, even though the legal minimum age for smoking is 18. This comes at a great cost to public health, with smoking being the leading cause of preventable deaths in the country, and parental smoking has been linked indirectly with stunting among children in poor families. Smoking also contributes to poverty, with cigarettes being the second largest household expenditure after rice for poor families.

Various factors contribute to high rates of smoking in Indonesia. These include that Indonesia is the only country in the Asia Pacific region that has not ratified the World Health Organization's (WHO's) Framework Convention on Tobacco Control. There are also few regulations that restrict the advertising of the tobacco industry from advertising, and weak enforcement of the control regulations that exist. In addition, tobacco companies have been successful in popularising the idea that smoking is part of culture, while religious organisations have been ambivalent, making it easier for smokers to ignore religious prohibitions. Taken together, this has normalised high rates of smoking in the country.

Moreover, tobacco companies continue to hold significant economic power and political influence. Tobacco companies are major investors, employers and taxpayers, and are very well-connected to politicians, often becoming a key source of campaign finance. They also have the ability to mobilise popular forces (such as tobacco farmers) to support their cause, meaning they are well-positioned to resist the efforts of the tobacco control lobby (Rosser 2015; Rosemary & Ciptaningtyas 2020).

Education

The education dimension in the HDI is measured by taking into account both the mean years of schooling for adults of 25 years and above and the expected years of schooling for children of school-entering age. For both, Indonesia has made significant improvements. The number of expected years of schooling climbed from 10.1 years in 1990 to 13.6 years in 2019. The mean years of schooling have increased from 3.3 years in 1990 to 8.2 in 2019 (UNDP 2020), though it is noteworthy that women tend to receive a year less education than men (7.8 years for females compared to 8.6 years for males). There has also been an increase in literacy rates from 81.5 percent in 1990 to 95.7 percent in 2020. Similarly, gross enrolment ratios have improved significantly across all educational sectors, particularly in secondary (from 47 percent in 1990 to 89 percent in 2020) and tertiary (from 8 percent in 1990 to 36 percent in 2020) education (UNDP 2021).

The improvements in the education dimension can be explained by investments in this sector. Under the New Order, the geographical reach of the education system was improved, which enhanced access to education. Once again, however, Indonesia invested less than neighbouring countries and the system itself was largely used as a tool to propagate the state ideology Pancasila (Rosser 2015). Thus, while the quantity of educational institutions and the years of schooling increased, the quality of education remained low. Following 1998, investment in educational infrastructure continued by building more and more schools, especially in rural areas where access to education has often been difficult. In addition, the government endeavoured to lower the costs of schooling and improve the quality of teachers. These efforts to expand supply, enhance access and improve the quality of education have been intertwined with rising income levels, which has also increased demand for education. As a result, there has been an increase in enrolment rates at all levels of the education system (Rosser 2018).

However, just like during the New Order, these improvements have not been matched by educational quality and learning outcomes, with studies suggesting that since the fall of authoritarianism, achievement levels have improved little and compare poorly to neighbouring countries like Malaysia, Thailand and Vietnam (Rosser 2018). A key problem is the low quality of educators at all levels. Teachers have few incentives to seek professional development and there is no reward system for innovative, successful educators. Government management of teachers is also poor, while absenteeism among teachers continues to be a problem, particularly in remote areas.

Moreover, there are deep inequalities in the educational system. These include a significant lack of schools for students with special needs, high dropout rates for children from poorer families at the end of (lower) secondary school and discrepancies between enrolment at schools between urban and rural areas (Purdey, Missbach & McRae 2020, pp. 115–116). Last but not least, meaningful reforms in the education sector have also been hampered by elite actors, including bureaucrats, political leaders and business figures, whose main interest has been to expand the scope of education in order to create a large labour market rather than improve the quality of learning (Rosser 2018).

Income

The final indicator of the Human Development Index is income. In this category, Indonesia has made enormous advances since the 1960s. According to Hill (2015, p. 286), average per capita income increased about sixfold between 1960 and 2015. Only during major upheavals such as the regime change from Guided Democracy to the New Order, the Asian financial crisis of 1997–1998 and the Covid-19 pandemic in 2020 has Indonesia recorded negative GDP growth, otherwise economic growth has been remarkably solid. In the first two decades of the democratic era, Indonesia's gross national income per capita increased from $4,202 in 1999 to $11,459 in 2020.

Back in 1998, the Asian financial crisis had hit Indonesia hard: by the end of that year, nearly 25 percent of the population was living below the poverty line and many people were forced to find other (and largely reduced) sources of income outside of urban areas, often in the informal sector. This in turn led to deteriorating health outcomes and education attendance, particularly for poor families (Perdana & Maxwell 2011, p. 276). The Habibie government sought to respond to these challenges through macroeconomic interventions aimed at stabilising the country's economy as well as a number of social welfare measures that included job creation programmes. Subsequent administrations continued poverty reduction initiatives, but it was only under the presidency of Susilo Bambang Yudhoyono that a direct cash assistance programme for poor households known as BLT (Bantuan Langsung Tunai or Direct Cash Assistance) was introduced. While the distribution of the programme left much to be desired (Purdey, Missbach & McRae 2020, p. 128), it was widely popular and both the BLT programme and other assistance packages (i.e. financial assistance for families to send their children to school and attend regular health checks) contributed to Yudhoyono's re-election in 2009 (Perdana & Maxwell 2011, p. 279). By the end of his second term in 2014, Yudhoyono had overseen a reduction in the national poverty rate from 16.7 percent in 2004 to 11.3 percent (Manning & Miranti 2015, p. 312).

The successes in reducing poverty, however, were offset by a sharp increase in inequality during the Yudhoyono years. While the Indonesian economy has long been dominated by an extremely rich and gradually expanding oligarchy (Winters 2011), more and more second-tier elites also increased their wealth substantially during the Yudhoyono period. According to Hill (2015, p. 318), the two main reasons for this were huge wage increases for skilled employees of multinational companies and the commodity boom of the mid-2000s which provided new regional elites with enormous profits and opened up wide-ranging opportunities for rent-seeking. As a result, Indonesia's Gini coefficient – the most commonly used measure of inequality – jumped from the mid-0.30s at the beginning of the *reformasi* era to 0.4 at the end of Yudhoyono's term in office.

Well aware of the widening gap between the rich and poor, current president Jokowi has focused his economic policies less on poverty reduction and more on large infrastructure projects, including airports, railways and roads, even though he did continue and in fact expand various social welfare programmes from the Yudhoyono era. Infrastructure projects are commonly believed to be a prerequisite for economic growth, particularly in developing countries (Davidson 2015) and in Indonesia, they may have helped reduce the wealth gap by providing economic benefits primarily to the growing middle class (Suryahadi & Al Izzati 2019). Indeed, during Jokowi's first term in office, Indonesia's Gini coefficient fell back to under 0.4 (Figure 8.2).

Whether or not that is related to Jokowi's infrastructure drive, however, is unclear, not least because several prestige projects stalled during or even before construction. In other words, the modest reduction in inequality during Jokowi's first term may well have had other reasons, for instance salary decreases at the top range after the end of the commodity boom. In any case, Jokowi seems to have convinced most of his supporters that inequality is contracting due to his policies

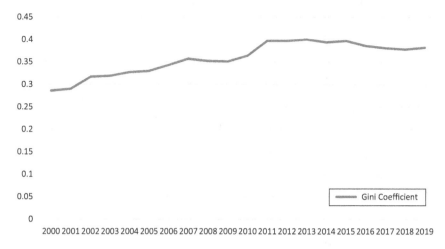

Figure 8.2 Inequality in Indonesia, according to the Gini coefficient

as survey analysis has shown strong correlations between perceptions of inequality and partisan support or opposition to Jokowi (Muhtadi & Warburton 2020).

These developments occurred within a broader context of solid but ultimately underwhelming economic growth. Throughout Jokowi's first term in office, growth rates remained below the government's target of 7 percent. Key obstacles that impeded higher growth rates included the power of entrenched rent-seeking networks, disputes between national and local governments and land conflicts between the government and communities affected by proposed infrastructure projects (Davidson 2015, p. 230). The most dramatic challenge to the Indonesian economy since the beginning of democratic rule, however, came in 2020 with the arrival of Covid-19 in Indonesia. Within just a few months after the first cases were confirmed, the pandemic had unravelled many earlier achievements in macroeconomic management and poverty alleviation.

The Politics of Containing the Covid-19 Pandemic

On 30 January 2020, the World Health Organization (WHO) declared the Covid-19 outbreak, which had originated in China but swiftly spread around the world, an international public health concern. As infections were reported from all over the world, many Southeast Asian countries began implementing containment measures such as mandatory face masks, mass testing, social distancing and lockdowns. By contrast, business as usual continued in Indonesia where the government claimed it had no cases until early March. Government officials attributed this to wide-ranging and often bizarre factors, including prayer, diet, traditional herbal remedies, Indonesia's climate and supposed immunity to the virus. When the government at last acknowledged that there were indeed cases of Covid-19 in Indonesia, it under-reported the number of infections and deaths. The government also failed to implement strict stay-at-home orders as recommended by medical experts. By the end of March 2020, the WHO demanded that Indonesia respond more seriously to the pandemic (Lindsey & Mann 2020; Mietzner 2020, p. 228).

By April 2020, the number of reported cases had risen to more than 2,700 per week. A spike of funerals in Jakarta, up 40 percent from the average prior to the pandemic, was a stark reminder of the human cost of the spread of the virus. It also underlined the possibility that many cases went undetected (Allard, Kapoor & Widianto 2020). Still, Indonesia conducted worryingly few Covid tests. It was not before July 2020 that the country finally met the WHO requirement of at least one swab test per 1,000 of the population, which amounts to 40,000 people per day (Souisa 2021). Even after meeting this testing guideline, however, the infection rate remained high and daily cases continued to grow. But while many countries imposed lockdowns and other restrictions on movement, Indonesian officials from the health ministry actually warned against new restrictions due to the high economic costs.

The *laissez-faire* response from the central government in Jakarta contrasted with the actions taken by provincial, municipal and district authorities in areas where the virus spread most rapidly. Local government responses in these regions often included large-scale social restrictions known as PSBB (*pembatasan sosial berskala besar*), even when the central government opposed these measures. In the lead up to the annual Ramadan holidays (*mudik*), most areas in fact implemented tighter lockdowns, which disrupted trade networks and employment. Soon after the holidays, however, restrictions were loosened again, which was criticised by epidemiologists who warned that the epidemic had not even peaked yet (McCarthy et al 2020, p. 46).

The second half of 2020 was characterised by frequently changing and unclear messaging from the government as to how to contain the virus. Local elections scheduled for September were postponed but eventually went ahead in December despite widespread concerns that even with restrictions on campaigning, people would gather in large groups, not least on voting day at the ballot booths. In early 2021, Indonesia recorded 1 million official cases of Covid-19, the most in Southeast Asia. The official death toll at this stage had reached nearly 30,000, including around 600 health professionals. Independent watchdog organisations, however, consistently estimated the total number of deaths and cases to be significantly higher than the official government statistics. Even when more and more people were turned away from hospitals because of overcapacity, President Jokowi still maintained that he believed that 'Indonesia is among the countries that control these two [health and economic] crises well' (Souisa 2021).

Despite government efforts to project the image of a successful response, the Jokowi administration has faced significant criticism for its handling of the pandemic. Many critics accused the government of prioritising economic growth over public health. In the early weeks of the pandemic, for example, when many countries started closing their borders to limit the spread of the virus, the Jokowi administration offered almost $8 million to travel influencers to promote domestic tourism. At the same time, many hospitals struggled to cope with the lack of personnel and equipment. With only 4 doctors and 12 hospital beds per

10,000 people, and less than 3 intensive care beds per 100,000, the deficiencies in Indonesia's health system were brutally exposed. The limited medical infrastructure was especially felt in regional areas, where there were significant shortages of essential medical equipment such as ventilators as well as protective equipment for health workers, with some having to use raincoats to protect themselves from infection (Lindsey & Mann 2020).

It would be an oversimplification, however, to explain Indonesia's ineffective response to the pandemic merely as a result of its status as a lower-middle income country or a lack of state capacity. In fact, countries that are poorer than Indonesia have had a more effective response to the pandemic, as have states with comparable levels of state capacity. Instead, as argued by Mietzner (2020, pp. 228–229), Indonesia's poor response to the health crisis can be explained more convincingly as a direct consequence of its specific political trajectory in the years before the pandemic, which has been characterised by a steady decline in democratic quality. In particular, sociopolitical trends such as rising populism, increasing religious conservatism, political polarisation and unfettered corruption have prevented a more effective Covid-19 strategy.

First, Indonesia's response to Covid-19 was reminiscent of the rhetoric and inaction found in other countries governed by populist leaders such as the United States or Brazil. Populist politics have been on the rise in Indonesia since at least the 2014 elections (Aspinall & Mietzner 2014; Aspinall 2015; Kenny 2019) and its impact could be felt acutely during the pandemic. Like populist leaders elsewhere, Jokowi and his cabinet ministers responded to the Covid-19 pandemic by downplaying the threat posed by the virus, openly challenging scientific evidence and accusing critics of interfering with the government.

The government's response therefore comprised a curious mix of executive aggrandisement and executive underreach. On the one hand, Jokowi and his cabinet followed the script of other populist and authoritarian leaders in clamping down on public dissent (Setiawan 2020) and spreading false and misleading information in order to undermine the credibility of scientific evidence. According to Power and Warburton (2020, p. 2), 'police harassment and arrests of ordinary citizens, activists and opposition figures then became a prominent and disturbing feature of the Jokowi government's pandemic response'. The flipside of the coin, however, was Jokowi's initial neglect of public health concerns and his subsequent failure to clearly communicate and implement restrictions once they were finally in place. This part of the Indonesian Covid-19 response can be categorised as 'executive underreach', which Pozen and Scheppele (2020) have defined as 'a national executive branch's wilful failure to address a significant public problem that the executive is legally and functionally equipped (though not necessarily legally required) to address'.

The second underlying factor behind Indonesia's initial reluctance to act decisively against the pandemic is the trend of increasing religious conservatism. As outlined in Chapter 6, conservative Islamic groups have grown into a powerful social force in post-Suharto Indonesia. Through alliances with political elites and adroit mobilisation of religious sentiment among ordinary citizens, Islamist groups have become increasingly influential in politics and contributed to a mainstreaming of religious intolerance. The 2016 demonstrations against the former Jakarta governor Ahok were particularly momentous events that galvanised support for the Islamist agenda, as evidenced in numerous public opinion surveys after Ahok's demise (Mietzner & Muhtadi 2019).

The growing influence of conservative Islam has had significant implications for Indonesia's political landscape. On the one hand, the Jokowi government framed radical Islamism as a threat to national unity and began to crack down on hardline Muslim groups and leaders, as illustrated by the 2017 ban of the Hizbut Tahrir (Gammon 2020). On the other hand, concessions were made to politically moderate yet socially conservative Islamic groups like Nahdlatul Ulama (NU), which was showered with patronage before and after the 2019 election.

Jokowi's selective embrace of conservative Islamic groups meant that when the pandemic broke out, he needed to take into consideration the position of these groups. NU initially took an ambivalent approach, issuing a *fatwa* stating that Friday prayers were obligatory provided that Muslims are healthy. NU issued this directive at a point when it had become clear that the virus could be spread even when an individual was not showing any symptoms of illness. Similarly, an ambivalent stance was taken to the question whether the government should ban the *mudik*, the annual holiday at the end of the fasting month Ramadan when millions of Indonesians go home from the cities where they work to the villages where they grew up. Both NU and Muhammadiyah refused to call a ban on *mudik*, while at the same time demanding the government to do so. The government, however, wanted NU and Muhammadiyah to issue a ban because it otherwise feared repercussions from the Muslim community. The unwillingness of the government to make decisions that could lead to opposition from the Muslim community thus had a significant impact on Indonesia's Covid-19 response (Mietzner 2020, pp. 234–235).

Third, while Jokowi forged close ties with NU and, to a lesser degree, Muhammadiyah in the aftermath of the 2016 Islamist mobilisation, the groups that were at the forefront of that mobilisation (FPI, Hizbut Tahrir and others) remained steadfast in their opposition to Jokowi. The deep rift between the two camps became a defining feature of Indonesian politics before and after the 2019 elections, so the pandemic hit Indonesia at a time of intense polarisation between Jokowi's moderate–pluralist coalition and the Islamist-linked opposition. At the societal level, this polarisation was reflected in very different public perceptions of the government response to the Covid crisis. In general, people in provinces that had voted against Jokowi in 2019 were more likely to consider the government response as too slow, while people in provinces where Jokowi had won decisively mostly believed the government had acted quickly (Warburton 2020).

At the elite level, meanwhile, polarisation translated into conflict between the Jokowi government and the governor of Jakarta, Anies Baswedan, who back in 2016 had played a key role in the mobilisations against his predecessor Ahok and who was supported by various hardline Islamic groups. The nature of polarisation was so significant that it led to Jokowi and Anies taking opposing approaches to the handling of the pandemic: where Jokowi argued for an approach that preserved the economy, Anies advocated for a strict lockdown of the capital. Islamist leaders quickly endorsed Anies' position, in a break from the initial anti-scientific approach they had taken earlier. In turn, Jokowi issued emergency regulations requiring all local governments that wanted to implement interventions to obtain permission from the Minister for Health (Mietzner 2020, Warburton 2020). Polarisation thus prevented a bipartisan and coordinated response between government and opposition, which has been crucial to contain the spread of the virus in other countries.

A fourth factor that has adversely impacted Indonesia's pandemic response has been the persistence of corruption and clientelism in the public health sector. Long before Covid-19 hit Indonesia, the health sector was already plagued by inadequate oversight of procurement processes which often led to corruption and purchases of poor-quality equipment for health service providers. As a consequence, many hospitals were utterly ill-prepared to respond to the pandemic. Once the virus was spreading in the community, corruption and clientelism also compromised the state's ability to obtain sufficient numbers of test kits, so Indonesia soon made headlines as the country with the lowest rates of testing in the Southeast Asian region. When the government eventually provided financial support for the procurement of much-needed equipment like testing kits, protective equipment and respirators health, private and state-owned enterprises took most of these funds, only to then sell the purchased equipment to the health services that needed them. Many of these products were of low quality and some of the firms engaged in these practices were closely aligned with high-ranking government officials, including former Vice-President Jusuf Kalla (Mietzner 2020, p. 239).

In December 2020, the Corruption Eradication Commission (Komisi Pemberantasan Korupsi, KPK) exposed the corruption at the highest level of the Covid-19 response when it arrested the then Social Affairs Minister Juliari Batubara for allegedly receiving 17 billion rupiah (US$1.18 million) in bribes from companies engaged in distributing social aid to millions of families in need. Reflecting on this case and the unfettered corruption in times of Covid, KPK commissioner Nurul Ghufron noted that 'the risk of corruption is higher today because there are people who try to take advantage of loosened regulations' (as quoted in Rayda 2021). In view of such assessments, it is little wonder that Indonesia's response to the pandemic has been so ineffective. This has come at a high cost: in July 2021, Indonesia became the epicentre of the pandemic in Asia, and a month later it reported more than 100,000 confirmed Covid-19 deaths.

Conclusion

Over the past few decades, Indonesia has made inroads in terms of its population's socio-economic development, as illustrated by its rising Human Development Index. Similarly, subsequent Indonesian governments have rolled out various initiatives to improve health care, increase access to education and reduce poverty. However, as this chapter has shown, many challenges remain. These are visible in persisting inequalities – particularly between the rich and poor, as well as those living in urban and rural areas. Given Indonesia's growing population, and the influence of health, education and income levels on overall economic development, it is crucial to address these inequalities.

However, there is no simple way to address these problems. This is not so much because there is a lack of initiatives – as this chapter has shown, subsequent administrations have rolled out various programmes to improve healthcare and education, as well as increase income levels. Budgetary spending on education and health has increased, even though it remains low compared to other countries in the region. Similarly, during the Covid-19 pandemic, the government rolled out support packages. If anything, the problem is not in the technocratic approach that has so often been characteristic of Indonesian politics. Rather, it is other features of Indonesian politics that have influenced, and will continue to influence, policymaking and its outcomes in these areas. These include, as particularly noticeable in the sectors of education and health, corruption and clientelism. Moreover, the Covid-19 pandemic has exposed how populism, polarisation and increased religious conservatism have not only negatively impacted the delivery of public health services in a time of crisis – with devastating effects on individuals and the wider community – but also laid bare the precarious state of Indonesian democracy.

References

Allard, T, Kapoor, K & Widianto, S 2020, 'Exclusive: jump in Jakarta funerals raises fears of unreported coronavirus deaths', viewed 5th February 2021, <https://www.reuters.com/article/us-health-coronavirus-indonesia-funerals-idUSKBN21L2XU>.

Arbi, IA 2019, 'Indonesia breaks into UNDP's high human development category', *Jakarta Post*, 14 December, viewed 1 April 2021, <https://www.thejakartapost.com/news/2019/12/14/indonesia-breaks-into-undps-high-human-development-category.html>.

Aspinall, E 2014, 'Health care and democratization in Indonesia', *Democratization*, vol. 21, no. 5, pp. 803–823.

Aspinall, E 2015, 'Oligarchic populism: Prabowo Subianto's challenge to Indonesian democracy', *Indonesia*, vol. 99, no. 1, pp. 1–28.

Aspinall, E & Mietzner, M 2014, 'Indonesian politics in 2014: democracy's close call', *Bulletin of Indonesian Economic Studies*, vol. 50, no. 3, pp. 347–369.

Badan Pusat Statistik 2020, *Informasi seputar SP 2020*, viewed 1 April 2021, <https://www.bps.go.id/>.

Berenschot, W, Hanani, R & Sambodho, P 2018, 'Brokers and citizenship: access to health care in Indonesia', *Citizenship Studies*, vol. 22, no. 2, pp. 129–144.

Birdsall, NM, Campos, JEL, Kim, CS, Corden, WM, MacDonald, L, Pack, H, Page, J, Sabor, R & Stiglitz, JE 1993, *The East Asian miracle: economic growth and public policy: Main report* (English). A World Bank policy research report, World Bank Group, Washington DC.

Davidson, JS 2015, *Indonesia's changing political economy: governing the roads*, Cambridge University Press, Cambridge.

Fossati, D 2017, 'From periphery to centre: Local government and the emergence of universal healthcare in Indonesia', *Contemporary Southeast Asia*, vol. 39, no. 1, pp. 178–203.

Gammon, L 2020, 'Is populism a threat to Indonesian democracy?', in T Power & E Warburton (eds), *Democracy in Indonesia: from stagnation to regression?*, ISEAS – Yusof Ishak Institute, Singapore, pp. 101–117.

Hill, H 1996, *The Indonesian economy since 1966: Southeast Asia's emerging giant*, Cambridge University Press, Cambridge.

Hill, H 2015, 'The Indonesian economy during the Yudhoyono decade', in E Aspinall, M Mietzner & D Tomsa (eds), *The Yudhoyono presidency: Indonesia's decade of stability and stagnation*, Institute of Southeast Asian Studies, Singapore, pp. 281–302.

Kenny, PD 2019, *Populism in Southeast Asia*, Cambridge University Press, Cambridge.

Lindsey, T & Mann, T 2020, 'Indonesia was in denial over coronavirus. Now it may be facing a looming disaster', *The Conversation*, 8 April, viewed 10 February 2021, <https://theconversation.com/indonesia-was-in-denial-over-coronavirus-now-it-may -be-facing-a-looming-disaster-135436>.

Mahendradhata, Y, Trisnantoro L, Listyadewi, S, Soewondo, P, Marthias, T, Harimurti, P & Prawira, J 2017, *The Republic of Indonesia health system review*, World Health Organization Regional Office for South-East Asia, New Delhi.

Manning, C & Miranti, R 2015, 'The Yudhoyono legacy on jobs, poverty and income distribution: a mixed record', in E Aspinall, M Mietzner & D Tomsa (eds), *The Yudhoyono presidency: Indonesia's decade of stability and stagnation*, Institute of Southeast Asian Studies, Singapore, pp. 303–324.

Mboi, N, Surbakti, IM, Trihandini I, Elyazar, I, Houston Smith K, Ali, PB, Kosen, S, Flemons, K, Ray, SE, Cao, J, Glenn, SD, Miller-Petrie, MK, Mooney, MD, Ried, JL, Ningrum, DNA, Idris, F, Siregar, KN, Harimurti, P, Bernstein, RS, Pangestu, T, Sidharta, Y, Naghavi, M, Murray, CJL & Hay, SI 2018, 'On the road to universal health care in Indonesia, 1990-2016: a systematic analysis for the global burden of disease study 2016', *The Lancet*, vol. 392, pp. 581–591.

McCarthy, JF, Winarto, YT, Sitorus, H, Kutanegara PM & Budianto, V 2020, 'COVID-19 and food systems in Indonesia', in L Robins, S Crimp, M van Wensveen, RG Alders, RM Bourke, J Butler, M Cosijn, F Davil, A Lal, JF McCarthy, A McWilliam, ASM Palo, N Thomson, P Warr & M Webb (eds), *COVID-19 and food systems in the Indo-Pacific: an assessment of vulnerabilities, impacts and opportunities for action*, Canberra, ACIAR, pp. 41–92.

Mietzner, M 2020, 'Populist anti-scientism, religious polarization, and institutional corruption: how Indonesia's democratic decline shaped its COVID-19 response', *Journal of Current Southeast Asian Affairs*, vol. 39, no. 2, pp. 227–249.

Mietzner, M & Muhtadi, B 2019, 'The myth of pluralism: Nahdlatul Ulama and the politics of religious tolerance in Indonesia', *Contemporary Southeast Asia*, vol. 42, no. 1, pp. 58–84.

Muhtadi, B & Warburton, E 2020, 'Inequality and democratic support in Indonesia', *Pacific Affairs*, vol. 93, no. 1, pp. 31–58.

Myrdal, G 1968, *Asian drama: an inquiry into the poverty of nations*, Pantheon Books, New York.

Perdana, A & Maxwell, J 2011, 'The evolution of poverty alleviation policies: ideas, issues and actors', in C Manning & S Sumarto (eds), *Employment, living standards and poverty in contemporary Indonesia*, Institute of Southeast Asian Studies, Singapore, pp. 273–290.

Pisani, E, Kok, MO & Nugroho, K 2017, 'Indonesia's road to universal health coverage: a political journey', *Health Policy and Planning*, vol. 32, no. 2, pp. 267–276.

Pozen, DE & Scheppele, KL 2020, 'Executive underreach, in pandemics and otherwise', *American Journal of International Law*, vol. 114, no. 4, pp. 608–617.

Purdey, J, Missbach, A & McRae, D 2020, *Indonesia: state and society in transition*, Lynne Rienner Publishers, Boulder.

Rayda, N 2021, 'Urgency of Covid-19 exacerbates corruption risk in Indonesia, says deputy chair of anti-graft commission', *Channel News Asia*, 9 March, viewed 1 April 2021, <https://www.channelnewsasia.com/news/asia/indonesia-corruption-commission-kpk-covid19-manipulation-14360582>.

Rosemary, R & Ciptaningtyas, R 2020, 'Up in smoke? Tobacco and Indonesia's efforts to reduce stunting', *Indonesia at Melbourne*, 23 January, viewed 1 February 2021, <https://indonesiaatmelbourne.unimelb.edu.au/up-in-smoke-tobacco-and-indonesias-efforts-to-reduce-stunting/>.

Rosser, A 2012, 'Realising free health care for the poor in Indonesia: the politics of illegal fees', *Journal of Contemporary Asia*, vol. 42, no. 2, pp. 255–275.

Rosser, A 2015, 'Contesting tobacco-control policy in Indonesia', *Critical Asian Studies*, vol. 47, no. 1, pp. 69–93.

Rosser, A 2018, *Beyond access: making Indonesia's education system work*, Lowy Institute & Victoria State Government, Melbourne.

Setiawan, KMP 2020, 'A state of surveillance? Freedom of expression under the Jokowi Presidency', in T Power & E Warburton (eds), *Democracy in Indonesia: from stagnation to regression*, ISEAS – Yusof Ishak Institute, Singapore, pp. 254–274.

Souisa, H 2021, 'Indonesia hits 1 million coronavirus cases as health experts criticise government's response', *ABC*, 26 January, viewed 27th January 2021, <https://www.abc.net.au/news/2021-01-26/indonesia-coronavirus-covid-19-cases-hit-1-million/13091968>.

Suryahadi, A & Al Izzati, R 2019, 'Middle class winners of economic growth under Jokowi', *East Asia Forum*, 19 February, viewed 4 February 2021, <https://www.eastasiaforum.org/2019/02/19/economic-growth-under-jokowi-benefits-the-middle-class-more-than-the-poor/>.

Sutrisno, B 2020, '2020 HDR: Indonesia retains 'high' HDI, but slips 16 ranks in new planetary pressures index', *Jakarta Post*, 17 December, viewed 10 February 2021, <https://www.thejakartapost.com/news/2020/12/17/2020-hdr-indonesia-retains-high-hdi-but-slips-16-ranks-in-new-planetary-pressures-index.html>.

United Nations 2017, *World population ageing 2017: highlights*, Department of Economic and Social Affairs, New York.

UNDP 2020, 'The next frontier: human development and the Anthropocene', UNDP, viewed 10 February 2021, <http://hdr.undp.org/sites/all/themes/hdr_theme/country-notes/IDN.pdf>.

UNDP 2021, 'Human development indicators – Indonesia', UNDP, viewed 15 January 2021, <http://hdr.undp.org/en/countries/profiles/IDN>.

Warburton, E 2020, *Indonesia: polarization, democratic distress, and the Coronavirus*, viewed 25th January 2021, <https://carnegieendowment.org/2020/04/28/indonesia-polarization-democratic-distress-and-coronavirus-pub-81641>.

Winters, J 2011, *Oligarchy*, Cambridge University Press, Cambridge.

World Bank 2021a, *Current health expenditure (% of GDP) – Indonesia*, viewed 1 April 2021, <https://data.worldbank.org/indicator/SH.XPD.CHEX.GD.ZS?locations=ID>.

World Bank 2021b, *Gini index (World Bank estimate) – Indonesia*, viewed 1 April 2021, <https://data.worldbank.org/indicator/SI.POV.GINI?locations=ID>.

9 Gender Equality and Sexual Politics

Introduction

On International Women's Day in 2006, a colourful parade of protestors marched through Jakarta. They demonstrated against the controversial anti-pornography bill which was under deliberation in the Indonesian parliament at the time. The bill aimed to ban not only the production and distribution of pornographic material but also so-called pornoactions, including seemingly harmless activities such as kissing on the lips and erotic dancing in public. Perhaps most controversially, it sought to enforce a conservative dress code for women. The 2006 Women's Day march was the most widely publicised but by no means the only protest against the bill (Allen 2009). In the end, however, the demonstrators could only delay, but not stop the bill from being passed. Conservative religious groups and ostensibly secular political elites banded together and passed the bill into law in 2008.

Since then, Indonesia has undergone a major religious turn and alliances between political elites and conservative Islamic groups have become a common feature of Indonesian politics. At times, these alliances have sought to constrict public space for women and sexual minorities in similar ways the anti-pornography bill intended to do. But progressive women's rights groups have not backed down and continued to struggle for greater gender equality based on international human rights norms. Indeed, gender equality is a fundamental human right that is closely linked to sustainable development. The advancement of gender equality is critical to the development of society as it reduces poverty, contributes to economic productivity and growth and supports health and education as well as the well-being of all persons regardless of their sexual identity.

Since the fall of authoritarianism in 1998, Indonesia has made some noteworthy progress towards gender equality. For instance, the country has ratified all major international conventions that uphold principles of gender equality and women's empowerment. It has passed a range of legislation pertaining to women's rights, including the 2004 Law on the Elimination of Domestic Violence and the 2009 Law on the Protection of Women and Anti-Gender-Based Violence. A gender quota for legislative elections was introduced, women's literacy rates have improved and a new universal healthcare system (Jaminan Kesehatan Nasional

DOI: 10.4324/9780429459511-9

or JKN) included a focus on enhancing women's access to maternal and neonatal care to reduce maternal and infant mortality.

At the same time, many challenges remain. In 2018, Indonesia ranked 111 out of 189 countries on the United Nations Development Programme's (UNDP) gender inequality index, which measures gender disparities in education, reproductive health and economic and political participation (Arbi 2019). Indonesia has one of the lowest rates of women's participation in the workforce in the Asian region (Cameron & Contreras Suarez 2019) and the gender pay gap is still substantial, with women on average almost earning 25 percent less than men (Rahman 2020). Indonesia's maternal mortality risk of 177 deaths per 100,000 live births is high in the region: in Thailand, this number is 37 and in Malaysia 29 (UNFPA 2017). Cases of domestic violence against women remain high, with over 430,000 reported cases in 2019 (Komnas Perempuan 2020). In addition, there are ongoing problems with discrimination and violence towards sexual minorities in Indonesia.

This chapter seeks to explain why these economic, social and political gender disparities persist in Indonesia. Following this introduction, it will begin with a discussion of state gender ideologies before focusing on a number of key issues, including women's political participation, education, health, marriage and polygamy, as well as violence and sexual identity. While this is not an exhaustive list of issues, together they provide an insight into some of the key challenges that Indonesians face in their struggle for gender equality.

State Gender Ideologies

Gender ideologies set out expectations of how men and women should behave according to their ascribed sex, while state gender ideologies refer to the state's assumptions and acts towards gender. These can be identified through state actions and policies that reveal what the state considers to be appropriate for men and women in society. It is important to recognise that in a country as diverse as Indonesia, many ethnic and religious groups have their own gender traditions. The matrilineal system of the Minangkabau in West Sumatra, for example, is well known for its inheritance system which follows the female line (Von Benda-Beckmann 1979). By contrast, Batak society in North Sumatra is strongly patrilineal, whereas in Java society tends to be organised around greater equality between men and women. Other ethnic groups do not clearly differentiate between two sexes, with the Bugis in South Sulawesi known for their recognition of a third sex (*bissu*). Frequently, these gender norms are inconsistent with religious norms: the inheritance practices of the Minangkabau, for instance, are at odds with Islamic notions that sons receive larger shares of inheritance.

In her seminal work on women and the state in Indonesia, Susan Blackburn (2004) has remarked that in sharp contrast to the diversity of ideas on gender in society, the Indonesian state's gender ideology has left far less space for diversity. This has had an impact on the development of the women's movement which has had to negotiate prevailing gender norms propagated by the state. Nevertheless, Indonesia has a long history of women's political organisations. Women's mobilisation can be traced back to colonial times when women were active in the nationalist movement and the workforce. This earned women credibility with the state, and principles of equality between men and women were laid down in the Constitution, which also rejected the applicability of Islamic law, that potentially limited the rights of women (Blackburn 2004).

In the early independence period, women's organisations flourished at national and local levels, even if there were disparities between the various regions. While no particular gender ideology was imposed by the state, government rhetoric designated women as 'weavers of national unity' and 'mothers of the nation' (Davies 2005, p. 232), roles that women were largely unable to contest. Even women's organisations that were considered more radical – such as Gerwani, affiliated with the Indonesian Communist Party (Partai Komunis Indonesia, PKI) – did not question women's maternal characteristics (Wieringa 2002). The 1955 general elections illustrated the limitations of women's political participation and influence, with many women actively involved in voting but very few (approximately 7%) elected (Blackburn 2004).

If women's activism was limited in the 1950s, it came to a virtual standstill during the New Order period. Under President Suharto, the state firmly entrenched a patriarchal gender ideology in its policies and practices. Indonesian feminist Julia Suryakusuma (1987) coined the term *state ibuism* to characterise the way in which the New Order state construed women's roles as limited to the domestic sphere. Women were designated as wives, mothers and managers of the household. In assigning women this role, the state preserved and promoted heterosexual family norms, and the family principle (*azas kekeluargaan*) was used to position heterosexual families as the basis of the nation-state. Consequently, heterosexual marriage and the reproductive function of the family became a marker of adulthood and an ideal citizen (Boellstorff 2016).

Unsurprisingly, under the New Order, women were virtually absent in political life – men held approximately 90 percent of parliamentary seats, and very few women were part of cabinet with the exception of the Women's Minister, a position that was created in 1975 in response to international demands (Robinson 2014). Women's organisations were limited to religious and other state-endorsed groups. All organisations in Indonesia were expected to adhere to the state ideology Pancasila, while women's state corporatist organisations were charged with supporting and disseminating the state's official gender ideology. In structure, they mirrored the male-dominated state with leaders being the wives of government officials. These state corporatist organisations offered women some form of representation and voice, but very rarely were they able to influence or change policy related to women (Diprose, Savirani, Setiawan & Francis 2020).

State gender ideology, however, did not completely suppress women's activism. Religious-based women's organisations such as 'Aisyiyah, affiliated with Muhammadiyah, and Muslimat, affiliated with Nahdlatul Ulama, continued with social work and tried to maintain their independence from the state. Moreover, as a result of economic growth and increased education levels in the mid-1980s, women became increasingly involved in broader movements and activist networks. In this period, many new non-governmental organisations for women were established. Built on feminist ideas and the global human rights movements, they countered the gender ideology of the regime, even though their political influence and geographical reach were limited at the time.

The end of the New Order in 1998 cannot be separated from gendered violence. In the wake of the economic downturn triggered by the Asian financial crisis, the regime attempted to blame Chinese Indonesians for the crisis (see also Chapter 2). This resulted in violence against Chinese Indonesians in Jakarta and other major cities. Hundreds of Chinese Indonesian women were raped and sexually assaulted under the orders of security forces and vigilante groups backed by them (Purdey 2006). Following the end of the regime, and in response to the violence, the Indonesian government established the National Commission on the Elimination of Violence Against Women (Komisi Nasional Anti Kekerasan Terhadap Perempuan, Komnas Perempuan) in 1998.

The *reformasi* period heralded a change in terms of gender politics. The Ministry for Women was renamed the Ministry for Women's Empowerment and became more outspoken on government policies on gender equality. Women's groups seized the opportunity for an increased political presence, which was reflected in new women's networks, unions and other non-governmental organisations. Women's state corporatist organisations also made changes to their structures, allowing for more democratic participation within the organisations and increasing their focus on women's participation in politics and gender equality. Women also became more prominent in government, and many women's organisations successfully advocated for new and revised legislation, policies and programs to help address gender inequalities.

Democratisation, however, has not meant that gender ideology has left the political stage. A particular challenge has come from conservative Islamic groups, some of which are inspired by Islamic fundamentalism in the Middle East. These groups have turned to populist strategies to build alliances with political parties and government representatives in order to craft a more religiously conservative state gender ideology. At the national level, this resulted in the 2008 anti-pornography law, while at the local level a range of regulations based on Islamic law (the so-called Perda Sharia) often placed restrictions on women's dress, sexuality and movement (Buehler 2016). Related to this has been an increase in discrimination and violence targeted against lesbian, gay, bisexual and transgender (LGBT) Indonesians. These developments highlight that contestations of sexuality and gender ideology are still very much part of state power. The following sections will illustrate how women have navigated this challenging sociopolitical environment, beginning with a discussion of women's participation in electoral politics.

Women's Political Participation

The end of the New Order in 1998 provided an impetus for increased women's political activism (Setiawan, Beech Jones, Diprose & Savirani 2020). Women not only established and joined NGOs and professional organisations, but also became active in political parties. Many were inspired by Megawati Sukarnoputri, a symbol of opposition against Suharto in the twilight years of the New Order and leader of the Indonesian Democratic Party-Struggle (Partai Demokrasi Indonesia-Perjuangan, PDI-P). In 1999, Megawati's PDI-P won Indonesia's first democratic election after the New Order with more than 30 percent of the votes.

Despite the emphatic victory, however, PDI-P was unable to form a coalition that would subsequently help Megawati win the presidency in the indirect presidential election in the People's Representative Assembly (Majelis Permusyawaratan Rakyat, MPR). Among the reasons why she failed in her bid for the presidency that year was resistance from Islamic parties against a female leader at the helm of the government. The controversy set the tone for a debate about women's electability as presidential or legislative candidates in a political environment marked by both greater female participation in politics and growing Islamic conservatism.

Megawati did eventually become president in 2001 when she succeeded Abdurrahman Wahid who had been impeached for alleged corruption. While she only stayed in the highest office for three years, she remained chairwoman of PDI-P and generally retained enormous influence in Indonesian politics. But her prominence is the exception rather than the norm for female politicians in Indonesia. Many other women have struggled to leave their mark as the costs of electoral campaigning have risen exponentially and party politics remains dominated by male power brokers. Nevertheless, some noteworthy progress has been made, thanks largely to the introduction of gender quotas for party lists in 2004.

In 1999, a meagre 7 percent of elected members of parliament were female (National Democratic Institute for International Affairs 1999). This gender imbalance prompted extensive lobbying from women's rights activists and female legislators to introduce a gender quota as a necessary measure to redress the gaps in female political representation in a short period of time. Against the background of ongoing electoral reform, the lobbying was successful. Law Number 12 of 2003 on the General Elections – enacted in preparation for the 2004 election – recommended that at least 30 percent of all candidates for national, provincial and local parliaments should be female. Five years later, the 2008 election law changed the wording of the quota, making it now compulsory for parties to adhere to the 30 percent minimum for female candidates. This law also provided for the introduction of a so-called zipper system in the 2009 elections: for every three candidates on a party list, there should be at least one female nominee. This zipper system was retained in subsequent elections, with notable consequences. In the 2019 elections, over 40 percent of legislative candidates were women, more than ever before (see Table 9.1).

The success of the gender quota in raising the number of female candidates can be in part attributed to its 'increasingly robust implementation' (Perdana & Hillman 2020, p. 159). Initially, parties were simply asked to consider nominating more women. Over time, however, the tightened rules not only made compliance compulsory but also introduced tougher sanctions, including the potential disqualification of a party from the elections. In addition, the General Election

Table 9.1 Women's representation in parliament

Election year	Female candidates (%)	Seats won by female candidates (%)
1999	n/a	7
2004	32.32	11.60
2009	35.49	18.04
2014	37.34	17.32
2019	41.16	20.52

Source: Prihatini (2020).

Commission (Komisi Pemilihan Umum, KPU) has improved its monitoring system. As a result, in 2019, many parties not only met, but also actually surpassed the 30 percent quota. The average percentage of female candidates for secular–pluralist parties such as PDI-P, PD (Partai Demokrat, Democratic Party) and Golkar was around 38 percent, whereas women made up 40 and 42 percent of all candidates respectively on lists of Islamic parties such as the Prosperous Justice Party (Partai Keadilan Sejahtera, PKS) and the United Development Party (Partai Persatuan Pembangunan, PPP). That Islamic parties nominated more women than secular parties demonstrates that religious conservatism does not necessarily constrain women's political participation (Prihatini 2020).

Significantly, it is not only the number of female candidates that has increased over time. The percentage of women in parliament has also risen as a result of the larger number of candidates, as Table 9.1 demonstrates. The likelihood of success for female candidates is strongly associated with their prior experience in political positions, their age, as well as kinship ties. In the last two elections, almost half of all women elected came from nationally or locally influential political families and many of these legislators relied on financial support from these families during their campaigns.

Apart from limited access to their own financial resources, another key impediment for women's electoral success is that male candidates tend to be allocated the top two positions on the party list more often, while women are commonly allocated third and sixth positions on the party list (so as to comply with the quota and the zipper system). The lower rankings mean that women are less likely to be elected because few voters actually go through the entire list of candidates. Especially voters with little knowledge about individual candidates are often inclined to tick the box at the top of the party list. According to Perdana and Hillman (2020, p. 164), almost every second female candidate who was listed at the top of the ballot paper in 2019 was elected, but the success rate then decreased progressively to 25 percent for candidates ranked second and 13 percent in the third position. Thus, the effectiveness of gender quotas is undermined by the ranking practices of male-dominated political parties (Pratiwi 2019, Prihatini 2020). As long as women are placed on these unfavourable ballot positions, female political representation will remain limited.

Education

Enhancing female representation in political institutions has long been a major focus of women activists in Indonesia. In addition, the struggle for gender equality has focused on a number of other key issues, with education particularly high on the agenda. Historically, Indonesia has a strong track record of promoting increased access to schooling and literacy for both boys and girls. Universal primary schooling was achieved at the end of the 1980s, which was a result of increased government spending facilitated by the 1970s oil boom. Foreign aid also contributed to further investment in education. By the mid-1990s, 95 percent of primary school–aged children were enrolled at school, although the target of nine years of basic education was not met, especially for girls (Blackburn 2004).

Since then, investment in the education system has continued, as is evident in more schools, government efforts to lower the costs of schooling and legislative reforms to improve the quality of teachers. These efforts to expand supply, enhance access and improve the quality of education have been intertwined with rising income levels, which has also increased demand for education. As a result, there has been an expansion of enrolment rates at all levels of the education system. Importantly, the growth in enrolment has also been reflected in increased female participation in education. As such, there is no longer a significant gender gap in enrolment percentages.

Indonesia has thus made substantial improvements in access to education. Children are starting school earlier and stay in school longer, while boys and girls have virtually equal access to education. However, these improvements have not been matched by educational quality and learning outcomes, and since the fall of authoritarianism achievement levels have improved little and compare poorly to neighbouring countries such as Malaysia, Thailand and Vietnam (Rosser 2018, p. 8). International development organisations such as the World Bank and the Asian Development Bank have commonly attributed this to inadequate funding, the low quality of educators at all levels, poor rewards and incentives for educators and poor government management. At the same time, however, the limitations of educational reform cannot be explained only through these factors. Elite actors including bureaucrats, political leaders and business figures have also directly impeded improvements in the education sector, as they favoured an expansion of the scope of education (in turn creating a large labour market) rather than improving the quality of education (Rosser 2018).

As for gender equality in education, progress towards gender parity in enrolments cannot conceal other gender-based problems. Many schools across the country, for example, continue to reinforce gender stereotypes in education. Girls also continue to be at a higher risk of dropping out of school, particularly at the secondary school level and in remote areas. This in turn affects women's position in the workforce where there continue to be stark differences between men and women: men's workforce participation is around 80 percent, while for women the rate is just over 50 percent, which is among the lowest in the region (Cameron & Contreraz Suarez 2019). Unsurprisingly, there is also a significant gender pay gap, with the ILO (International Labour Organisation) reporting in 2020 that Indonesian women earn 23 percent less than men. This pay gap is particularly significant as more women workers have a tertiary degree compared to male workers, indicating that higher education has not succeeded in narrowing the gender pay gap. Women also continue to be overrepresented in the informal sector, with less than half of all women in the labour force working as professionals. And, according to the ILO (2020), 'only 30 percent of those occupy managerial positions where they are also paid less than men'.

There are a range of reasons that contribute to gender disparities in education and its impact on economic inequalities. These include pervasive gender ideologies that continue to regard women's roles as being primarily in the domestic sphere. Poverty levels and sociocultural norms may also result in the education of boys being prioritised over that of girls. Similarly, in some areas, there are high incidences of early and child marriage. While this can impact both boys and girls, girls are most likely to miss out on education as a result. While there are no regulations that prohibit married girls from going to school, many do drop out, especially if they become pregnant.

Women's Reproductive Health and Sexual Politics

Female biological functions of pregnancy and childbirth intersect with gender inequalities and poverty, exposing women to maternal health risks. A lack of women's autonomy to make informed decisions about their healthcare, limited control over financial resources and restricted mobility to access health services may all prevent women from obtaining quality care essential during pregnancy and delivery.

One particular area of concern in Indonesia is its maternal mortality rate, which remains high compared to its neighbours (UNFPA 2017). Maternal health has, in fact, been a priority area for Indonesia's health policy since the late 1980s, through the introduction of a village midwife program to ensure adequate care in every Indonesian village. Despite investment in service provision, however, the quality of and access to maternal health services remain relatively low. There are also sharp geographical inequalities in access to healthcare services: in Java and Bali, the maternal mortality numbers are considerably lower than in other areas (Table 9.2) (Badan Pusat Statistik 2018).

One reason for Indonesia's high maternal mortality rates is that up to the mid-2010s, public spending on health was relatively low. However, the introduction of universal healthcare in 2014 is expected to lead to a reduction in maternal mortality. At the same time, however, this is not only a budgetary issue. Poor access to quality health services – particularly in remote areas – as well as socio-economic and cultural factors also contribute to maternal mortality (Cameron, Contreraz Suarez & Cornwell 2019). Even though a high proportion of deliveries is done by ostensibly skilled birth attendants, maternal mortality in Indonesia remains high – a reflection of the low quality of attendance care. In fact, the use of traditional birth attendants, who often lack formal education and training,

Table 9.2 Maternal mortality rate (MMR) by region per 100,000 live births (2015)

Region	MMR
Sumatra	344
Java and Bali	247
Sulawesi	282
Nusa Tenggara, Maluku and Papua	489
Indonesia (average)	305

Source: Badan Pusat Statistik (2018).

remains widespread in Indonesia, with many women and their families preferring to use traditional attendants because of social norms and the high costs associated with seeing a trained midwife or going to hospital. Finally, many women also have limited knowledge about how they can access basic and emergency obstetric services.

The challenges Indonesia faces in terms of reducing maternal mortality rates are therefore a reflection of broader patterns of gender inequality. High maternal mortality rates are caused by dominant expectations on women's roles, limited education and substandard investment in social services that benefit all people – but especially women. This also indicates that addressing this problem requires more than simply enhanced funding or training of personnel. Instead, systematic changes to gender norms are key to achieving gender equality in health. How difficult it is to achieve such structural change, however, can be seen in other areas of gender politics, for example in the limited progress in the struggle against child marriage and polygamy.

Marriage

Marriage and divorce in Indonesia are regulated through the 1974 Marriage Law. Drafted in the early years of the New Order, the law was initially envisaged as a reflection of the regime's secular developmentalism which regarded the control of marriage age as a crucial instrument to slow down population growth. Accordingly, the initial draft noted that jurisdiction over marital affairs of Muslims would be largely transferred from the Islamic to the general courts, women and men would hold equal rights to initiate divorce and the minimum marriage age was to be set at 18 years for females and 21 for males. Polygyny, a form of marriage where a man is married to more than one wife simultaneously (more commonly known as polygamy, even though that is in fact a broader term which refers to practices where a person, irrespective of their gender, has more than one spouse), was made conditional upon permission from the general court.

These proposals, however, resulted in a strong backlash from Islamic groups. In response, the government revised the law. In the final draft, women retained equal rights to initiate divorce, but the Religious Courts were granted jurisdiction in all Muslim marital matters and polygamy for Muslim men was permitted as long as they took no more than four wives simultaneously. The minimum age for marriage was lowered from 18 for females and 21 for males to 16 and 19 years, respectively. Importantly, the law also stated that permission could be granted to allow marriage before this age, without specifying the circumstances under which this may occur.

After the end of authoritarianism, women's groups once again started actively advocating for higher marriage ages. Increased advocacy was intertwined with international debates on reproductive health, drawing attention to high maternal mortality rates, especially among teenage women, and to the need to extend basic education for all Indonesians, but especially girls. The growing engagement and adherence to international norms on gender equality exposed discrepancies between Indonesia's marriage practices and international standards defining 'child marriage' as marrying before the age of 18. This means that some marriages in Indonesia, while in line with local legislation, are considered as child marriage under international law. Moreover, many girls continue to be married young outside of state law through religious or customary marriages, including in non-Muslim areas.

Indeed, early marriage is a pressing problem in Indonesia. In 2016, Indonesia ranked seventh in the global top ten countries with the highest absolute numbers of child marriage, and it is estimated that nearly 25 percent of all Indonesian women were married as girls (Grijns & Horii 2018, Sumner 2020). Slowly though, the Indonesian government has acknowledged the detrimental impacts of child marriage on development and now supports eliminating child marriage as part of the Sustainable Development Goals (SDGs). Government subsidies to support students from lower socio-economic backgrounds and universal healthcare, for example, have all contributed to preventing child marriage. In 2016, the Ministry for Women's Empowerment and the Protection of Children developed a proposal for a Government Regulation in Lieu of Law (Peraturan Pemerintah Pengganti Undang, Perppu) to eliminate child marriage, in collaboration with civil society organisations. However, regulating against and preventing child marriage is highly complex in view of prevailing contestations over gender norms and ideologies.

This became apparent in 2014 when a coalition of women's and youth organisations in Indonesia sought a review of the Marriage Law at the Constitutional Court in order to raise the minimum age for marriage. During the proceedings, judges heard the opinions of a range of experts and all major religious organisations, but in the end the application was rejected. In the verdict, the panel, which only included one female and non-Muslim judge, disregarded the views of moderate Islamic and non-Muslim experts who had put forward evidence about the negative consequences of early marriage, especially for girls. Instead, the panel referred to the Islamic standard of *akil baligh* (mental and physical maturity) as a measure of marriageability (Grijns & Horii 2018). The ruling thus showed that conservative Islamic interpretations have a strong hold over judicial decision-making.

Significantly, however, in 2018, the Constitutional Court allowed another judicial review, in which it ruled that the minimum age of 16 for women and 19 for men was a form of gender-based discrimination. In response to this decision, the following year parliament revised the Marriage Law, raising the minimum age to 19 for both men and women. While this is an important step towards the elimination of child marriage, challenges remain. The Marriage Law still allows dispensation to marry prior to this age, with no minimum age set. In virtually all cases in which dispensation has been given, it was granted by Religious Courts. In addition, it is estimated that 97 percent of marriages involving underage girls take place without court approval as they are unregistered (Sumner 2020). Legal change alone therefore will be insufficient as long as conservative religious and sociocultural norms continue to condone early marriage and many families living in poverty regard marriage as a way to alleviate material concerns.

Apart from child marriage, another contentious issue that has pitched secular and progressive women's rights activists against conservative religious groups, including conservative women activists, is polygamy. Discourses in favour of the practice have in fact risen sharply since the end of the New Order. This can be understood as a result of both increased public space for conservative Islamic discourses in general and a response from Islamists to heightened women's emancipation in the post-Suharto era (Nurmila & Bennett 2015, p. 72). It is, however, difficult to determine to what extent polygamy is practised in Indonesia due to the high number of unregistered marriages which many men prefer for their second and subsequent unions. The prevalence of unregistered polygamous marriages indicates that the restrictions placed on polygamy in the Marriage Law have not actually stopped this form of marriage.

Empirical research on women's lived experiences in polygamous marriages shows that – although there are exceptions – many women suffer from a lack of economic and emotional support. Moreover, second (and subsequent) wives are often disadvantaged as their marriages are rarely officially registered and, thus, they have no legal recourse in the event of a dispute. There is also some evidence that suggests that domestic violence is more likely to occur in polygamous marriages (Nurmila 2009).

While human rights activists and Islamic feminists have pushed for a revision to the Marriage Law and a ban on polygamy, considerable support for the practice continues. Monogamy may be the norm in Indonesia, but the majority of Indonesian Muslims consider polygamy as religiously permitted. This has led many members of Muslim women's organisations and political parties to refuse possible prohibitions on polygamy, even if they personally disagree with the practice. Similarly, there is limited support to ban the practice among political elites and religious organisations. The Indonesian Council of Ulama (Majelis Ulama Indonesia, MUI), for instance, has stated it has not received any complaints about polygamy and does not plan to discourage the practice. All in all, many politicians seem unwilling to address the issue for fear of an electoral backlash.

Violence

Violence against women is a relatively new issue of concern for the Indonesian women's movement, only rising to prominence in the late 1990s. Cultural resistance towards the matter meant that there was both a strong denial of gender violence and a general perception that domestic violence, including marital rape and abuse, was a private matter. Many women, too, were reluctant to speak out. In part this can be explained by a lack of faith in the justice system, but also because reporting gendered violence has an effect on others. For example, in the case of domestic violence, women are often reluctant to lay charges against their husbands and the father of their children, on whom they tend to be economically dependent. Therefore, addressing violence against women is highly complex.

Perhaps the most important event to bring the topic into public view was the anti-Chinese violence in May 1998. Especially the involvement of the state and security apparatus in perpetrating the violence against Chinese Indonesian women led to a public shock, which in turn generated some positive developments, including the establishment of Komnas Perempuan. Subsequently, greater political freedom helped women's organisations to lobby successfully for legislative change. The 2004 Law on the Elimination of Domestic Violence was a groundbreaking achievement as it brought violence that occurs in the private sphere into the public arena and designated it as a criminal act. Perpetrators of such violence were now subject to fines and imprisonment, and a broad definition of domestic violence was used to encompass physical, psychological, sexual and economic neglect. The law also covered all members of the household, including the extended family and domestic helpers (*pembantu*). In addition to this key legislation, in 2009 a law was passed on the Protection of Women and Anti Gender-Based Violence.

Nevertheless, the elimination of violence against women remains a highly contentious issue in Indonesia. This was evident in the prolonged efforts to pass a Bill on the Elimination of Sexual Violence. First introduced to the Indonesian parliament in 2016, the bill defines nine forms of sexual violence: sexual harassment, exploitation, rape, sexual slavery, torture, forced abortion, contraception, marriage and prostitution. Advocates for the bill include a wide range of women's organisations who have argued that the bill offers Indonesia a specific legal framework that emphasises the importance of prevention of sexual violence, as well as the protection and recovery of the rights of victims.

However, there has been widespread resistance to the bill, with conservative Islamic groups arguing that the bill promotes feminist values that are in contradiction to Islamic teachings and that the bill, if passed, would encourage adultery and 'LGBT behaviour'. Among the most outspoken organisations that opposed the bill was the Family Love Alliance (Aliansi Cinta Keluarga, AILA), an Islamic group whose members are predominantly women. As part of a new wave of 'anti-feminist' groups, AILA has focused on religious and legal advocacy on women's and children's issues and on promoting conservative religious values in collaboration with other Islamic organisations and parties. According to Kartika (2019), 'one thing that makes AILA more influential than other conservative organisations is the support of its intellectuals in criticising gender policies within the existing legal system, an approach that has never been used before by proponents of Indonesia's anti-feminist agendas'.

Nationalist and pluralist parties have bowed to the pressure from AILA and others, showing ambivalence towards the bill and not taking a clear position in support of the legislation. In the context of these pressures, the bill was removed from the list of legislative priorities in July 2020, to be discussed again in 2021. Yet, the Bill on Family Resilience, proposed by the PKS with support from AILA in response to the Bill on Sexual Violence, has continued to be discussed. This bill, which controversially states that husbands and wives must perform their individual roles in accordance with religious norms and social ethics, and that LGBT people must undergo rehabilitation, has been widely criticised by progressive women's and LGBT activists for interfering with personal matters and for promoting traditional gender roles. The bill remained under deliberation at the time this manuscript was completed.

Sexual Identity

One of the major points of contention in the public debate about sexual violence and family resilience has been the place of the LGBT community in Indonesian society. The renewed attention to LGBT rights came on the back of a major anti-LGBT panic that had gripped the country in 2016 after the Minister for Research, Technology and Higher Education at the time, Muhammad Natsir, had claimed that members of the LGBT community should be barred from university campuses. Senior politicians did not condemn Natsir's statement, but instead supported him publicly. His cabinet colleague Ryamizard Ryacudu, who then served as Defence Minister, even likened LGBT Indonesians to a threat that is 'worse than nuclear warfare'. Media outlets willingly reproduced these statements, continuously warning Indonesians against the 'threat' posed by LGBT people.

From thereon, there was increasing pressure on the LGBT community and associated events and groups, which in some cases led to the forced cancellation of events including those that focused on healthcare (i.e. HIV/AIDS prevention awareness). That the push against LGBT Indonesians came from the highest political circles became evident once again when the then Vice-President Jusuf Kalla asked the UNDP not to fund LGBT community programs. Meanwhile, conservative Islamic groups started calling for legislation to criminalise LGBT activities. These groups also placed increasing pressure on more liberal Islamic groups, leading to the closure of an Islamic boarding school where transgender students had been attending. In addition, the LGBT community became the target of censorship. Online content relevant to the LGBT community was regularly blocked, and the Ministry of Communication and Information ordered internet services to block social networking apps used by the LGBT community, citing 'sexual deviance'. In 2018, Google removed 14 applications from the Google Play store with LGBT-related content (Jakarta Post 2018).

LGBT and human rights groups, as well as some public figures, condemned the events and discourses, calling instead for tolerance and respect. Some academics and journalists also pointed to the history of homosexuality and transgenderism in Indonesia in order to counter discourses that depict the LGBT community as a threat to Indonesian culture. These appeals, however, fell largely on deaf ears. Anti-LGBT sentiment is widespread in Indonesia, transcending religious and social divisions. Merely attributing the events to rising Islamism is therefore inaccurate – even if anti-LGBT acts were often perpetrated by Islamic vigilante groups.

Instead, the state-backed moral panic that gripped Indonesia in 2016 should be seen in the broader context of sexual politics and questions of national belonging in Indonesia (Boellstorff 2016). Much of the debate in 2016 and thereafter was framed around contentions that being LGBT is inconsistent with Indonesian culture and constitutes a threat to the Constitution and the nation itself. This cannot be separated from global and regional developments that demand equal rights for LGBT people, including in marriage. In the eyes of many Indonesians, LGBT communities and discourses about same-sex marriage threaten the heteronormative basis of the Indonesian state as expressed in the family principle (*azas kekeluargaan*) that underpins Indonesia's state philosophy Pancasila – which assumes heterosexuality. This assumption feeds into beliefs that heterosexuality is superior, thereby facilitating an environment of discrimination and violence towards LGBT persons.

Conclusion

This chapter has turned the focus to a number of pressing issues with regard to gender equality in contemporary Indonesia, ranging from women's political participation, education and health to marriage, gendered violence and increasing pressures on individuals' rights to express and live their sexual identity. Overall, there have been some noteworthy achievements in Indonesia's track record on gender equality, especially in regard to political participation and education. But challenges not only remain but, arguably, are becoming increasingly difficult to tackle as Indonesia's conservative religious turn impedes efforts to push for more institutional and structural change that would protect women and sexual minorities.

While the various topics covered in this chapter have many specific characteristics, they also share certain commonalities that cannot be separated from broader political dynamics. A key way to understand these is to consider the development of state gender ideology, and the manner in which the state has acted towards gendered identities. The chapter has highlighted that despite increasing public space for women's activists since 1998, Indonesia's state gender ideology remains tied to gender norms that emphasise traditional roles for women as well as heterosexual marriage and sexual relations. Accordingly, women's roles are primarily confined to the domestic sphere, while the LGBT community is regarded as deviant from the norm. Today, such deviance is increasingly scrutinised and even denunciated. For as long as these gender norms remain entrenched at high levels of political power, the struggle for gender equality will continue to face enormous obstacles.

References

Allen, P 2009, 'Women, gendered activism and Indonesia's anti-pornography bill', *Intersections*, vol. 19, viewed 25 March 2021, <http://intersections.anu.edu.au/issue19/allen.htm>.

Arbi, IA 2019, 'Indonesia breaks into UNDP's high human development category', *The Jakarta Post*, viewed 7 April 2021, <https://www.thejakartapost.com/news/2019/12/14/indonesia-breaks-into-undps-high-human-development-category.html>.

Badan Pusat Statistik 2018, 'Angka Kematian Ibu Menurut Pulau (per 100.000 kelahiran hidup), 2015', *Badan Pusat Statistik*, viewed 7 April 2021, <https://www.bps.go.id/dynamictable/2018/06/05%2000:00:00/1439/angka-kematian-ibu-menurut-pulau-per-100-000-kelahiran-hidup-2015.html>.

Blackburn, S 2004, *Women and the state in modern Indonesia*, Cambridge University Press, Cambridge.

Boellstorff, T 2016, 'Against state straightism: five principles for including LGBT Indonesians', *E-International Relations*, viewed 7 April 2021, <https://www.e-ir.info/2016/03/21/against-state-straightism-five-principles-for-including-lgbt-indonesians/>.

Buehler, M 2016, *The Politics of shari'a law: Islamist activists and the state in democratizing Indonesia*, Cambridge University Press, Cambridge.

Cameron, L & Contreraz Suarez, D 2019, 'Why do millions of Indonesian women still quit work after marriage and kids?', *Indonesia at Melbourne*, viewed 7 April 2021, <https://indonesiaatmelbourne.unimelb.edu.au/why-do-millions-of-indonesian-women-still-quit-work-after-marriage-and-kids/>.

Cameron, L, Contreraz Suarez, D & Cornwell, K 2019, 'Understanding the determinants of maternal mortality: an observational study using the Indonesian Population Census', *PLoS ONE*, vol. 14, no. 6, pp. 1–18 <https://doi.org/10.1371/journal.pone.0217386>.

Davies, SG 2005, 'Women in politics in Indonesia in the decade post-Beijing', *International Social Science Journal*, vol. 57, no. 184, pp. 231–242.

Diprose, R, Savirani, A, Setiawan, KMP & Francis, N 2020, *Women's collective action and the village law: how women are driving change and shaping pathways for gender-inclusive development in rural Indonesia*, University of Melbourne with Universitas Gadjah Mada and MAMPU.

Grijns, M & Horii, H 2018, 'Child marriage in a village in West Java (Indonesia): compromises between legal obligations and religious concerns', *Asian Journal of Law and Society*, vol. 5, no. 2, pp. 453–466.

International Labour Organisation 2020, *Indonesia supports the global movement toward equal pay*, Press Release, 17 September, ILO, Jakarta, viewed 25 March 2021, <https://www.ilo.org/jakarta/info/public/pr/WCMS_755550/lang--en/index.htm>.

Jakarta Post 2018, 'Google bows to Ministry's request to remove LGBT apps', 30 January, viewed 25 March 2021, <https://www.thejakartapost.com/life/2018/01/30/google-bows-to-ministrys-request-to-remove-lgbt-apps.html>.

Kartika, DA 2019, 'An anti-feminist wave in Indonesia's election?', *New Mandala*, 14 April, viewed 25 March 2021, <https://www.newmandala.org/an-anti-feminist-wave-in-indonesias-election/>.

Komnas Perempuan 2020, *Kekerasan Meningkat: Kebijakan Penghapsan Kekerasan Seksual Membangun Ruang Aman bagi Perempuan dan Anak Perempuan. Catatan Kekerasan Terhadap Perempuan Tahun 2019*, Komnas Perempuan, Jakarta.

National Democratic Institute for International Affairs (NDI) 1999, *The 1999 presidential election and post-election developments in Indonesia: a post-election assessment report*, NDI, Jakarta.

Nurmila, N 2009, *Women, Islam, and everyday life: renegotiating polygamy in Indonesia*, Routledge, London & New York.

Nurmila, N & Bennett, LR 2015, 'The sexual politics of polygamy in Indonesian marriages', in LR Bennett & SG Davies (eds), *Sex and sexualities in contemporary Indonesia: Sexual politics, health, diversity and representations*, Routledge, London, pp. 69–87.

Perdana, A & Hillman, B 2020, 'Quotas and ballots: the impact of positive action policies on women's representation in Indonesia', *Asia & the Pacific Policy Studies*, vol. 7, no. 2, pp. 158–170.

Pratiwi, AM 2019, 'The policies, practices, and politics of women representation in political parties: a case study of women members of parliament in regency/city-level legislative council period 2014–2019', *Jurnal Perempuan*, vol. 24, no. 2, pp. 151–163.

Prihatini, ES 2020, 'Islam, parties, and women's political nomination in Indonesia', *Politics & Gender*, vol. 16, no. 3, pp. 637–659.

Purdey, J 2006, *Anti-Chinese violence in Indonesia 1996–1999*, NUS Press, Singapore.

Rahman, DF 2020, 'Female workers in Indonesia earn 23% less than their male peers', *The Jakarta Post*, viewed 7 April 2021, <https://www.thejakartapost.com/news/2020/09/20 /female-workers-in-indonesia-earn-23-less-than-their-male-peers.html>.

Robinson, K 2014, 'Masculinity, sexuality and Islam. The gender politics of regime change in Indonesia', in LR Bennett & SG Davies (eds), *Sex and sexualities in contemporary Indonesia: Sexual politics, health, diversity and representations*, Routledge, London, pp. 51–68.

Rosser, A 2018, *Beyond access: making Indonesia's education system work*, Lowy Institute, Sydney 7 Victoria State Government.

Setiawan, K, Beech Jones, B, Diprose, R & Savirani, A 2020, *Women's journeys in driving change: women's collective action and village law implementation in Indonesia*, The Australia-Indonesia Partnership for Gender Equality and Women's Empowerment (MAMPU), The University of Melbourne and Universitas Gadjah Mada.

Sumner, C 2020, *Ending child marriage in Indonesia: the role of courts*, Centre for Indonesian Law, Islam and Society, University of Melbourne.

Suryakusuma, J 1987, *State Ibuism: The social construction of womanhood in the Indonesian New Order*, Master's thesis, The Institute of Social Studies, The Hague.

UNFPA 2017, 'Maternal health', United Nations Population Fund, viewed 7 April 2021, <https://www.unfpa.org/maternal-health#:~:text=According%20to%20the%20most %20recent,related%20to%20pregnancy%20and%20childbirth.&text=For%20every %20woman%20who%20dies,and%20injuries%20are%20entirely%20preventable.>.

Von Benda-Beckmann, F 1979, *Property in social continuity: continuity and change in the maintenance of property relationships through time in Minangkabau, West Sumatra*, Springer Science and Business Media, Dordrecht.

Wieringa, S 2002, *Sexual politics in Indonesia*, Palgrave Macmillan, Houndmills, Basingstoke.

10 Human Rights

Introduction

Since 2007, every Thursday afternoon a group of protestors dressed in black has been gathering in front of the presidential palace in Jakarta. Carrying black umbrellas and banners, the protest, which is Indonesia's longest-running human rights protest, is widely known as Kamisan ('thursdays'), and over the years has spread to many other Indonesian cities. While initially staged as a protest by survivors and relatives of victims of the New Order regime in response to the deadlock in obtaining justice for violations committed in that period, the protest nowadays asks attention for a wide range of human rights issues, including the protection of religious minorities, the dispossession of farmers from their land to make way for development projects and repression of journalists. Irrespective of the specific human rights issue that is addressed during a protest, Kamisan is consistent in that it demands that human rights laws are upheld, and that perpetrators of violations are held to account in court. In so doing, Kamisan draws attention to one of the most pressing democratic challenges Indonesia faces: impunity.

The many challenges that Indonesia faces in terms of its human rights record stand in sharp contrast with the rapid development of human rights law in the post-authoritarian context. While this legal framework is far from perfect, on paper Indonesia is certainly well-positioned to protect human rights. As this chapter will show, the realisation of human rights remains an uphill battle, due to a combination of at least three factors: first, the prevalence of powerful politico-economic and military structures that are at best disinterested in the implementation of human rights or at worst directly involved in human rights violations; second, the impact of both religious and social conservatism; and third, the lack of presidential leadership. These three factors not only have a direct impact on the protection of individual rights, but also have ramifications for the character of democracy in Indonesia, which has become increasingly illiberal.

This chapter will start by discussing the country's human rights framework that was rapidly developed after Suharto's resignation in 1998 in response to the systemic human rights abuses under authoritarianism. The chapter then will discuss the various challenges to human rights protection by focusing on a number of key issues, starting with addressing past human rights violations. The chapter

DOI: 10.4324/9780429459511-10

continues with a discussion of the protection of religious minorities, pressures on the freedoms of expression and association and a discussion of ongoing human rights violations in Papua. Based on these brief case studies, the chapter will argue that structural factors at levels of state and society, as well as the agency of individual political leaders, hamper the implementation of human rights norms.

Indonesia's Human Rights Framework

Suharto's New Order was born from violence and saw the entrenchment of the military as a political and social force (see Chapter 2). Under authoritarianism, the military gained territorial control across the country and was able to monitor civilians at every level of government, while political organisations and activities were tightly controlled (Eldridge 2002, p. 129). Under the New Order, human rights violations were entrenched in state behaviour and particularly pronounced in regions with separatist movements such as East Timor, Papua (known at the time as Irian Jaya) and Aceh.

Internationally, there was limited scrutiny of Indonesia's human rights record as a consequence of the Cold War and the country's strongly anti-communist stance. However, as the Cold War waned, criticism of military conduct increased, especially in the context of East Timor. This led to some concessions from the Suharto government, including the 1993 establishment of the National Human Rights Commission (Komisi Nasional Hak Asasi Manusia, Komnas HAM) which, to the surprise of many, became an outspoken critic of the Suharto regime in the late New Order (Setiawan 2016). Nonetheless, anyone critical of the regime was at risk of retaliation by the security forces. Prominent examples include the attacks on supporters of opposition leader Megawati Sukarnoputri in 1996 and the disappearances of pro-democracy activists in 1997-1998 (McGregor & Setiawan 2019, p. 843). Indeed, 'fear and violence were constant elements of the New Order state' (Heryanto & Mandal 2003, p. 4).

The final days of the New Order once again brought to the fore the role of the military in violent crackdowns on civilians. On 12 May, 4 students were killed by security forces during demonstrations against the regime, while more than 1,000 people were believed to have been killed in subsequent riots. Suharto's successor B.J. Habibie understood that in order to gain support as president, amongst other things his government needed to respond to the regime's poor human rights record. Within days, Habibie released all remaining political prisoners of the New Order and established a Joint Fact Finding Team to investigate the violence of May 1998 and the role of the security forces. This team's conclusion that highly trained provocateurs were behind the looting and violence increased public scrutiny of the military (Purdey 2006, pp. 127-128) and placed pressure for it to rescind its *dwifungsi* role.

Habibie's time as president may have been short (May 1998–October 1999) but his tenure was characterised by an impressive array of legal reforms. Many of these touched on human rights issues, including freedom of expression (and the abolition of the Ministry of Information) and labour rights (Eldridge 2002).

In addition, specific human rights legislation was also enacted. In November 1998, the foundation for Indonesia's current human rights framework was drawn up by the People's Consultative Assembly (Majelis Permusyawaratan Rakyat, MPR). The three main elements of the relevant decree passed by the MPR were:

- The government apparatus and state bodies are responsible for the respect, implementation and promotion of human rights;
- A human rights commission will be tasked to provide education, investigation, research and mediation of human rights;
- The implementation of human rights will be guaranteed and regulated by law.

This decree was the precursor to Indonesia's main Human Rights Law that was enacted in 1999. The law expanded on the human rights provisions included in the decree and encompassed a broad range of human rights, including civil and political rights such as the right to equality before the law and the right to association and freedom of opinion, as well as the freedom of religion. Economic, social and cultural rights included in the law guarantee the rights to education and employment, the right to adequate housing and the protection of indigenous cultures. The law reiterates that the protection, promotion, implementation and realisation of human rights are the responsibility of the government. It also stipulates that international human rights law ratified by Indonesia becomes national law, and as such reflects Indonesia's commitment to a society that is based on respect for fundamental human rights (Herbert 2008).

In addition to the Human Rights Law, the 2000 amendments to the Constitution also saw the inclusion of many human rights provisions, thereby firmly embedding human rights norms in Indonesian law. These constitutional amendments were a response to the original 1945 Constitution, which included very few of these guarantees and mainly emphasised citizens' duties towards the state. Modelled on the Universal Declaration of Human Rights (UDHR), the human rights chapter in Indonesia's amended Constitution now includes a wide range of human rights guarantees, including the principle of non-discrimination and the right of equal opportunity, the right to education and freedom from torture and other degrading or inhumane treatment or punishment. The human rights provisions in the Constitution have been lauded as a 'lengthy and impressive passage, formally granting a full range of protections extending well beyond those guaranteed in many developed states' (Lindsey 2008, p. 29).

In addition to the development of national law on human rights, Indonesia also ratified all major international human rights treaties. In 2006, Indonesia's integration into the international human rights framework culminated in the ratification of the International Covenant on Civil and Political Rights (ICCPR) and the International Covenant on Economic, Social and Cultural Rights (ICESCR), which together with the UDHR constitute the International Bill of Rights. Indonesia's swift ratification of international treaties is all the more remarkable considering that prior to 1998 it had only accepted a handful of international instruments, and historically had been ambivalent to embrace universal concepts of human rights (Eldridge 2002).

Human rights norms were not only enshrined in law, however. There was also swift action to develop human rights policy, with the first five-year National Human Rights Action plan passed in 1998. Existing institutions were also strengthened, including the establishment of a Directorate General for Human Rights within the Ministry of Law and Human Rights. Furthermore, Indonesia's Human Rights Commission was empowered through its inclusion in the Human Rights Law, thereby strengthening its legal status, while also expanding its mandate and bringing its appointment procedures in line with international standards for these bodies (Setiawan 2016). A National Commission on the Elimination of Violence Against Women (Komisi Nasional Anti Kekerasan Terhadap Perempuan, Komnas Perempuan) was established in 1998.

Other reforms enabled the creation of new specialised courts to address gross human rights violations. The jurisdiction of these Human Rights Courts, which were established in 2000, concerns the crime of genocide and crimes against humanity. There are both permanent and ad hoc Human Rights Courts, with the latter established by parliament to address cases of human rights violations that occurred prior to 2000 (Setiawan 2019). However, as will be discussed below, these courts have largely been unable to live up to expectations from activists that they could offer an avenue for redress for the most serious human rights crimes.

It is thus evident that since 1998, Indonesia has gone through a remarkable process of legal and institutional reform, including the establishment and strengthening of organisations charged with the promotion and protection of human rights. Transforming this framework into tangible results in promoting and protecting human rights, however, has proven challenging, as the following sections will outline.

Addressing Past Human Rights Violations

Since the end of authoritarianism, the immense legacy of past human rights issues has been a highly contentious political issue. Organisations and individuals favourable to a transitional justice process have argued that accountability will break the cycle of military impunity, which in turn is regarded as crucial to strengthening democracy and the rule of law (Linton 2006, p. 202). Internationally, some pressure was also exerted on the Indonesian government to face the past, largely as a result of a context where many other countries had transitioned from authoritarianism to more democratic forms of governance (McGregor & Setiawan 2019).

Transitional justice refers to justice measures during periods of political changes that address the wrongdoings of predecessor regimes (Teitel 2003, p. 69). These measures are commonly conceptualised as including both judicial (i.e. court processes) and non-judicial (i.e. truth commissions) approaches. It is believed that the combination of these strategies is important to meet the diverse needs of victims of human rights violations (Hayner 2001, p. 12–15).

As discussed above, in the early *reformasi* years, a legal human rights framework was developed, including the establishment of the Human Rights Courts, which are specifically charged with addressing past human rights violations. Komnas HAM has played a key role in the process of bringing cases to court as it is the sole body that can conduct a preliminary investigation where it expects gross human rights violations (Setiawan 2019). Since 2000, Komnas HAM has investigated eight cases of human rights violations that occurred under the New Order (Komnas HAM 2014). Only one of these cases, the 1984 Tanjung Priok killings, proceeded to the Human Rights Courts. The security forces actively interfered during the proceedings and all defendants were acquitted at different stages of the process (Setiawan 2019). All other investigations initiated by Komnas HAM were abandoned by the Attorney General's Office (AGO), citing vague procedural reasons. Independent observers, however, believed that the AGO effectively budged to pressure from political and military interest groups (Setiawan 2016, p. 24).

Non-judicial efforts have not been more successful, either. In 2004, a Truth and Reconciliation Commission (TRC) was established, with the mandate to settle cases of human rights violations outside the court system. Already during the drafting process it became apparent that there was significant resistance from some political parties and the security forces (Kimura 2015). This led to compromises in the law's provisions, including a passage stating that compensation of victims would only be awarded in exchange for amnesty for perpetrators, which carried a significant risk of entrenching impunity. In response, a number of human rights organisations then brought the TRC's establishing law to the Constitutional Court for review in 2006. The court decided in favour of the human rights organisations, maintaining that the provision was in contradiction with rights guaranteed in the Constitution. However, instead of dismissing the provision in question, the court cancelled the entire law (Lindsey & Butt 2018, p. 264). To date, there has been no serious attempt to revise the law and thereby reinstate the TRC, leaving Indonesia without a formal non-judicial mechanism to resolve past human rights abuses.

As for political leadership, most Indonesian presidents have offered lip service to addressing past human rights violations, but to date none have been able or willing to push the agenda significantly further. As part of the 1998 Independence Day speech, for instance, Habibie apologised for widespread human rights violations under the Suharto regime and stated that these had been perpetrated by 'individuals from the state apparatus' (Gittings 2019). Habibie's successor Abdurrahman Wahid, who was also a prominent leader of Nahdlatul Ulama (NU), offered a personal apology for the role of NU in the 1965 violence, which led to parts of the organisation starting to examine its role in the violence.

While the Megawati presidency entailed no serious efforts to address past human rights abuses (Human Rights Watch 2002), there were indications that Susilo Bambang Yudhoyono would offer a national apology for all cases of past human rights abuses. However, due to sustained political and public pressure, Yudhoyono's strong ties to the military and his father-in-law's own involvement in the 1965 violence, this did not eventuate. When Jokowi became president in 2014, there were some hopes judicial initiatives would be reinstated, but instead his government opted for a number of non-judicial initiatives, including a public dialogue on the 1965 massacres involving both victims of the violence and representatives of the military. Over time, however, all these initiatives ran out of steam, and they have largely served to shield those responsible from accountability (McGregor & Setiawan 2019).

Indonesian civil society organisations have responded to the deadlock in transitional justice by persistent activism, including at the local level where there have been some successful reconciliation processes. A difficulty with these local initiatives though is that they do not result in broad socialisation, and as they are tied to local environments the past role of the state in perpetuating violence tends to be obscured (McGregor & Setiawan 2019). In addition, a significant challenge to obtain justice for past crimes is that there is very limited societal interest and sometimes outright hostility towards addressing past human rights violations (Kuddus 2017).

All in all, in the area of transitional justice, Indonesia set out to provide both judicial and non-judicial mechanisms for redress of past crimes. But in practice these initiatives have not been able to deliver justice for past human rights crimes. The reasons for this failure are complex and include weaknesses in the judicial system, active opposition from military and political elites, including in the legal process, and limited societal support for issues of historical justice (McGregor & Setiawan 2019). Taken together, there is little backing – whether institutionally, politically or socially – to pursue justice for past human rights crimes.

Religious Minorities

In 2017, President Jokowi called upon Indonesians to combat discrimination 'pertaining to race, religion and ethnicity', warning that 'intolerance will only weaken our nation' (Lumanauw 2017). Indonesia likes to profile itself as a highly diverse and tolerant nation, yet religious intolerance is widespread and the state has not only often failed in protecting its citizens but, in some cases, has also been actively involved in violations of the rights to religious freedom.

The Indonesian Constitution guarantees the freedom of religion, including the freedom of citizens to choose a religion and to worship in accordance with that faith. At the same time, the Constitution states that individuals must accept limitations by law to protect the rights of others and to meet 'just demands based upon considerations of morality, religious values, security and public order in a democratic society'. Central to those limitations is the 1965 Blasphemy Law. Intended to allow religious leaders to protect the privileged status and conventional interpretations of recognised religions (Islam, Catholicism, Protestantism, Hinduism and Buddhism, with Confucianism added in 2000), the law also allows for religious practice to be monitored and controlled by the state, identifying 'deviant' beliefs as a threat to social order (Setiawan 2020, p. 265). Since 1998, the Blasphemy Law has been increasingly used, especially against citizens who belong to minority religions for so-called religious deviancy or insulting a religion, specifically

Islam (Crouch 2012). This has had far-reaching effects on minority groups and raises concerns about their protection and treatment.

In 2016, for instance, a joint decree of the Ministers of Religious Affairs and Home Affairs banned activities of the Gafatar (Gerakan Fajar Nusantara) community, which supposedly combines teachings of Islam, Judaism and Christianity, and was therefore declared heretical. Not only did Gafatar leaders face life imprisonment, but the community was also torched by Islamic vigilantes, forcing members to return to their home villages to be 're-educated' by religious leaders (Topsfield 2016).

The most conspicuous example of the use of the Blasphemy Law came in 2017 when it was used against former Jakarta governor, Basuki Tjahaja Purnama ('Ahok'). Ahok had made comments about a Quranic verse, which made him an easy target for Islamic hard-line groups that accused him of blasphemy and organised mass demonstrations against him. The Indonesian Council of Ulama (Majelis Ulama Indonesia, MUI) weighed in by stating that Ahok deserved to be punished for his remarks, and the prosecutorial services budged to this pressure. The court found Ahok guilty and convicted him to two years imprisonment, despite weak evidence – a common pattern in blasphemy cases (Butt 2018). While the use of the Blasphemy Law served political purposes, in Ahok's case they were also based on his double-minority status, both as an ethnic Chinese and a Christian (Hadiz 2017, p. 264).

The law is also used frequently against ordinary citizens. In 2018, Meliana, a Chinese Buddhist woman from North Sumatra was sentenced to 18 months imprisonment after she had complained about the volume of the call to prayer of the local mosque (Harsono 2018). Islamic vigilante groups retaliated by attacking her house and burning down at least 14 Buddhist temples. The MUI's branch in North Sumatra in 2017 issued a fatwa against Meliana, which pressured the police into investigating her, eventually leading to her trial and conviction (A'yun 2019).

The above examples illustrate that in limiting the rights and freedoms of religious minorities, the state often budges to pressure from conservative Islamic groups and organisations. This has been particularly pronounced in what has now been the nearly two decades of persecution against the Ahmadiyah Muslim minority group. Part of a movement founded at the end of the 19th century by Mirza Ghulam Ahmad, Ahmadis have been part of Indonesian social and religious life since the 1920s. In 1953, the Ahmadiyah were recognised as a legal entity, and in 2003 as a social organisation. But while Ahmadis consider themselves Muslims, their views are controversial among many mainstream Muslims, in particular the view of Ahmadis that Muhammad is not Islam's final prophet. This led the MUI to issue two *fatwas* against the Ahmadi, stating that the group is deviant. The first of these decrees was issued in 1980, and the second in 2005. The 2005 *fatwa* stated that Ahmadi are apostates and called upon the government to ban the organisation and close its places of worship (Colbran 2010, p. 681).

While the MUI has thus long targeted the Ahmadiyah, it has only been since the 2005 *fatwa* that violence and discrimination against Ahmadis have increased. These include physical attacks on homes and places of worship that forced hundreds of Ahmadis to flee. The authorities have not guaranteed their safety, with local governments asking Ahmadis to assimilate to mainstream Islamic teachings instead. While there has been no outright ban of the Ahmadiyah, in 2008 an inter-departmental government body issued a decree prohibiting the community from promoting its beliefs. The MUI has persistently denied any responsibility in the violence against the group (Colbran 2010, p. 689).

While the Indonesian Constitution provides for the right to freedom of religion, it is evident from the examples above that the fulfilment of freedom of religion leaves much to be desired. The Blasphemy Law is highly problematic from this perspective, as by 'recognising' official religions it gives much leeway to limiting the rights of followers who are considered to be outside these religions or beliefs. In addition, at a local level, decentralisation and the promulgation of local regula-tions (*peraturan daerah*), known as Perda, also pose threats to the rights of reli-gious minorities. These developments reflect broader struggles between Islamist forces and the state over the rightful place of religion in public life as well as the growing presence of Islamist forces in mainstream politics (Aspinall 2010, p. 20), which has had far-reaching effects on the protection of religious minorities.

Freedom of Expression and Association

Closely related to religious freedom are the freedoms of expression and associa-tion. Following the end of the New Order, much attention was paid to undoing the strong restrictions placed on freedom of expression under authoritarianism. A wide array of laws and regulations were reviewed, and rights to freedom of expression were also included in the Constitution. Particularly under the presi-dencies of Habibie and Wahid significant progresses were made in the areas of freedom of expression, association and assembly, while politically motivated tri-als also appeared to be a relic of the past.

Indeed, Indonesia's burgeoning civil society and media (see Chapter 7) are often regarded as evidence of the improvements that have taken place since 1998. At the same time, however, Indonesia's new-found freedoms were also contested from the outset. Like the limitations on freedom of religion, constitutional guar-antees for freedom of expression were limited by what was vaguely described as 'political, moral, religious and security considerations'. During the presidency of Megawati, the first indicators of backsliding became apparent as media edi-tors were brought to court for alleged defamation of politicians, while under Yudhoyono violent attacks on journalists increased (Setiawan 2020, p. 257).

In 2008 – during Yudhoyono's tenure – the so-called Electronic Information and Transactions (ITE) Law was passed. This law was designed to protect busi-nesses and individuals in electronic transactions but has increasingly been used by powerful political and economic actors to intimidate and coerce critics. Activists, lawyers, researchers, journalists and even 'ordinary' social media users have been disproportionally targeted through the law (Hamid 2017). While during the Jokowi presidency the ITE Law was amended, lowering prison sentences from six to four years, prosecutions have become far more frequent, and the penalties for online defamation remain harsher than those committed offline. Moreover, the ITE Law has also been used to block websites that are deemed radical or offensive. To this end, the government has established a specialised task force that monitors and identifies sites to be blocked. Of course, in some cases limitations can be justified – for instance in the case of terrorism-related content – but in many others, restrictions are far more dubious, including the limitations placed on online content relevant to the LGBT community (Setiawan 2020).

During the Jokowi presidency, new restrictions on freedom of association were introduced in response to the mass protests against Ahok. In 2017, the government passed a Government Regulation in Lieu of Law (Peraturan Pemerintah Pengganti Undang-Undang, Perppu) on Societal Organisations whose main purpose was to give the government a legal tool to ban the transnational Islamist organisation Hizbut Tahrir Indonesia (HTI). But the Perppu was worded in such a way that the executive can now unilaterally ban any organisation that is believed to contravene the state ideology of Pancasila. Furthermore, the Perppu also removed the possibility for organisations to contest bans in court, thereby taking away a crucial path to check the executive (Power 2018).

In addition, a renewed push to revise the Criminal Code also saw the introduction of new defamation clauses which criminalised defamation of the president and vice-president with penalties of up to five years imprisonment. Similarly, other proposed revisions criminalise the broadcasting of fake news or hoaxes that lead to social disturbances. A major concern related to these proposed revisions is that they are ambiguously worded and therefore open to a wide range of interpretations. Due to this ambiguity, critics call them *pasal karet*, or 'rubber clauses', in Indonesian. While defamation and the spreading of fake news certainly are issues that need to be addressed, criminalisation – especially when crimes are poorly defined – threaten the freedom of the press and journalists (Tapsell 2020).

Similarly, it has been increasingly difficult for academics to do their work, with seminars, book launches and film screenings on topics that are considered politically or socially sensitive often forced to be cancelled following pressure from local governments, police or conservative community groups. In some cases, university leadership demanded events to be cancelled (Setiawan 2020). In 2015, this was particularly noticeable in a harsh crackdown on academic and other public events related to the 1965-1966 mass violence (Kuddus 2017). The attacks on open debate culminated in September 2017 in an attack on the head office of the Legal Aid Foundation (Lembaga Bantuan Hukum, LBH), one of Indonesia's oldest and most influential civil society organisations. The protestors either represented or were mobilised by Islamic hard-line groups which had the backing of Kivlan Zen, a former chief of the Army Strategic Reserve Command (Komando Strategi Angkatan Darat, Kostrad). No charges were laid against the attackers.

Other government critics and activists have also come under growing pressure, with dramatic increases in prosecutions of anti-corruption and land reform activists. Physical and social media surveillance as well as wiretapping by the security forces have become increasingly common. At the same time, the state does not act in isolation, as the role of conservative and vigilante groups illustrates. State institutions, including the police, often turn a blind eye or even endorse the repressive and illiberal agendas of these groups – rather than upholding the right to freedom of expression and association. The close ties between law enforcement organisations and hard-line community groups have provided an enabling environment for the unlawful harassment of journalists, academics and activists, as well as impunity for transgressors (Jaffrey 2017).

Taken together, the restrictions on political freedoms and civil liberties during the Jokowi presidency are to a large extent unprecedented in the *reformasi* era. Like no other president since the end of the New Order, Jokowi has used legal instruments to silence oppositional, and more broadly critical, expressions of political views. There is, however, one region in Indonesia where such democratic deficits are not new at all. In Papua and West Papua, Indonesia's two westernmost provinces on the island of New Guinea, the human rights situation has been a major cause for concern basically throughout the democratic era, due to the Indonesian government's heavy-handed approach to dealing with a long-running independence struggle.

Papua

The roots of this independence struggle date back to 1961, when Papuan nationalists initially declared independence and raised their flag, the Morning Star. The territory then known as Netherlands New Guinea or West New Guinea had not been part of Indonesia at the time of the transfer of sovereignty from the Dutch in 1949 (see Chapter 2) and Papuans had steadily developed their own national identity throughout the 1950s. The Dutch continued to administer the territory during this time with no intention of relinquishing sovereignty to Indonesia. Instead, they slowly prepared it for full independence which Papuan nationalists duly declared in 1961.

Indonesian President Sukarno, however, strongly believed that Netherlands New Guinea should be part of Indonesia, and soon made its 'integration' into Indonesia a priority of foreign policy (Setiawan 2018, p. 196). In the context of the Cold War and Sukarno's growing anti-Western stance, the United States chose to appease Sukarno in the hope that it would prevent further alienation of Jakarta. Following extensive negotiations between the United States, the Netherlands and Indonesia from 1960 to 1962, the three parties eventually agreed to hand over Netherlands New Guinea to Indonesia, under the condition that Papuans would be able to decide their own future through a public vote in an 'act of free choice' by 1969. When this act was eventually held in 1969, however, it was a 'stage-managed whitewash' (Webster 2013, p. 10) in which Papuan elders were coerced by the Indonesian military to vote for integration into Indonesia.

Having been left out from the negotiations in the early 1960s, some Papuans took matters into their own hands through the declaration of independence and the subsequent formation of the Free Papua Organisation (Organisasi Papua Merdeka, OPM) in 1963. With little access to weapons and no large popular support base, however, the OPM struggled to mobilise resistance against Indonesian forces which had already begun to enter Papuan territory (Timmer 2005). The dramatic regime change in Jakarta from Sukarno to Suharto had no bearing on developments in Papua and so, in 1969, the staged referendum, called the 'act of no choice' by Papuan nationalists, formally finalised Indonesia's annexation of West New Guinea.

Under the New Order regime, many resources were directed into the province which was renamed Irian Jaya in 1973. But the implementation of development programs largely failed. At the same time, the military – which only received 25 percent of its budget from the government – had its eyes on Papua's rich natural resources to increase its funds. Soon, the armed forces gained political and economic control of the province, leading to the economic dislocation of Papuans. Moreover, under the New Order's transmigration policy to ease overpopulation on other islands, immigrants from Java and elsewhere started to fill labour and business opportunities, intensifying tensions between 'Papuans' and 'Indonesians' (Timmer 2005, p. 2). Papuans also lived under continuous threat from the Indonesian military which used torture and other brutal techniques to control the population. These practices were institutionalised in the 1980s when Papua was declared a Military Operation Zone (Daerah Operasi Militer, DOM) which would last until the fall of the New Order in 1998 (Hernawan 2016, p. 8).

The power of the military in Papua is also illustrated by its collaboration with big business. For example, in 1972 Freeport Indonesia, a subsidiary of a US-based mining giant, opened the Grasberg mine in the highlands north of Timika, which became one of the biggest gold mines – and third largest copper mine – in the world. Protected by the military, the mining operations forced local tribes to relocate from the highlands, altered the local ecosystem and affected the livelihoods of local communities as well as their traditional and spiritual rights (Prihandono 2013). The security contracts with Freeport were highly lucrative for the military: it was estimated that in the late New Order, Freeport paid the military US$ 35 million, followed by annual payments of several million dollar, though the exact amount of these annual payments is contested (Global Witness 2005, p. 10–11).

After 1998, there was a significant shift in civil-military relations in Indonesia, but in Papua the military's presence and conduct hardly changed (Mietzner 2009), even after the province was granted special autonomy in 2001. While violence and other serious human rights abuses became more sporadic, they never really disappeared. Merely three weeks after the special autonomy law was passed, for example, one of Papua's most prominent proponents of independence, Theys Eluay, was killed by Indonesian special forces. The murderers were later called 'heroes' by the then army chief of staff.

As calls for independence grew louder in the wake of East Timor's separation from Indonesia in 2001, the government instead split Papua into two provinces, Papua and West Papua. For many Papuans, this decision felt like a betrayal as it was clearly designed to erode unity among Papuans. Meanwhile, skirmishes between security forces and Papuans continued, though as the International Crisis Group (2006, p. 9) noted in a report, 'this violence by security forces against civilians is more the product of a culture of impunity than any systematic campaign of killings'. This culture of impunity has effectively persisted until today, with military personnel rarely held accountable for human rights abuses. At the same time, other conflicts in Papua have also repeatedly erupted, including conflicts over natural resources, frictions between different Papuan ethnic and religious groups, as well as between migrants and locals.

The last two presidents, Yudhoyono and Jokowi, have both taken a prosperity and development-based approach to Papua, and to achieve this have increased central government funding into both provinces. Under Jokowi, there has been a particular focus on developing infrastructure and connectivity. The Trans- Papua Road, for instance, which is over 4,000 kilometres long, means to end the isolation of many Papuan communities. Similarly, a national standard price for fuel aims to bring down the cost of petrol in Papua, which can be nearly ten times more than the average national (Ruhyanto 2018). In addition, Jokowi ordered the release of five political prisoners in early 2015 and hinted at lifting travel restrictions for foreign journalists who want to visit Papua (Chauvel 2015).

By and large, however, these actions have had limited success. At the end of Jokowi's first term, travel for foreign media remained tightly regulated (Setiawan 2020) and despite increased investment, Papua was still poorly developed. In terms of health, for instance, Papua has the lowest life expectancy in Indonesia, and the highest infant, child and maternal mortality rates (Harsono 2017). Nor has the Jokowi government been able to put a halt to violence, with regular reports of torture and extrajudicial killings involving the security forces (Amnesty International 2020, Human Rights Watch 2020). The power of the military in Papua became once again blatantly clear when early during Jokowi's tenure the security forces killed six peaceful protestors, including five high school students, in what is known as the Paniai killings.

In late 2019 and early 2020, the OPM once again intensified its guerrilla activities around the Freeport mine. Several attacks on Freeport staff and facilities were reported, including an assault inside Freeport's office complex in Kuala Kencana on 30 March 2020. OPM gunmen also attacked a number of villages in the area around the Freeport mine, displacing around 1,600 residents who were evacuated by the military (IPAC 2020a). Significantly, these attacks took place at a time when the number of military personnel in Papua had just been substantially increased. All in all, the situation in Papua remains as tense as ever, with violence perpetrated by both the security forces and guerrilla groups like the OPM.

At the same time, little progress has been made towards a political solution to the situation. Even though some Papuan political prisoners have been released, many others remain behind bars. In 2019, the government had no qualms to block internet access in Papua in response to protests following the arrests and racist treatments of Papuan students in Java (Idris 2019). While the Jokowi administration has framed its actions as solving the conflict in Papua, the 'prosperity approach' effectively only addresses the symptoms rather than the substance of anti-Indonesian sentiment (Chauvel 2015).

As Jakarta's focus on infrastructure, education and healthcare has failed to rebuild trust and foster reconciliation, discussions arose in 2020 about the future of the special autonomy arrangement. With both Jakarta and Papuan leaders dissatisfied with the legislation, it appeared as if these discussions might offer a valuable opportunity to finally address the reasons behind the ongoing demands for self-determination – the suffocating military and police presence in Papua, the lack of accountability for past human rights violations and the ongoing internal migration into Papua. Observers, however, were sceptical about the outlook for these discussions. As a report from mid-2020 notes, 'the revision of Otsus [special autonomy] could be an opportunity, but nothing suggests the Jokowi government will seize it' (IPAC 2020b).

Conclusion

More than two decades after the fall of authoritarianism, Indonesia continues to struggle with the effective protection of human rights. Through case studies of transitional justice, the position of religious minorities, freedom of expression and association and human rights issues in Papua, this chapter has shown that explanations for Indonesia's human rights challenges are complex and differ between issues. Nonetheless, three factors can be identified that are at the root of Indonesia's poor human rights record: structural factors at the state level that impede implementation of legislation, limited societal support for the idea of universal human rights and last but not least the agency of political leaders, in particular the president (Setiawan 2020, p. 268).

First, there are structural issues at the level of the state and political institutions. As discussed in this chapter, after 1998 many human rights reforms were introduced. At the same time, these progressive changes were immediately contested in both legal provisions and practice. This raises questions about the nature and extent of Indonesia's democratic transition, where commitment to liberal ideals such as human rights ultimately was minimal. This lack of broad elite support for human rights has over time proven to allow for limited implementation and ongoing violations.

Second, the implementation of human rights is also hampered by limited societal support. Scholars have long noted 'creeping' religious and political conservatism among Indonesian citizens (Van Bruinessen 2013), which amongst others is evident in the powerful resistance from Islamic hard-line groups against quintessential human rights such as religious freedom. Indeed, survey data from the Asian Barometer has shown that while Indonesians are committed to procedural elements of a democracy, such as free and fair elections, they are far more ambivalent about individual rights, including freedom of religion and freedom of expression (Warburton & Aspinall 2019).

Third, the effective protection of human rights is also constrained by the agency of political leaders. While Indonesian presidents in the post-authoritarian era have all, to different extents, engaged with human rights issues, none have been able to achieve structural changes. This stems partially from leaders' own ambivalence towards human rights, but also from their reliance on support from powerful political, military and religious actors, all of whom have their own agendas to undermine efforts to protect human rights.

Taken together, these three factors have continuously chipped away at the many steps forward that Indonesia has taken in human rights policies and practices since 1998. They do not only place the realisation of human rights in Indonesia in a precarious position, but also raise questions about the broader state of democracy in Indonesia. Even if in the last two decades Indonesia has shown commitment to relatively free and fair elections, the protection of citizens' rights leaves much to be desired. As such it appears that Indonesia is firmly on the path to illiberal democracy, where electoral democracy is combined with serious limitations on individual rights and the rule of law.

References

Amnesty International Indonesia 2020, *Civil and political rights' violations in Papua and West Papua. List of Issues Prior to Reporting (LOIPR) for Indonesia CCPR session 129, June-July 2020*, Amnesty International, Jakarta, viewed 2 April 2020 <https://www.amnesty.id/wp-content/uploads/2020/06/ASA2124452020ENGLISH.pdf>.

Aspinall, E 2010, 'The irony of success', *Journal of Democracy*, vol. 21, no. 2, pp. 20–34.

A'yun, RQ 2019, 'Blasphemy on the rise', *Inside Indonesia*, viewed 20 March 2020, <https://www.insideindonesia.org/blasphemy-on-the-rise.

Butt, S 2018, 'Religious conservatism, Islamic criminal law and the judiciary in Indonesia: a tale of three courts', *Journal of Legal Pluralism and Unofficial Law*, vol. 50, no. 3, pp. 402–434.

Chauvel, R 2015, 'Dialogue missing in Jokowi's Papua policy', *Indonesia at Melbourne*, 30 June, viewed 2 April 2020, <https://indonesiaatmelbourne.unimelb.edu.au/dialogue-missing-in-papua-policy/>.

Colbran, N 2010, 'Realities and challenges in realising freedom of religion or belief in Indonesia', *The International Journal of Human Rights*, vol. 14, no. 5, pp. 678–704.

Crouch, M 2012, 'Law and religion in Indonesia: the Constitutional Court and the Blasphemy Law', *Asian Journal of Comparative Law*, vol. 7, no. 1, pp. 1–46.

Eldridge, P 2002, 'Human rights in post-Suharto Indonesia', *The Brown Journal of World Affairs*, vol. 9, no. 1, pp. 127–139.

Gittings, J 2019, 'B.J. Habibie obituary', *The Guardian*, 17 September, viewed 1 April 2020, <https://www.theguardian.com/world/2019/sep/17/bj-habibie-obituary>.

Global Witness 2005, 'Paying for protection: the Freeport mine and the Indonesian security forces', Global Witness, viewed 3 April 2020, <https://cdn2.globalwitness.org/archive/files/import/missing%20docs/paying%20for%20protection.pdf>.

Hadiz, VR 2017, 'Indonesia's year of democratic setbacks: towards a new phase of deepening illiberalism?', *Bulletin of Indonesian Economic Studies*, vol. 53, no. 3, pp. 261–278.

Hamid, U 2017 'Laws, crackdowns and control mechanisms: digital platforms and the state', in E Jurriëns & R Tapsell (eds), *Digital Indonesia: connectivity and divergence*, ISEAS Yusof Ishak Institute, Singapore, pp. 93–109.

Harsono, A 2017, 'Indonesia permits rare Papua access to UN health rights expert', Human Rights Watch, viewed 3 April 2020, <https://www.hrw.org/news/2017/04/07/indonesia-permits-rare-papua-access-un-health-rights-expert>.

Harsono, A 2018, 'The human cost of Indonesia's Blasphemy Law', Human Rights Watch, viewed 29 March 2020, <https://www.hrw.org/news/2018/10/25/human-cost -indonesias-blasphemy-law>.

Hayner, P 2001, *Unspeakable truths: confronting state terror and atrocity*, Routledge, London.

Herbert, J 2008, 'The legal framework of human rights in Indonesia', in T Lindsey (ed.), *Indonesia: law and society*, 2nd edn, The Federation Press, Annandale, pp. 456–482.

Heryanto A & Mandal, KS 2003, 'Challenges to authoritarianism in Indonesia and Malaysia', in A Heryanto & KS Mandal (eds.), *Challenging authoritarianism in Southeast Asia: comparing Indonesia and Malaysia*, RoutledgeCurzon, London, pp. 1–23.

Hernawan, B 2016, 'Torture as theatre in Papua', *International Journal of Conflict and Violence*, vol. 10, no. 1, pp. 77–92.

Human Rights Watch 2002, 'Human Rights Watch world report Asia: Indonesia', Human Rights Watch, viewed 30 March 2020, < https://www.hrw.org/legacy/wr2k2/asia7 .html>.

Human Rights Watch 2020, 'Indonesia: events of 2020', Human Rights Watch, viewed 3 April 2020, < https://www.hrw.org/world-report/2021/country-chapters/indonesia>.

Idris, IK 2019, 'The internet shutdown in Papua threatens Indonesia's democracy and its people's right to free speech', *The Conversation*, 23 August, viewed 1 April 2020, <https://theconversation.com/the-internet-shutdown-in-papua-threatens-indonesias -democracy-and-its-peoples-right-to-free-speech-122333>.

International Crisis Group 2006, *Papua: answers to frequently asked questions*, Asia Briefing no. 53, ICG, Jakarta/Brussels.

IPAC 2020a, *Covid-19 and conflict in Papua*, IPAC Short Briefing no. 2, IPAC, Jakarta.

IPAC 2020b, *Renewing, revising or rejecting special autonomy in Papua*, IPAC Report no. 64, IPAC, Jakarta.

Jaffrey, S 2017, 'Justice by numbers', *New Mandala*, viewed 25 March 2020, <https:// www.newmandala.org/justice-by-numbers/>.

Kimura, E 2015, 'The struggle for justice and reconciliation in post-Suharto Indonesia', *Southeast Asian Studies*, vol. 4, no. 1, pp. 73–93

Komnas, HAM 2014, *Ringkasan eksekutif laporan penyelidikan pelanggaran HAM yang berat*, Komnas HAM, Jakarta.

Kuddus, R 2017, 'The ghosts of 1965: politics and memory in Indonesia', *New Left Review*, no. 104, pp. 45–92.

Lindsey, T 2008, 'Constitutional reform in Indonesia: muddling towards democracy', in T Lindsey (ed.), *Indonesia: law and society*, 2nd edn, The Federation Press, Annandale, pp. 23–47.

Lindsey, T & Butt, S 2018, *Indonesian law*, Oxford University Press, Oxford.

Linton, S 2006, 'Accounting for atrocities in Indonesia', *Singapore Year Book of International Law*, no. 10, pp. 199–231.

Lumanauw, N 2017, 'Jokowi calls on the nation to combat racial and religious intolerance', *Jakarta Globe*, 18 April, viewed 28 March 2020, <https://jakartaglobe.id/news/jokowi -calls-nation-combat-racial-religious-intolerance/>.

McGregor, K & Setiawan, K 2019, 'Shifting from international to 'Indonesian' justice measures: two decades of addressing past human rights violations', *Journal of Contemporary Asia*, vol. 49, no. 5, pp. 837–861.

Mietzner, M 2009, *Military politics, Islam and the state in Indonesia: from turbulent transition to democratic consolidation*, ISEAS, Singapore.

Power, TP 2018, 'Jokowi's authoritarian turn and Indonesia's democratic decline', *Bulletin of Indonesian Economic Studies*, vol. 54, no. 3, pp. 307–338.

Prihandono, I 2013, 'Transnational corporations and human rights violations in Indonesia', *Australian Journal of Asian Law*, vol. 14, no. 1, pp. 1–23.

Purdey, J 2006, *Anti-Chinese violence in Indonesia 1996–1999*, National University of Singapore Press, Singapore.

Ruhyanto, A 2018, 'Papua: how Indonesian president Jokowi is trying - and failing - to win hearts and minds', *The Conversation*, 5 December, viewed 3 April 2020, <https://theconversation.com/papua-how-indonesian-president-jokowi-is-trying-and-failing-to-win-hearts-and-minds-107826>.

Setiawan, K 2016, 'From hope to disillusion: the paradox of Komnas HAM, the Indonesian National Human Rights Commission', *Bijdragen tot de Taal-, Land- en Volkenkunde*, vol. 172, no. 1, pp. 1–32.

Setiawan, K 2018, 'On the periphery: human rights, Australia and Indonesia', in T Lindsey & D McRae (eds), *Strangers next door?: Indonesia and Australia in the Asian century*, Hart Publishing, Oxford, pp. 193–210.

Setiawan, KMP 2019, 'The Human Rights Courts: embedding impunity', in M Crouch (ed.), *The politics of court reform: judicial change and legal culture in Indonesia*, Cambridge University Press, Cambridge, pp. 1–28.

Setiawan, KMP 2020, 'A state of surveillance? Freedom of expression under the Jokowi presidency', in T Power & E Warburton (eds), *Democracy in Indonesia: from stagnation to regression?*, ISEAS Yusof Ishak Institute, Singapore, pp. 254–274.

Tapsell, R 2020, 'The media and democratic decline', in T Power & E Warburton (eds), *Democracy in Indonesia: from stagnation to regression?*, ISEAS Yusof Ishak Institute, Singapore, pp. 210–227.

Teitel, RG 2003, 'Transitional justice genealogy', *Harvard Human Rights Journal*, vol. 16, pp. 69–94.

Timmer, J 2005, 'Decentralisation and elite politics in Papua', *State, society and governance in Melanesia*, discussion paper 2005/6, viewed 1 April 2020, <https://openresearch-repository.anu.edu.au/bitstream/1885/10137/1/Timmer_Decentralisatio nElite2005.pdf>.

Topsfield, J 2016, 'Ex-Gafatar leaders charged with blasphemy and treason in Indonesia', *Sydney Morning Herald*, 7 June, viewed 1 April 2020, <https://www.smh.com.au/world/exgafatar-leaders-charged-with-blasphemy-and-treason-in-indonesia-20160607 -gpd9h5.html>.

Van Bruinessen, M 2013, *Contemporary developments in Indonesian Islam: explaining the conservative turn*, ISEAS, Singapore.

Warburton, E & Aspinall, E 2019, 'Explaining Indonesia's democratic regression: structure, agency and popular opinion', *Contemporary Southeast Asia*, vol. 41, no. 2, pp. 255–285.

Webster, D 2013, 'Self-determination abandoned: the road to the New York Agreement on West New Guinea (Papua), 1960–62', *Indonesia*, no. 95, pp. 9–24.

11 Environmental Challenges

Introduction

On 5 October 2020, two local residents living near a forest in South Kalimantan photographed a bird they did not recognise from their regular forages into the woods. Curious about the bird's identity, they sought help from a local birdwatching group and professional ornithologists further away. Upon studying the images, the experts concluded that the two men had just rediscovered a bird species that had not been seen for more than 170 years. Remarkably, the discovery came less than a year after an international team of researchers had provided the very first scientific description of five other new bird species from the remote islands of Taliabu, Peleng and Batudaka in the provinces of Central Sulawesi and North Maluku (Rheindt et al. 2020).

These major ornithological breakthroughs illustrate just how much of Indonesia's enormously diverse fauna remains underexplored. According to 2003 data from the country's National Planning Board, Indonesia at the turn of the century was home to 515 species of mammal, 511 species of reptile, 1,531 species of bird, 1,400 species of fish and 38,000 species of plants (Bappenas 2003). Some new species have been added to the list since then, but many more, including some of those that have only just been discovered, are at risk of extinction due to rapidly expanding human activity that encroaches ever faster on the country's last remaining natural habitats. In particular, deforestation, unsustainable fishing, poaching and wildlife trafficking are driving the depletion of Indonesia's natural resources and the decline in biodiversity. Moreover, the effects of climate change and global warming are also posing significant threats to the environment as well as the people who depend on forests and marine environments for their livelihoods.

This chapter will outline both the challenges to environmental conservation in Indonesia and the policies and institutional reforms devised to tackle these challenges. It will highlight that environmental problems such as deforestation, climate change and wildlife trafficking have only fairly recently received broader attention in Indonesia and, so far, governmental responses have been largely ineffective. The chapter argues that in order to understand the reasons behind this ineffectiveness, a combination of structural, institutional and attitudinal

DOI: 10.4324/9780429459511-11

factors needs to be considered. Structurally, natural resources are a key pillar of Indonesia's patronage-driven political economy, with the forestry sector particularly deeply enmeshed in the corrupt practices that underpin this political economy. Institutionally, environmental policies and the organisations established to implement these policies lack resources and coherence, which allows powerful interests opposed to conservation to continuously contest conservation standards and exploit loopholes in the policy framework. Attitudinally, many Indonesians remain either unaware or indifferent to the consequences of poaching, hunting and habitat destruction. In Java, the deeply engrained tradition of keeping wild birds in cages adds further obstacles to attempts to protect Indonesia's avifauna.

After this brief introduction, the chapter will begin by outlining some of the main environmental problems in contemporary Indonesia. First, it will sketch the contours of deforestation, highlighting both the magnitude and the impact of forest loss in Indonesia, including the fact that due to the large-scale burning of its forests, Indonesia is now one of the biggest producers of greenhouse gas emissions in the world. The second section shifts attention from the causes of climate change to some of its consequences, emphasising in particular Indonesia's susceptibility to flooding and other extreme weather events. Third, the chapter sheds light on poaching and the illicit wildlife trade, which threaten many iconic species as well as less well-known songbirds. The fourth part discusses what the Indonesian government and non-governmental organisations (NGOs) have done to address these key environmental issues. The last section of the chapter, finally, analyses why so many of these initiatives have failed to be effective in protecting the environment.

Deforestation

There can be little doubt that deforestation is one of Indonesia's most pressing environmental problems. Along with Brazil and the Democratic Republic of Congo, Indonesia has some of the largest areas of tropical rainforest in the world (Food and Agriculture Organisation 2016, p. 17), yet it is also losing large parts of these forests every year due to logging, burning and other means of conversion into agricultural land. Back in 1950, forests had covered more than 80 percent of the total land area of the Indonesian archipelago (Forest Watch Indonesia & Global Forest Watch 2002), but by 2015 it was estimated that only around 50 percent of land remained forested. Significantly, only about half of these forests are natural primary forests, while secondary and plantation forests account for the remainder (Tsujino et al 2016, p. 345).

Deforestation in Indonesia began on a grand scale during the authoritarian New Order period when the Suharto regime began issuing logging concessions to the president's business cronies and international investors. Driven by regional demand for wood and pulp, and further fuelled by domestic population growth, the timber industry quickly expanded to cover massive logging and plywood operations in Sumatra, Kalimantan and Sulawesi. One of Suharto's most notorious cronies, Bob Hasan, quickly took control of the sector through the Indonesian

Wood Panel Association (Asosiasi Panel Kayu Indonesia, Apkindo), which he turned into a 'collective marketing apparatus with cartel-like control over the nation's plywood exports' (Barr 1998, p. 16). With Hasan at the helm of Apkindo, deforestation accelerated in the 1990s as growing international demand for palm oil opened up new lucrative incentives to decimate forests and turn them into oil palm plantations.

The end of the New Order and the onset of regional autonomy in the wake of the Asian financial crisis shifted the authority to grant logging concessions from Jakarta to the district level. While this ended the corrupt centralised control of the forestry sector, many newly empowered local governments viewed forests in very much the same way as the authoritarian Suharto regime had done, namely 'as an easy source of financial revenue to be exploited rather than managed' (Wollenberg, Moeliono & Limberg 2009, p. 17). Thus, the logging and burning of Indonesia's forests initially continued virtually unabated, made worse by an increase in illegal logging practices as a result of institutional uncertainty and economic hardship in the aftermath of the regime change (McCarthy 2002). Only when the broader political and economic situation stabilised during the presidency of Susilo Bambang Yudhoyono (2004–2014) did the demise of Indonesia's forests slow down a bit (Food and Agriculture Organisation 2010). Nevertheless, deforestation has continued under the watch of Yudhoyono and his successor Jokowi, with devastating consequences not only for biodiversity but also for millions of people who depend on the forests for their livelihoods.

Arguably, the most direct effect of deforestation is the threat to biodiversity. Since the mid-1980s, iconic large mammal species such as the Sumatran rhinoceros, the Sumatran tiger and the orangutan have been among those most severely affected by the loss of forest habitat. As population numbers declined, the International Union for Conservation of Nature (IUCN) progressively upgraded the conservation status of all three species to 'critically endangered'.

Meanwhile, the shrinking of forested areas has also led to more and more human–animal conflicts, often with deadly outcomes for wildlife. For example, in the first half of 2018, at least seven high-profile cases of cruelty against animals occurred across the archipelago, including the torture of orangutans and the killings of tigers, bears and elephants (Heriyanto 2018). In most of these cases, the animals were killed in the immediate vicinity of villages or plantations.

But deforestation not only affects animals. It also has severe impacts on the multitude of local communities that used to rely on forests for food and shelter. In many parts of Indonesia, the massive spread of plantations and mining operations in recent years has driven countless members of these communities out of their traditional ways of life. To be sure, many farmers have embraced palm oil as a lucrative new income opportunity (Murray Li 2014). But processes of agrarian change are complex and not all smallholders have reaped tangible benefits from their engagement in the palm oil industry (McCarthy 2010). In some cases, resistance from local communities against the encroachment of large plantations on their villages has led to outright conflict with palm oil, timber and mining companies. Apart from the direct threat to the land, another source of conflict has been the fact that these companies often bring migrant labour from Java and elsewhere to work on the plantations and mines while systematically excluding local communities. Thus, deforestation not only destroys the natural environment, but it can also bring sustained economic hardship and social conflict to formerly forest-dependent communities. Conflict resolution mechanisms are often ineffective, so few communities receive adequate compensation for the loss of land (Afrizal & Berenschot 2020).

Beyond the communities that live around deforested areas, Indonesians further afield as well as people from neighbouring countries have also felt the consequences of deforestation, especially when highly combustible peat forests were burned down for quick conversion into oil palm plantations. This widespread practice first came to the attention of a wider international audience in 1997–1998 when massive forest fires on the islands of Sumatra and Borneo caused a regional haze crisis. In 2006 and 2015, fires again raged out of control, blanketing large parts of Indonesia as well as neighbouring Singapore and Malaysia in thick smoke. Scientists subsequently linked the 2015 haze crisis to the premature deaths of an estimated 100,000 people in the three affected countries (Koplitz et al 2016). Beyond the severe impact on people's health, the forest fires also carried a significant economic cost. According to the World Bank (2016, p. 1), sectors like agriculture, forestry, trade, tourism and transportation all suffered severe losses in 2015 and if expenses for emergency responses, fire suppression and school closures are added on, the overall cost of the 2015 crisis was estimated to be around US$16.1 billion (IDR 221 trillion).

Finally, it is important to note that the shrinking of Indonesia's tropical rainforests also has global implications as the country is now one of the ten largest emitters of greenhouse gases and therefore a major contributor to climate change and global warming (Friedrich, Ge & Pickens 2020). Forests like the Indonesian peat forests store large amounts of carbon, but the relentless degradation and destruction has released large parts of this carbon into the atmosphere as carbon dioxide. Over time, tropical forests have increasingly lost their ability to function as a 'carbon sink' because they now emit more carbon than they capture (Baccini et al 2017). In Indonesia, in particular, the widespread use of fire as a mode of converting forest into oil palm plantations has exacerbated the impact of deforestation on the global climate. The 2015 fires, for example, produced emissions that were estimated to be equal to Japan's entire annual CO_2 output in that year (Mooney 2015). Thus, both the process and the outcomes of deforestation contribute to Indonesia's enormous carbon footprint.

Impacts of Climate Change

Indonesia is not only a large producer of greenhouse gas emissions. It is also among the countries that are likely to face some of the most significant consequences from climate change, due to its location in the tropics and its archipelagic geography. These twin factors make Indonesia particularly vulnerable to a broad range of observable consequences of climate change, including rising sea levels, extreme weather events such as storms, floods and droughts as well as related disruptions to agriculture and fishery (Jotzo et al. 2009). Like elsewhere in the world, the people who are most at risk from these impacts of climate change are the poor and marginalised, especially those living in low-lying coastal communities. However, Indonesia is also facing the prospect of losing entire sections of its capital city, as Jakarta is one of the fastest sinking cities in the world (Lin & Hidayat 2018).

Box 11.1: Indonesia's Sinking Capital

Located on the northwest coast of Java, Indonesia's capital Jakarta is infamous for its floods. Virtually every year during the rainy season, streets turn into rivers, forcing residents to wade through knee-deep water as they try to go about their daily business. In particularly bad years, the city basically comes to a standstill when the floods hit. Rising sea levels as a consequence of climate change are no doubt contributing to the problem, but at its core, Jakarta's floods are more about the sinking ground than the rising sea. As a matter of fact, Indonesia's capital is sinking, and not just by a few millimetres a year. According to a report by BBC reporters Mayuri Mei Lin and Rafki Hidayat (2018), the northern part of the city 'has sunk 2.5 m in 10 years and is continuing to sink by as much as 25 cm a year in some parts'. That makes the 10 million metropolis one of the fastest sinking cities in the world.

A key reason for this high rate of land subsidence is that Jakarta's residents are extracting unsustainable amounts of ground water from the aquifers underneath the city to make up for shortages in reliable water supplies for drinking, bathing and other purposes. In addition, inadequate waste management and a lack of sewers exacerbate the problem as Jakarta's rivers have become so polluted over the years that rainwater can no longer flow freely out of Jakarta. At the same time, reservoirs lack capacity to store the water that falls onto the city during heavy downpours while uncontrolled development, poor urban planning and political deadlock over potential solutions also add to the imbroglio (Kimmelman 2017). When former Jakarta governor Basuki Tjahaja Purnama (Ahok) finally took decisive action to clear the rivers and expand the city's water pump system, flooding decreased noticeably and Ahok's popularity soared, yet the incumbent still lost the election because voting behaviour for most residents was shaped more by religious and ethnic sentiment than by appreciation for the track record of Jakarta's first ethnic Chinese governor.

Some water management experts believe that unless city authorities are prepared to soon evacuate large numbers of citizens at its northern coastline, the only solution to prevent the sea from inundating the city further is to build a massive sea wall in the Jakarta Bay. Former governor Ahok as

Box 11.1 continued

well as the central government supported this idea and approved permits to start building a range of artificial islands in 2014. But such reclamation projects are controversial because they damage existing coastal ecosystems and usually favour upmarket development rather than accommodate the needs of impoverished fishing communities. Siding with the opponents, Ahok's successor Anies Baswedan revoked the permits for the sea wall in October 2018, declaring that 'the reclamation is a part of the history of Jakarta, but it will not be a part of its future' (Gokkon 2018a). Meanwhile, President Jokowi's response to the problem was to propose a new purpose-built capital in Kalimantan. And while Covid-19 stalled the construction plans throughout 2020, a spokesman for the president announced in early 2021 that works on a new presidential palace would resume that year. He did not reveal how this plan would help tackle Jakarta's annual floods.

As an archipelagic state with one of the longest coastlines in the world, Indonesia is particularly susceptible to the risks of rising sea levels. While estimates of the likely extent of sea level rise over the next few decades vary depending on the projected extent of greenhouse gas emissions, the Intergovernmental Panel on Climate Change (IPCC) warned in its 2021 report that relative to 1995–2014, even under a *very low* emissions scenario, sea levels are likely to rise between 0.28 and 0.55 m by 2100. In other, more dire scenarios presented in the same report, these figures increase dramatically, culminating in a warning that under conditions of *very high* greenhouse gas emissons, sea levels may rise by 0.63–1.01 m by 2100 (IPCC 2021, p. SPM-28). For Indonesia, the rising seawaters pose a direct threat as up to 2,000 of its islands are at risk of being swallowed by the sea. According to World Bank analyst Susmita Dagupta (2018), 'a one-meter rise would inundate more than 13,800 square kilometres and may displace 2.8 million people'. But regular flooding and inundation is not just a future scenario. In many coastal communities, it is already a part of daily life, especially where the removal of mangroves and poor infrastructure planning are further exacerbating the consequences of climate change.

Apart from the loss of land due to rising sea levels, climate change also threatens the livelihoods of millions of Indonesians who depend on agriculture and fishery. As extreme weather events such as droughts and floods increase in frequency and intensity, Indonesia faces the prospect of severe disruptions to water supplies, decreasing soil fertility and an overall decline in land productivity (Jotzo et al. 2009, p. 253). In addition, changing rainfall patterns have already altered availability and access to drinking water in many parts of the country. Meanwhile, fishing communities on Java's northern coast are struggling to cope with the growing salinity in their brackish shrimp and fish ponds as rising sea levels result in more and more saltwater finding its way into the artificially created ponds.

Finally, climate change poses a direct threat to biodiversity, both on land and in Indonesia's extensive marine waters where, according to a 2018 report by the

Indonesian Institute of Sciences (Lembaga Ilmu Pengetahuan Indonesia, LIPI), more than a third of all Indonesian coral reefs were in bad condition (Jakarta Post 2018). Due to its archipelagic geography, Indonesia has large numbers of endemic plant and animal species (species that occur nowhere else on earth), but many of these species only occur on small and remote islands whose ecosystems are extremely vulnerable to climate change. The newly discovered bird species mentioned in the introduction of this chapter, for example, live only on small islands in Eastern Indonesia that have suffered not only from logging, but also extensive forest fires, which Rheindt et al. (2020, p. 170) presume were 'caused by recent climate change'. For one of the new species on Taliabu, suitable habitat is already confined to just a few mountaintops. Changes to the islands' ecosystem triggered by climate change threaten this species with extinction as there are no backup populations elsewhere.

Hunting, Poaching and the Illegal Wildlife Trade

In addition to deforestation and the consequences of climate change, another huge threat to Indonesia's environment and its biodiversity comes from hunting and poaching. A study into the decline of Bornean orangutans between 1999 and 2015, for example, found that while the rate of decline was highest in areas of Kalimantan that were affected by deforestation, absolute losses were actually largest in areas where forests were still intact (Voigt et al. 2018). As the authors point out, this finding supports a range of other studies from Indonesia and other tropical regions that have highlighted the significance of hunting as a major threat to biodiversity. Apart from large mammals such as orangutans or tigers, songbirds are particularly vulnerable to hunting and trapping pressure in Indonesia, due to deeply engrained cultural traditions that make the keeping of songbirds in cages socially desirable (Felbab-Brown 2017, p. 6).

According to a famous Javanese proverb, a man is regarded as successful if he has a horse, a house, a wife, a *keris* (ceremonial dagger) and a bird in a cage. Keeping birds in cages thus has deep cultural roots in Indonesia, especially in Java and Bali. In recent decades, however, the long-established cultural esteem for songbirds has reached new dimensions as highly competitive bird-singing contests have attained immense popularity. With huge amounts of prize money at stake at these competitions, the keeping of songbirds is no longer just a matter of social status, but it has also morphed into serious business. At the most prestigious national competitions, winning birds can attract buyers willing to spend thousands of dollars (Paddock 2020).

A dense network of bird clubs now exists to organise these bird-singing competitions from the village to the national level while massive bird markets supply the birdkeepers with a broad range of species, including many that are listed as threatened by the IUCN. At the turn of the century, some researchers estimated that more than 20 percent of all households in Indonesia's five biggest cities owned at least one bird (Jepson & Ladle 2005). Semarang and Surabaya were the cities with the highest proportion of households that kept birds (34.4 and

29.5 percent, respectively), while numbers in Jakarta, Bandung and Medan were below the average of 21.8 percent. More recently, a nationwide survey conducted by polling institute Indikator Politik on behalf of one of the authors in November 2020 found very similar results for the whole of Indonesia. Asked if they had ever owned a pet bird, 21.8 percent of respondents answered 'yes'. Like in the earlier study, there was substantial regional variation, with 31.7 percent of respondents from East Java answering yes, but only 16.1 percent of Jakarta residents answering yes. These regional trends are also echoed by Marshall et al. (2020), but worryingly, their comprehensive study estimates that overall songbird ownership in urban areas on Java has actually increased in recent years, with an estimated 66–84 million birds now being kept in cages across the island.

In order to feed the enormous demand, Indonesian bird markets are selling staggering numbers of birds, including many threatened songbird and parrot species. For example, Chng et al. (2015) surveyed the three biggest bird markets in Jakarta over a three-day period and found more than 19,000 birds on offer, while Chng and Eaton (2016) found more than 22,000 birds on five markets in Central and Eastern Java. Significantly, many of the birds that are sold on these markets, including threatened species, are not bred in captivity but caught in the wild (Lucas 2011). In fact, the trapping of wild birds is so extensive that some conservationists now regard the cage bird trade as the most serious threat to Indonesia's avifauna apart from habitat loss. In Java in particular, wild populations of many songbird species have been so depleted that large tracts of forest have virtually fallen silent. As trappers find it increasingly difficult to catch the most sought-after species on Java, they have recently intensified their efforts in the outer islands. According to Rentschlar et al. (2018), for example, Kalimantan now has a thriving bird trade where popular songbirds such as Straw-headed or Olive-winged Bulbul fetch average prices of more than US$400 and 200, respectively. With much larger rewards beckoning at the various singing contests, few serious birdkeepers will hesitate to pay such prices.

While most birds that are traded on these traditional bird markets are songbirds for the domestic market, Indonesia also supplies large numbers of birds and other animals for the global illegal wildlife trade, which is widely believed to be among the most lucrative illicit trades in the world alongside drugs, arms and human trafficking (Sollund & Maher 2015, p. 1). In fact, Indonesia has become a major hotspot for the global trade in wildlife and wildlife products, partly because of the growing demand for bush meat in various Asian countries and partly because followers of traditional Chinese medicine believe that certain body parts of tigers, rhinos, pangolins and hornbills have extraordinary medicinal or sexual powers.

Pangolins, also known as scaly anteaters, fit both patterns. Their meat is a highly sought-after delicacy in some countries, while their scales are supposed to heal a range of body ailments. As a result of the huge demand, pangolins are now estimated to be one of the most trafficked mammals in the world (Hogenboom 2016). In 2016, their plight came to global attention when a photo called 'The Pangolin Pit' by Paul Hilton won the Wildlife Photographer of the Year Award. Taken in Sumatra, the photo showed about 4,000 dead, defrosting pangolins that had been found hidden in a shipping container. Shocking though it was, this case was only one of many extraordinary pangolin seizures that year; according to conservation organisation Annamiticus (2016), no less than 18,670 tonnes of pangolin scales were seized across 19 countries in the first nine months of 2016 alone.

The poachers and hunters who catch these and other animals in the wild are often, though not always, poor and barely benefit from the trade. As Felbab-Brown (2013) wrote in her study about wildlife trafficking in Indonesia, poachers in Maluku or Papua 'are sometimes paid as little as a bowl of noodles for a day's hunting, or a pack of cigarettes for a rare bird'. In Kalimantan, Dayak hunters can earn US$20 per gram for delivering the head of a rare Helmeted Hornbill, but the carved products made from the casques on top of the birds' bills are sold for thousands of dollars in China, Vietnam or Laos (Lazarus 2018), handing the trafficking syndicates enormous profits. Meanwhile, the species has become so rare in the wild that the IUCN upgraded its conservation status in 2015 to critically endangered. As numbers of Helmeted Hornbills have plummeted, rainforest ecosystems in Kalimantan and Sumatra are suffering because the birds can no longer fulfil their important role of seed dispersal. Thus, the example of the Helmeted Hornbill shows that the environmental impact of poaching can extend far beyond the potential extinction of just one species.

Policy Initiatives to Protect the Environment

Concerns about Indonesia's environmental problems have been documented since the New Order period (Cribb 1990, MacAndrews 1994, McCarthy 1998). But the country was initially rather slow in responding to the various challenges. Early government initiatives such as the establishment of a State Ministry for the Environment in 1978 and the passing of the Environmental Management Act in 1982, for example, were mainly window-dressing intended to appease the regime's international donors. Even when deforestation rose to prominence as a global environmental issue in the 1990s, President Suharto showed little interest in addressing the concerns from conservationists because members and close allies of his family directly profited from the assault on the country's forests. In effect, neither the ministry nor the law, which was revised in 1997, was designed to protect Indonesia's natural habitat against the rampant exploitation driven by Suharto's inner circle.

When the New Order regime collapsed in 1998 – incidentally just a year after a major environmental disaster, the 1997 haze crisis – timber tycoon Bob Hasan was one of the few Suharto cronies to be prosecuted and jailed. Despite this important signal, however, reforms to environment policy were not immediately forthcoming. Preoccupied with constitutional change and the struggle to stay in power, none of the first three post-Suharto presidents paid much attention to issues such as deforestation, climate change or wildlife trafficking. Only under President Susilo Bambang Yudhoyono (2004–2014) did the environment gradually move from the margins of policymaking to a more prominent place in the presidential administration. Especially in his second term, Yudhoyono put forward a range of proposals that aimed to improve the state of Indonesia's environment.

From an institutional perspective, perhaps the most important reform was the passing of a new environmental law (Law 32/2009) which provided a stronger legal framework for sustainable development and climate change policy in Indonesia. The new law not only incorporated good governance principles such as accountability and transparency into environmental policy, but also linked environmental protection to the rights of indigenous communities, which often depend on forests and pristine marine environments for food, shelter and livelihood (Anderson, Firdaus & Mahaningtyas 2015, p. 260). Moreover, Yudhoyono also put Indonesia on the global map of the fight against climate change when he pledged to drastically reduce Indonesia's carbon emissions at the G20 conference in Pittsburgh in 2009. A year later, he set up a new taskforce to prepare Indonesia for the implementation of its commitments under the UN-backed REDD+ (Reducing Emissions from Deforestation and Degradation) framework. To help Indonesia achieve its emission reduction goals, Yudhoyono issued a moratorium on new land conversion permits in 2011, thus protecting large tracts of forests from logging and burning.

This moratorium was extended three times (in 2013, 2015 and 2017) and eventually made permanent in 2019. However, it still contains a number of loopholes that allow deforestation to continue. Yudhoyono's successor Jokowi has sought to close at least some of these loopholes by adding new restrictions on land clearance and the construction of drainage systems for drying carbon-rich peatland (Alisjahbana & Busch 2017, p. 129). In addition to strengthening the formal moratorium, Jokowi also took more unconventional steps to address the notorious failure of the security forces to prevent forest and peatland fires. In a direct reaction to the devastating fires of 2015, which drew global condemnation for Indonesia, Jokowi threatened to discharge military and police officers who failed to prevent the burning of forested areas in regions under their command.

Taken together, these new measures appeared to have a positive effect. In 2016 and 2017, Indonesian authorities counted far fewer fire hotspots than in 2015. According to an expert from the Center for International Forestry Research (CIFOR), 'the threat [to dismiss military and police officers] worked because a lot of the fires were deliberately lit by local residents who colluded with security officers. Now the police and the military don't want to be in on it anymore' (Jakarta Globe 2018). Meanwhile, in cases where fires did occur and threaten to rage out of control, local governments quickly declared a state of emergency to bring them under control more efficiently.

Beyond the efforts to rein in the forest fires, Jokowi also reorganised the institutional structure tasked with implementing and financing REDD+ by folding the Ministry of Forestry, the Ministry of Environment, the formerly independent REDD+ agency and the Indonesian National Council on Climate Change into a new Ministry of Environment and Forestry (Alisjahbana & Busch 2017, p. 127). The merger could be seen as an attempt by Jokowi to streamline and improve environmental governance, especially in regard to climate change policy, as in the past the Ministry of Forestry often seemed to undermine rather than support environmental policy initiatives. In fact, many REDD+ projects in Indonesia have faltered due to resistance from the Ministry of Forestry (Bachelard 2012) and by the time of writing, there was still no reliable data on the extent of emission reductions since Yudhoyono and Jokowi pledged their commitments to the international community.

Finally, the Jokowi government has also attempted, if only half-heartedly, to address the songbird crisis and general decline in biodiversity. In June 2018, the government updated and expanded its list of nationally protected plant and animal species from 677 to 919 species. It was the first update in nearly 20 years and, significantly, many of the newly added species were birds (Gokkon 2018b). The move was widely welcomed by conservationists, but bird traders and clubs immediately protested, arguing that the new list had neither a scientific nor a cultural basis. Moreover, they claimed that many people involved in the songbird trade would lose their livelihoods if certain species were not removed from the list (Gokkon 2018c). In the end, their lobbying was successful, and the government did remove some of the most popular songbird species from the list again.

Obstacles to Environmental Protection

All in all, it is clear that Indonesia's recent record in trying to improve its framework for environmental governance has produced some noteworthy results. Laws were revised, moratoriums extended and important institutions restructured. President Jokowi even challenged the security forces to come on board for better environmental protection. In 2020, the combined effects of these measures and other developments out of the government's direct control (for example, extraordinarily wet weather due to the La Nina climate pattern as well as reduced global demand for timber and palm oil due to the economic fallout from the Covid-19 pandemic) helped Indonesia achieve its lowest deforestation rate on record (Jong 2021). And yet, many conservationists fear that this is just a temporary relief and that significant obstacles to long-term environmental protection in Indonesia persist. In accounting for these concerns, analysts have suggested a number of explanations, ranging from institutionalist to structuralist and culturalist approaches.

To begin with, liberal institutionalist and neoliberal approaches point to the shortcomings in the institutional framework and seek improvements through reforms to this framework. For example, when Indonesia announced the revised threatened species list in 2018, the initial version was widely hailed as an important step towards better conservation, yet subsequent amendments in response to pressure from the birdkeeping lobby resulted in a much watered down version which leaves a number of globally threatened species unprotected in Indonesia. Similar loopholes can be found in other important regulations and laws. The moratorium on land conversion permits, for example, only put an end to the issuance of new permits but allowed the continuation of land clearance by existing permit holders. Likewise, the 2009 environmental law contained a number of strong commitments to good environmental governance and acknowledged the risks associated with climate change, but then the government was extremely slow in issuing the necessary implementing guidelines to put the law into practice. As Anderson,

Firdaus and Mahaningtyas (2015, pp. 260–261) show in their assessment of environmental governance during the Yudhoyono era, out of 19 government regulations mandated by the 2009 environmental law, the president issued only one.

Due to this 'one step forward, two steps backward' approach, the institutional framework for environmental governance in Indonesia remains full of ambiguity, loopholes and missing regulations. Lax enforcement of existing laws further exacerbates institutional inefficiency. To address these shortcomings, institutions like the World Bank advocate better integration of environmental considerations into planning processes for land and resource usage. The underlying idea is that the institutional framework itself needs to be reformed in order to achieve better environmental governance. Thus, the government should invest in strengthening the legal tools for conservation and boost resources for law enforcement. At the same time, accountability in conservation agencies should be enhanced through incentives that reward good performance while penalising malfeasance (Meijaard 2014).

For critical political economists, however, the prospects for such reforms to be successful are dim because they fail to take into account the basic structure of Indonesia's political economy which is shaped by rent-seeking and the commodification of nature (Maxton-Lee 2018). Palm oil and timber constitute key pillars of Indonesia's growth strategy, contributing billions of dollars in revenue to the Indonesian economy every year. While the bulk of the profits goes to oligarchic conglomerates and their global trading partners, millions of smallholders also benefit through their integration into the complex supply chains of global capitalism. As long as Indonesia's economic development strategy remains so heavily dependent on the rampant exploitation of the natural environment, further degradation of land and forests is much more likely than successful conservation, regardless of the institutional framework.

The structural and institutional obstacles to environmental protection that were described above are further exacerbated by a lack of environmental awareness among many Indonesians and the concurrent persistence of some deeply rooted cultural traditions which perpetuate environmental destruction and the demand and supply of wildlife and wildlife products. The cage bird trade is but one example where these factors intersect to pose a huge threat to biodiversity. Many hunters and poachers who supply birds to the markets in Java and beyond catch the increasingly rare creatures within the boundaries of national parks but claim to be unaware of park boundaries and the fact that some of the birds they catch are protected by law. At the same time, there are also those poachers, as well as many buyers, who are no doubt aware of the threat yet prefer to prioritise cultural tradition and financial gain over science (Lucas 2011). In fact, as rarity in the wild increases the value of a bird, many birdkeepers deliberately seek out threatened species rather than those that are more common or bred in captivity.

In the aforementioned public opinion survey conducted by Indikator Politik, respondents were asked whether they were aware and/or concerned about the fact that many of the animals that are sold on Indonesian markets are threatened or endangered. Worryingly, only a minority of 43.9 percent stated that they were both aware and concerned; 16.3 percent said that they were aware of the issue but not concerned, while 9.8 percent claimed to be neither aware nor concerned. A further 20.4 percent responded they were indifferent and 9.5 percent did not answer the question. These numbers indicate an urgent need to raise awareness about the long-term costs of continued environmental damage through better education. Some dedicated environmental NGOs are keenly involved in such activities, but their reach is often limited.

Another way to address the twin problems of ignorance and adherence to tradition would be to integrate the environment and the importance of protecting it into the national school curriculum. But according to Parker (2017), both curriculum and textbooks for high school students 'are almost bereft of environmental education'. It is therefore hardly surprising that many Indonesians remain indifferent towards wildlife and natural resources. To complicate matters further, external criticism or even just advice on environmental issues, especially in relation to the sustainability of Indonesia's palm oil industry, are often framed by the Indonesian government as attacks on the national interest. This was evident, for example, in Indonesia's strong reaction to the European Union's plans to phase out biofuel by 2030. In Indonesia's current political climate, which is shaped by an increasingly populist nationalism, natural resources and the right to exploit them have become heavily politicised (Warburton 2017), with dire consequences for the prospects for conservation.

Conclusion

The politics of environmental protection in Indonesia are fraught with complex challenges. Not only are there considerable cultural and attitudinal barriers to conservation, but an ineffective institutional framework for conservation and structural factors related to the nature of Indonesia's political economy also constitute formidable obstacles to better environmental protection. Recognising this mix of interrelated factors is crucial to understanding why observers like Meijaard (2014) believe that conservation in Indonesia is more difficult than in other middle- and low-income countries.

To illustrate the complexity of the challenges, this chapter focused on three of the most pressing environmental issues in Indonesia. First, deforestation is wreaking havoc on Indonesia's natural heritage, with millions of hectares lost every year due to the rampant expansion of the palm oil, mining and logging industries. Given the central importance of these industries to Indonesia's economic growth strategy, it is unlikely that the loss of forest will be halted any time soon, despite the recent decline in Indonesia's deforestation rate. Second, the chapter identified consequences of climate change such as rising sea levels and extreme weather events as major threats to Indonesia as the country's geography makes it particularly prone to flooding, droughts and fires. And third, the chapter demonstrated how hunting and poaching have diminished biodiversity in Indonesia over the years, due to persistent demand for Indonesian wildlife and wildlife parts from both within and outside the country. Each of these three factors constitutes a major environmental challenge in itself, yet, as Symes et al. (2018) have pointed out, impacts of various individual environmental problems frequently act together and thus further exacerbate the threats to biodiversity.

The Indonesian government has taken some cautious steps towards better conservation in recent years, but environmental policymaking is often hampered by the tensions between the needs for economic development and growth on the one hand and conservation on the other hand. Nowhere is this tension more obvious than in Indonesia's reluctance to get tough on deforestation. Although the government has repeatedly extended the moratorium on new concession permits, loopholes remain and palm oil, the main driver of deforestation, remains an important pillar of Indonesian exports. Without a change in its economic development strategy, Indonesia is unlikely to provide better protection for its embattled environment.

References

Afrizal & Berenschot, W 2020, 'Resolving land conflicts in Indonesia', *Bijdragen tot de Taal-, Land- en Volkenkunde*, vol. 176, pp. 561–574.

Alisjahbana, AS & Busch, JM 2017, 'Forestry, forest fires, and climate change in Indonesia', *Bulletin of Indonesian Economic Studies*, vol. 53, no. 2, pp. 111–136.

Anderson, P, Firdaus, A & Mahaningtyas, A 2015, 'Big commitments, small results: environmental governance and climate change mitigation under Yudhoyono', in E Aspinall, M Mietzner & D Tomsa (eds), *The Yudhoyono presidency: Indonesia's decade of stability and stagnation*, Institute of Southeast Asian Studies, Singapore, pp. 258–278.

Annamiticus 2016, 'Shocking figures reveal deadly reality for pangolins', 27 September, viewed 6 September 2018, <http://annamiticus.com/2016/09/27/shocking-figures -reveal-deadly-reality-for-pangolins/>.

Baccini, A, Walker, W, Carvalho, L, Farina, M, Sulla-Menashe, D & Houghton, RA 2017, 'Tropical forests are a net carbon source based on aboveground measurements of gain and loss', *Science*, vol. 358, no. 6360, pp. 230–234.

Bachelard, M 2012, 'Indonesia's forests of corruption', *Sydney Morning Herald*, 10 June, viewed 12 September 2018, <https://www.smh.com.au/environment/indonesias-forests -of-corruption-20120610-203sk.html>.

Bappenas 2003, *Indonesian biodiversity strategy and action plan 2003–2020*, Bappenas, Jakarta.

Barr, CM 1998, 'Bob Hasan, the rise of Apkindo, and the shifting dynamics of control in Indonesia's timber sector', *Indonesia*, vol. 65, pp. 1–36.

Chng, SC & Eaton, JA 2016, *In the market for extinction: Eastern and Central Java (Tech. Rep. No. August)*, TRAFFIC, Petaling Jaya, Malaysia.

Chng, SC, Eaton, JA, Krishnasamy, K, Shepherd, CR & Nijman, V 2015, *In the market for extinction: An inventory of Jakarta's bird markets (Tech. Rep.)*, TRAFFIC, Petaling Jaya, Malaysia.

Cribb, R 1990, 'The politics of pollution control in Indonesia', *Asian Survey*, vol. 30, no. 12, pp. 1123–1135.

Dasgupta, S 2018, 'Risk of sea-level rise: high stakes for East Asia & Pacific region countries', viewed 21 October 2018, <http://blogs.worldbank.org/eastasiapacific/risk -of-sea-level-rise-high-stakes-for-east-asia-pacific-region-countries>.

Food and Agriculture Organisation 2010, *Global forest resource assessment 2010: Main report*, FAO, Rome.

Food and Agriculture Organisation 2016, *Global forest resources assessment 2015: How are the world's forests changing?*, 2nd edn, FAO, Rome.

Felbab-Brown, V 2013, *Indonesia field report IV: the last twitch? Wildlife trafficking, illegal fishing, and lessons from anti-piracy efforts*, Brookings Institution, Washington DC.

Felbab-Brown, V 2017, *The extinction market: wildlife trafficking and how to counter it*, Hurst & Company, London.

Forest Watch Indonesia & Global Forest Watch 2002, *The state of the forest: Indonesia*, Forest Watch Indonesia and Global Forest Watch, Bogor and Washington.

Friedrich, J, Ge, M & Pickens, A 2020, 'This interactive chart shows changes in the world's Top 10 emitters', *World Resources Institute blog*, 10 December, viewed 19 March 2021, <https://www.wri.org/blog/2020/12/interactive-chart-top-emitters>.

Gokkon, B 2018a, 'Jakarta cancels permits for controversial bay reclamation project', *Mongabay*, 2 October, viewed 21 October 2018, <https://news.mongabay.com/2018/10/jakarta-cancels-permits-for-controversial-bay-reclamation-project/>.

Gokkon, B 2018b, 'Indonesia adds hundreds of birds to protected species list', *Mongabay*, 3 August, viewed 12 September 2018, <https://news.mongabay.com/2018/08/indonesia-adds-hundreds-of-birds-to-protected-species-list/>.

Gokkon, B 2018c, 'Indonesia gives in to bird traders, rescinds protection for 3 species', *Mongabay*, 7 September, viewed 12 September 2018, <https://news.mongabay.com/2018/09/indonesia-gives-in-to-bird-traders-rescinds-protection-for-3-species/>.

Heriyanto, D 2018, 'Indonesia sees 7 brutal animal killings in 2018', *Jakarta Post*, 18 July.

Hogenboom, M 2016, 'Pangolins are the world's most trafficked mammal', *BBC.com*, 8 October, viewed 6 September 2018, <http://www.bbc.com/earth/story/20161006-pangolins-are-the-worlds-most-trafficked-mammal>.

IPCC 2021, *Climate Change 2021: The Physical Science Basis. Contribution of Working Group I to the Sixth Assessment Report of the Intergovernmental Panel on Climate Change* [Masson-Delmotte, V., P. Zhai, A. Pirani, S.L. Connors, C. Péan, S. Berger, N. Caud, Y. Chen, L. Goldfarb, M.I. Gomis, M. Huang, K. Leitzell, E. Lonnoy, J.B.R. Matthews, T.K. Maycock, T. Waterfield, O. Yelekçi, R. Yu, and B. Zhou (eds.)], Cambridge University Press, In Press.

Jakarta Globe 2018, 'Jokowi's threat proved effective to prevent forest fires', 22 February, viewed 11 September 2018, <http://jakartaglobe.id/environment/jokowis-threat-proved-effective-prevent-forest-fires/>.

Jakarta Post 2018, 'Over one third of Indonesia's coral reefs in bad state: Study', 29 November, viewed 19 March 2021, <https://www.thejakartapost.com/news/2018/11/29/over-one-third-of-indonesias-coral-reefs-in-bad-state-study.html>.

Jepson, P & Ladle, RJ 2005, 'Bird-keeping in Indonesia: conservation impacts and the potential for substitution-based conservation responses', *Oryx*, vol. 39, no. 4, pp. 442–448.

Jong, HN 2021, 'Deforestation in Indonesia hits record low, but experts fear a rebound', *Mongabay*, 9 March, viewed 2 July 2021, <https://news.mongabay.com/2021/03/2021-deforestation-in-indonesia-hits-record-low-but-experts-fear-a-rebound/>.

Jotzo, F, Resosudarmo, IAP, Nurdianto, DA & Sari, AP 2009, 'Climate change and development in Eastern Indonesia', in BP Resosudarmo & F Jotzo (eds), *Working with nature against poverty: development, resources and the environment in Eastern Indonesia*, Institute of Southeast Asian Studies, Singapore, pp. 248–266.

Kimmelman, M 2017, 'Jakarta is sinking so fast, it could end up underwater', *New York Times*, 21 December, viewed 21 October 2018, <https://www.nytimes.com/interactive /2017/12/21/world/asia/jakarta-sinking-climate.html>.

Koplitz, SN et al 2016, 'Public health impacts of the severe haze in Equatorial Asia in September–October 2015: demonstration of a new framework for informing fire management strategies to reduce downwind smoke exposure', *Environmental Research Letters*, vol. 11, no. 9, pp. 1–10.

Lazarus, S 2018, 'Why Chinese demand for 'red ivory' dooms Helmeted Hornbill bird to extinction unless poaching can be stopped', *South China Morning Post Magazine*, 13 January, viewed 6 September 2018, <https://www.scmp.com/magazines/post -magazine/long-reads/article/2127802/why-chinese-demand-red-ivory-dooms -helmeted>.

Lin, MM & Hidayat, R 2018, 'Jakarta, the fastest-sinking city in the world', *BBC Indonesian*, 13 August, viewed 21 October 2018, <https://www.bbc.com/news/world -asia-44636934>.

Lucas, A 2011, 'Catching songbirds in a national park', *Inside Indonesia*, no. 106, viewed 10 April 2021, <https://www.insideindonesia.org/catching-songbirds-in-a-national -park-3>.

MacAndrews, C 1994, 'Politics of the environment in Indonesia', *Asian Survey*, vol. 34, no. 4, pp. 369–380.

Marshall, H, Collar, NJ, Lees, AC, Moss, A, Yuda, P and Marsden, SJ 2020, 'Spatio-temporal dynamics of consumer demand driving the Asian Songbird Crisis', *Biological Conservation*, vol. 241, January 2020, 108237, pp. 1–8.

Maxton-Lee, B 2018, 'Material realities: why Indonesian deforestation persists and conservation fails', *Journal of Contemporary Asia*, vol. 48, no. 3, pp. 419–444.

McCarthy, J 1998, 'Rare birds die in West Java', *Inside Indonesia*, no. 54, viewed 10 April 2021, <https://www.insideindonesia.org/rare-birds-die-in-west-java>.

McCarthy, JF 2002, 'Turning in circles: district governance, illegal logging, and environmental decline in Sumatra, Indonesia', *Society and Natural Resources*, vol. 15, no. 10, pp. 867–886.

McCarthy, JF 2010, 'Processes of inclusion and adverse incorporation: oil palm and agrarian change in Sumatra, Indonesia', *The Journal of Peasant Studies*, vol. 37, no. 4, pp. 821–850.

Meijaard, E 2014, 'Why is conservation so much harder in Indonesia than elsewhere?', *Jakarta Globe*, 12 December.

Mooney, C 2015, 'Indonesian fires are pouring huge amounts of carbon into the atmosphere', *Washington Post*, 20 October, viewed 3 September 2018, <https://www.washingtonpost .com/news/energy-environment/wp/2015/10/20/fueled-by-el-nino-carbon-emissions -from-indonesian-peat-fires-are-rising-fast/?utm_term=.d04fe4fb384a>.

Murray Li, T 2014, *Land's end: capitalist relations on an indigenous frontier*, Duke University Press, Durham, NC.

Paddock, RC 2020, 'Bought for a song: an Indonesian craze puts wild birds at risk', *New York Times*, 18 April, viewed 10 April 2021, <https://www.nytimes.com/2020/04/18/ world/asia/indonesia-songbirds-competition.html>.

Parker, L 2017, 'A write-off', *Inside Indonesia*, no. 127 (January-March 2017), viewed 6 November 2018, <https://www.insideindonesia.org/a-write-off>.

Rentschlar, KA, Miller, AE, Lauck, KS, Rodiansyah, M, Bobby, Muflihati & Kartikawati 2018, 'A silent morning: the songbird trade in Kalimantan, Indonesia', *Tropical Conservation Science*, vol. 11, pp. 1–10.

Rheindt, FE, Prawiradilaga, DM, Ashari, H, Suparno, Gwee, CY, Lee, GWX, Wu, MY & Ng, NSR (2020), 'A lost world in *Wallacea*: Description of a montane archipelagic avifauna', *Science*, vol. 367, no. 6474, pp. 167–170.

Sollund, R & Maher, J 2015, *The illegal wildlife trade: A case study report on the illegal wildlife trade in the United Kingdom, Norway, Colombia and Brazil*, A study compiled as part of the EFFFACE, University of Oslo and University of South Wales, Oslo and Cardiff.

Symes, WS, Edwards, DP, Miettinen, J, Rheindt, FE & Carrasco, LR 2018, 'Combined impacts of deforestation and wildlife trade on tropical biodiversity are severely underestimated', *Nature Communications*, vol. 9, article no. 4052, <https://doi.org/10.1038/s41467-018-06579-2>

Tsujino, R, Yumoto, T, Kitamura, S, Djamaluddin, I & Darnaedy, D 2016, 'History of forest loss and degradation in Indonesia', *Land Use Policy*, vol. 57, pp. 335–347.

Voigt, M et al 2018, 'Global demand for natural resources eliminated more than 100,000 Bornean Orangutans', *Current Biology*, vol. 28, no. 5, pp. 761–769.

Warburton, E 2017, 'Resource nationalism in Indonesia: ownership structures and sectoral variation in mining and palm oil', *Journal of East Asian Studies*, vol. 17, no. 3, pp. 285–312.

Wollenberg, E, Moeliono, M & Limberg, G 2009, 'Between state and society: decentralisation in Indonesia', in M Moeliono, E Wollenberg & G Limberg (eds), *The decentralisation of forest governance: politics, economics and the fight for control of forests in Indonesian Borneo*, Earthscan, London and Sterling, pp. 3–24.

World Bank 2016, *The cost of fire: an economic analysis of Indonesia's 2015 fire crisis*, World Bank Group, Jakarta.

12 Foreign Policy

Introduction

As the largest and most populous country in Southeast Asia, Indonesia may, at first sight, appear destined to be a regional hegemon. Indeed, some scholars have argued that in the first 50 years after independence, Indonesia did at least for certain periods of time act like a regional hegemon in maritime Southeast Asia as it exercised both benevolent and coercive power to achieve its goals (Emmers 2005). However, the Asian financial crisis of 1997–1998 and the subsequent political turmoil that resulted in regime change and loss of territory – East Timor seceded after voting for independence in 1999 – weakened Indonesia's standing in the region temporarily. But once the new democratic regime began to stabilise, proponents of Indonesia's hegemonic ambitions quickly revived the discourse about Indonesia's power and influence. At the end of the Yudhoyono era, one prominent International Relations scholar proclaimed that 'Indonesia matters', describing it as an 'emerging democratic power' (Acharya 2014).

Yet, others are more cautious. While acknowledging that democratisation and economic development during the Yudhoyono years lifted Indonesia's status in the world, observers like McRae (2014) or Ciorciari (2018) maintained that even Indonesia's most outward-looking president found it difficult to translate that elevated status into real influence on concrete policy initiatives at the regional or global level. And under Yudhoyono's successor Jokowi, Indonesia has not only taken a lower international profile once again, but its democratic credentials have also deteriorated, undermining claims of an emerging democratic power.

Thus, against the background of the ongoing debate about Indonesia's place in the world, this chapter will review the key features of Indonesia's foreign policy and the country's strategic engagement with the wider world. It echoes the more cautious assessments, arguing that Indonesia is yet to demonstrate real leadership qualities, either at the regional or global level. Rather than leading, Indonesia has mainly resorted to hedging as it seeks to avoid close alignment with either of the two great powers in the Indo-Pacific, the United States and China. Moreover, the chapter also argues that the biggest security threats for Indonesia in the current environment do not emanate from the rivalry between the United States and China

DOI: 10.4324/9780429459511-12

but from a lack of preparation for non-traditional security threats such as climate change or, as became evident in 2020, pandemic diseases.

The chapter begins with a brief historical overview of Indonesian foreign policy during the Sukarno and Suharto eras. It then proceeds to analyse how the democratisation process of 1998 changed both the dynamics of foreign policy-making as well as the standing of Indonesia in the region and the wider world. The next sections zoom in on the role of Islam in Indonesian foreign policy and the country's relations with the major powers, the United States and China, as well as some important multilateral organisations. The chapter ends with a discussion of some of the most pressing non-traditional security threats, highlighting the need to dedicate more resources to confronting these threats.

Indonesian Foreign Policy under Sukarno and Suharto

Indonesia declared independence in 1945, but it was not before 1949 that the international community recognised the sovereignty of the new state. By that time, the bipolar contours of the Cold War were already taking shape and it was against the background of this emerging world order that Indonesian Vice-President Mohammad Hatta formulated what would become the enduring principles of Indonesian foreign policy – at least on paper. In an article in the prestigious journal *Foreign Affairs*, Hatta wrote that 'Indonesia will pursue a policy of peace and of friendship with all nations on a basis of mutual respect and non-interference with each other's structure of government' (Hatta 1953, p. 442). Pointing to Indonesia's geographic location in a part of the world that was strategically important yet sufficiently distant from the great powers, he indicated that Indonesia would not align itself with either of the two warring blocs but would instead devise an 'independent' and 'active' foreign policy (Hatta 1953, p. 444).

Two years later, Indonesia demonstrated to the world what this independent and active foreign policy might look like when it hosted a large conference for newly independent states from Asia and Africa. The Bandung Conference, as it became known, took place in April 1955 and brought together leaders from 29 states, including, among others, China, India, Egypt and Saudi Arabia. Though it did not produce any tangible outcomes apart from a 'Final Declaration on the Promotion of World Peace and Cooperation', the conference paved the way for the formation of the Non-Aligned Movement in 1961 and was of enormous psychological importance for Indonesia as it placed the country firmly on the map of international affairs. As Shimazu (2014, p. 234) put it, 'the national pride of the newly created Republic of Indonesia was at stake in hosting the Asia-Africa Conference' and 'Indonesians were determined to play the "good host" at the historic event'. Indeed, by mastering the feat of hosting the conference in the midst of the ongoing Islamist Darul Islam rebellion and by orchestrating the highly symbolic notion of Asian-African solidarity despite numerous frictions and hostilities between attendees (Abraham 2008, p. 208), Indonesia managed to exhibit its diplomatic prowess to a worldwide audience.

Purdey, Missbach and McRae (2020, p. 199) have called the Bandung Conference 'the high point' of Indonesia's free and active foreign policy. Not long afterwards, President Sukarno effectively began to abandon the principle of non-alignment in favour of a more radical anti-Western foreign policy. Sukarno's increasingly aggressive agitation against imperialist, colonial and neo-colonial forces eventually culminated in armed conflict with Malaysia (1963–1966), which the president regarded as a neo-colonial British puppet state that threatened Indonesian interests (Poulgrain 1998). In 1965, Indonesia even withdrew from the United Nations (UN). Many of the more moderate post-colonial states that had attended the Bandung Conference felt alienated by these policies, so by the end of the Guided Democracy period in 1965 Indonesia was left with only a handful of allies – most notably China, with whom Sukarno had forged the so-called Beijing-Jakarta Axis.

Indonesia's informal diplomatic alliance with China was short-lived, however. Following the change of power from Sukarno to Suharto in 1965–1966 and the subsequent obliteration of the left, Indonesia embarked on a dramatic shift in its foreign policy orientation. Diplomatic relations with China were frozen in 1967, UN membership restored and security and economic interests aligned with the previously despised Western bloc. The Suharto regime pledged to restore the Hatta doctrine of an independent and active foreign policy as its main principle for engaging with the outside world, but in reality Indonesian foreign policy during the New Order period was neither independent nor active. Close military ties with the United States and massive economic aid from Western European countries made a mockery of claims about independence, while the regime's preoccupation with real and perceived domestic security threats such as communism, Islamism and secessionism prevented a more active foreign policy.

Internationally, Indonesia only made headlines in 1975 when it invaded and subsequently occupied East Timor, which was deemed a security risk after achieving its independence from Portugal (Simpson 2005). Otherwise, the Suharto regime focused its limited foreign policy attention primarily on the Association of Southeast Asian Nations (ASEAN), a regional organisation formed in 1967 by a group of anti-communist regimes from Thailand, Malaysia, Singapore, the Philippines and Indonesia as a buffer against China and, more broadly, against great power competition in the region. ASEAN suited Indonesia's interests not only because it comprised like-minded regimes, but also because it adopted a range of fundamental principles cherished by the Suharto regime, including mutual respect for territorial integrity and national identity, non-interference in the internal affairs of other states and peaceful dispute resolution (ASEAN 1976).

It was not before the late 1980s and the early 1990s that Indonesia at last became a bit more proactive in international affairs. By this time, Suharto had eliminated all major domestic challenges to his presidency and felt confident enough to project his power beyond Indonesia's borders. Some noteworthy diplomatic initiatives of this period included Indonesia's mediation in the Cambodia conflict in 1988 (Widyaningsih & Roberts 2014, p. 107), the resumption of diplomatic ties with China in 1990 (Sukma 2009) and the signing of a security agreement with

Australia in 1995 (Sukma 1997). But then the Asian financial crisis struck and forced the Indonesian government once again to focus its attention on domestic politics. The turbulent democratic transition that followed the financial crisis triggered significant reforms to the process and substance of foreign policy in Indonesia.

Democratisation and Its Effects on Foreign Policy

The fall of Suharto and subsequent democratisation process had a major impact on Indonesian foreign policy. With regard to the process of policymaking, for example, it brought a more diverse range of actors to the table, including the parliament and civil society which had been largely marginalised during the New Order (Rüland 2009). Moreover, the transition to democracy provided an opportunity to alter the country's strategic orientation and give the foreign policy narrative a more global and especially a more democratic outlook. Finally, once political stability was re-established with the election of Susilo Bambang Yudhoyono in 2004, it paved the way for a gradual return to the core of the Hatta doctrine of an independent and active foreign policy. This section will outline these consequences of the democratisation process in more detail.

First, democratisation opened up the process of foreign policymaking to a new set of political actors. If in the past the strong presidents Sukarno and Suharto had virtually monopolised decision-making in their hands, the presidents of the democratic era have had to contend with a range of newly assertive actors keen to be involved in determining the new direction of Indonesian foreign policy. In particular, the People's Representative Council (Dewan Perwakilan Rakyat, DPR) has sought to extend its authority over foreign policy as constitutional amendments gave it the mandate to ratify treaties and endorse or reject ambassadorial nominees (Rüland 2009, p. 380). An important pillar of the DPR's involvement in foreign policy decisions has been Parliamentary Commission I on Defence, Foreign Affairs, Information and Intelligence, which regularly exercises its oversight function by questioning state officials over proposed government policies.

Significantly, many of these government policies of the post-Suharto period were devised not only in the presidential palace but also in the Ministry of Foreign Affairs where prominent ministers like Hassan Wirajuda (2001–2009) and Marty Natalegawa (2009–2014) were instrumental in reforming the ministry (Nabbs-Keller 2013). One of the flagship reforms was the revision of Indonesia's strategic narrative which now depicted Indonesia as a successful Muslim democracy (Natalegawa 2018). Under Susilo Bambang Yudhoyono and his energetic ministers, Indonesia invested enormous effort into attempts to strengthen its international democratic credentials. Examples included the establishment of the Bali Democracy Forum in 2008 as well as its endeavours to embed human rights and democracy more prominently in ASEAN. At the same time, Yudhoyono also sought to use Indonesia's membership in the G20 and its regular contributions to international peacekeeping missions to reposition the country as a mediator and bridge-builder between the Islamic world and the West (Fitriani 2015).

By and large, however, these efforts yielded few if any tangible results. By the end of the Yudhoyono era, McRae (2014) for example described Indonesia's record as a foreign policy actor as 'more talk than walk'. Karim (2017) also only saw limited achievements and attributed the shortcomings to the oftentimes conflicting expectations and aims associated with the various roles Indonesia sought to perform simultaneously. But Yudhoyono was also constrained by domestic political forces who did not share his vision of a model Muslim democracy with 'a million friends and zero enemies', even if this emphasis on good relations was in line with Hatta's original dictum. Parliament in particular often sought to push Indonesia in a more nationalist direction (Purdey, Missbach & McRae 2020, p. 195) and Yudhoyono's averseness to conflict meant that he tended to give in to these pressures.

Under Yudhoyono's successor Jokowi, this gap between rhetoric and reality persisted and, arguably, widened. While Jokowi's foreign minister Retno Marsudi has reiterated Indonesia's commitment to democracy on several occasions (Rüland 2021, p. 248), the country's foreign policy has also drifted in an increasingly nationalist and protectionist direction. This was particularly evident in the early years of the Jokowi presidency, for example in the execution of foreign drug convicts, the public spectacle of sinking foreign vessels accused of illegal fishing in Indonesian waters and a range of protectionist economic policies (McRae 2019, p. 761). When asked about the reasons for his abandonment of Yudhoyono's mantra of 'a million friends and zero enemies', Jokowi argued that he sought to make Indonesian foreign policy more benefit-oriented, asking provocatively 'what's the point of making friends if we are always on the losing end?' (as quoted in Bland 2020).

Despite the slightly changed rhetoric, however, Jokowi's foreign policy has also shown some continuity with the Yudhoyono era. McRae (2019) has delineated this continuity with regard to territorial disputes in the South China Sea, while another area of continuity has been Indonesia's approach to relations with the Islamic world. Even though Indonesia is the country with the largest Muslim population in the world, Islam has never played a particularly prominent role in Indonesia's foreign policy (Sukma 2004). Relations with most other Muslim-majority countries are good, but the shared faith has not led to particularly close ties with any of them. In fact, in large parts of the Islamic world, Indonesia is regarded as an outpost, due to its geographic location, its lack of globally influential Islamic intellectuals and its long tradition of syncretism (Van Bruinessen 2012).

Nevertheless, domestic pressure from Muslim groups has ensured that Indonesia does occasionally speak out on behalf of discriminated or persecuted Muslim populations in other parts of the world. It has, for instance, repeatedly called for the recognition of Palestinian statehood, while at the same time remaining steadfast in its refusal to establish diplomatic ties with Israel. When former US President Donald Trump announced in December 2017 that the United States would move their embassy from Tel Aviv to Jerusalem, Indonesia protested vehemently, if unsuccessfully, alongside other Muslim-majority states (King 2017).

About a year later, Indonesia protested even more vehemently when Australian Prime Minister Scott Morrison announced he would follow the US decision and move the Australian embassy as well. And this time, the protests had the desired effect. After the Indonesian Foreign Ministry threatened to 'adjust' its policies towards Australia (Karp 2018), Morrison cancelled the plan.

By and large, however, such determined defence of fellow Muslims elsewhere in the world has not been a regular occurrence, especially not when calls for Muslim solidarity clashed with Indonesia's main foreign policy principles such as territorial integrity and non-intervention in the domestic affairs of other ASEAN states. In the protracted Rohingya crisis in Myanmar, for instance, Indonesia long avoided any open criticism of the regime in Myanmar, even after the International Court of Justice (ICJ) declared in January 2020 that the Rohingya Muslims in Myanmar faced the real and imminent risk of genocidal violence and that the Myanmar government should 'take all measures within its power' to prevent such genocidal violence (International Court of Justice 2020). Rather than join the chorus of condemnation, Indonesia instead continued with its preferred approach of quiet diplomacy, even though this policy approach had yielded 'no presentable results' (Adiputera & Missbach 2021, p. 93) in the years prior to the ICJ ruling. The Rohingya crisis thus confirmed that Muslim solidarity does not constitute a primary concern for Indonesian foreign policy.

Trade and Foreign Economic Policy

The diplomatic spat between Indonesia and Australia over the embassy in Israel was one of many between these two neighbours in recent years (Lindsey & McRae 2018), but its quick resolution highlighted the importance of economic concerns for Indonesia and its foreign policy, especially under the Jokowi administration. At the time when the Australian Prime Minister declared his intention to move the embassy, the two countries were on the cusp of signing a bilateral trade deal that had been in the making for more than eight years. The embassy debacle derailed the negotiations once again, but both sides eventually signed the agreement in March 2019 and ratified it in November 2019 and February 2020, respectively. It came into force on 5 July 2020, finally opening up new opportunities to increase the bilateral trade volume which has been lagging for decades despite the geographic proximity and similar size of the two economies (Busch 2018).

The sense of unfulfilled potential is not only palpable in Indonesia's relations with Australia. Even though Indonesia had the 16th largest economy in the world in 2019 (see Table 12.1), domestic consumption, rather than international trade, is the main driver of Indonesia's GDP. Its overall trade volume, in fact, is comparatively low. Figures for 2018 ranked the country at 28th for exports and 27th for imports, respectively (Observatory of Economic Complexity 2020), with exports dominated by coal briquettes, palm oil and petroleum gas, whereas top imports were refined and crude petroleum as well as vehicle parts and telephones.

In order to explain these somewhat underwhelming trade statistics, it is useful to take a look at the global 'Ease of Doing Business' (EODB) index, an annual

Table 12.1 Gross domestic product (GDP) per country (2019)

Rank	Country	Millions of US dollars
1	United States	21,427,700
2	China	14,342,903
3	Japan	5,081,770
4	Germany	3,845,630
5	India	2,875,142
6	United Kingdom	2,827,113
7	France	2,715,518
8	Italy	2,001,244
9	Brazil	1,839,758
10	Canada	1,736,426
11	Russia	1,699,877
12	South Korea	1,642,383
13	Spain	1,394,116
14	Australia	1,392,681
15	Mexico	1,258,287
16	**Indonesia**	**1,119,181**
17	Netherlands	909,070
18	Saudi Arabia	792,967
19	Turkey	754,412
20	Switzerland	703,082

Source: World Bank (2020a)

report published by the World Bank. The index measures a range of regulations to assess whether they enhance or constrain business activity. It covers areas such as starting a business, dealing with construction permits, getting electricity, registering property, getting credit, protecting minority investors, paying taxes, trading across borders, enforcing contracts and resolving insolvency. Indonesia has long performed poorly on this index and even though it has advanced in the ranking in recent years, it was still only ranked 73rd out of 190 economies in the 2020 report (World Bank 2020b), roughly on par with Vietnam (70) but far below Malaysia (12) and Thailand (21). More importantly, in the category 'trading across borders', which records the time and cost associated with the logistical process of exporting and importing goods, it only came in at number 116.

Improving Indonesia's position in these rankings has been a declared goal of President Jokowi. Early on in his presidency, he made 'economic diplomacy' a pillar of his foreign policy (Rosyidin 2017, p. 183), while domestically he announced a number of economic policy packages aimed at deregulation and boosting investment. In 2017, when Indonesia had just climbed from position 91 to 72 in the EODB index, Jokowi stated that his aim was for Indonesia to be ranked in the top 40 by 2019 (Sugianto 2017). However, counter pressure from nationalists and entrenched elites, along with unfettered corruption and ongoing coordination problems between the national and sub-national governments, have thwarted further advances on the index since.

Likewise, economic growth figures have also stagnated during the Jokowi presidency. Even before the 2020 pandemic began to wreak havoc on the Indonesian economy, growth rates were well below the president's targets, hovering just around the 5 percent mark throughout Jokowi's first term. In 2020 then, the pandemic-ravaged economy slumped into recession, with negative growth rates of –5.3 percent and –3.5 percent in the first two quarters (Trading Economics 2020). This prompted Jokowi to push for sweeping new legislation in the form of the controversial Omnibus Bill on Job Creation, a massive piece of legislation that amended nearly 80 existing laws when it was passed into law on 5 November 2020. Though touted by the government as a boost for Indonesia's economic development prospects, the law's blatant disregard for environmental sustainability standards and the rights of workers and indigenous peoples triggered widespread protests and criticism (Argama 2020).

Whether or not the Omnibus Law will lead to more trade and foreign direct investment remains to be seen. Even before this law was passed, some of Indonesia's trading partners had already criticised the country for its human rights record and its refusal to make palm oil production more sustainable. With the Omnibus Law, this criticism is only going to get louder. The EU has been particularly outspoken in the past, announcing in 2018 that it would phase out palm oil from biofuels because of the link between palm oil production and deforestation. But the EU is not actually a major trading partner for Indonesia. Far more important than European countries are China, the United States, Japan and India, as well as a number of Southeast Asian economies, as Table 12.2 shows.

China is not only Indonesia's largest trading partner, but it has in fact further expanded its two-way trade with Indonesia in recent years. China's Belt and Road initiative, which aims to revive the ancient silk trade routes via land and sea lanes, has played a major part in this as its objectives align well with President Jokowi's ambition to improve Indonesia's dilapidated infrastructure and transform Indonesia into a global maritime fulcrum (Gindarsah & Priamarizki 2015). Trade with the other great power, on the other hand, has been far less dynamic. As Suoneto (2020) points out, the trade volume between the United States and Indonesia never reached the US$30 billion mark in the last ten years. But while Indonesia's economic fortunes have become increasingly tied to China's, the country has also reached out to other economic partners in its infrastructure drive (for example Japan and Singapore), not least because it remains wary of China's strategic ambitions. This wariness is reflected even more clearly in Indonesia's approach to national and regional security.

National Security and Relations with Great Powers

When Mohammad Hatta formulated Indonesia's foreign policy principles in the 1950s, his vision for an independent and active foreign policy was informed by Indonesia's position within the emerging bipolar world order dominated by the United States and the Soviet Union. Today, China has replaced the Soviet Union as the United States' main adversary in the Indo-Pacific and, in contrast to the

Table 12.2 Indonesia's main trading partners

Partner name	Export US$ thousand		Export partner share (%)		Import US$ thousand		Import partner share (%)	
	2017	2018	2017	2018	2017	2018	2017	2018
China	23,049,295.90	27,126,932.42	13.65	15.05	34,520,725.30	45,537,814.91	21.93	24.13
United States	17,810,479.99	18,471,771.38	10.55	10.25	8,216,316.74	10,212,388.45	5.22	5.41
Japan	17,790,812.13	19,479,892.02	10.54	10.81	14,133,608.27	17,976,711.41	8.98	9.53
India	14,083,572.99	13,725,675.91	8.34	7.62	3,965,349.98	5,016,912.13	2.52	2.66
Singapore	12,767,192.92	12,991,592.74	7.56	7.21	16,992,133.22	21,439,514.47	10.80	11.36
Malaysia	8,467,527.30	9,436,721.37	5.02	5.24	9,058,604.61	8,602,839.08	5.76	4.56
South Korea	8,186,977.15	9,532,500.32	4.85	5.29	7,874,212.00	9,088,875.76	5.00	4.82
Philippines	6,627,221.69	6,825,460.23	3.93	3.79	832,743.64	958,432.33	0.53	0.51
Thailand	6,462,142.40	6,818,948.87	3.83	3.78	9,035,564.32	10,952,798.16	5.74	5.80
Netherlands	4,038,084.31	3,898,165.83	2.39	2.16	995,369.71	1,239,253.47	0.63	0.66
Vietnam	3,587,475.44	4,583,936.60	2.13	2.54	3,075,870.16	3,794,629.97	1.95	2.01
Germany	2,669,462.48	2,709,811.64	1.58	1.50	3,271,891.00	3,972,966.53	2.08	2.11
Australia	2,509,185.23	2,800,076.35	1.49	1.55	7,055,497.22	5,825,541.41	4.48	3.09

Source: https://wits.worldbank.org/CountryProfile/en/Country/IDN/Year/2017/TradeFlow/EXPIMP/Partner/by-country

1950s, the broader strategic environment in the region is also embedded in a dense network of multilateral institutions such as ASEAN, the ASEAN Regional Forum (ARF), ASEAN+III and the East Asia Summit (Beeson 2014). For Indonesia, these institutions form an important pillar of the regional order, especially since the strategic competition between the United States and China intensified in the 2010s. As a middle power with limited capabilities, Indonesia has sought to use these organisations to 'entangle the United States, China, and others in a web of interdependent economic and diplomatic relations in the hopes of forestalling aggressive action' (Murphy 2017, p. 170).

The emphasis on multilateralism is part of a broader strategy which International Relations scholars call hedging. Regarded as a sophisticated risk management strategy for smaller and middle powers (Haacke 2019), hedging is most commonly defined as a foreign policy approach that combines a mix of cooperative and confrontational strategies directed at powerful states (Chen & Yang 2013, Kuik 2016, Tunsjø 2017). These strategies can encompass both economic and security aspects, ranging from efforts to diversify economic and defence partnerships to the upgrading of military capacity. According to Kuik (2016, p. 502), hedging is 'a form of alignment behaviour', characterised by 'its ambiguous, mixed and "opposite" positioning, which exhibits elements of *both* power acceptance (manifest in some forms of selective partnership, collaboration and even deference vis-à-vis a power) and power rejection (some signs of selective resistance and defiance vis-à-vis the same power)'.

Indonesia's hedging strategy manifests in both its bilateral relations with the two great powers as well as its attempts to diversify its economic and security ties beyond these two powers. To begin with, Indonesia's relations with China have shown some clear signs of power acceptance in recent years, driven primarily though not exclusively by the desire to benefit from China's economic might. Formal diplomatic relations were only re-established in 1990, but as trade and investment began to grow rapidly, Indonesia also sought to forge closer political and even limited military ties with China. During the Yudhoyono presidency, the two countries first signed a strategic partnership in 2005 and later upgraded that agreement to the level of comprehensive strategic partnership in 2013 (McRae 2014, p. 7). Current President Jokowi sent a strong symbolic message about the importance of China when he met his counterpart Xi Jinping no less than five times within the first two years of his presidency. And despite deeply rooted anti-Chinese sentiment among the general population and recurring diplomatic tensions over China's conduct in the South China Sea, the foreign ministry has repeatedly insisted that Indonesia has no conflicts with China.

Other foreign policy actors, however, have not always toed this line. In fact, key members of Indonesia's political, military and business elite continue to regard China as a threat to Indonesia's national interest. Political and business elites, for example, are fearful about the economic implications of Indonesia's trade deficit with China and have called for greater protectionism (Fukuoka & Verico 2016, p. 54). In terms of security, meanwhile, China's increasingly assertive behaviour in the South China Sea has heightened concerns among sections of the military and some ministries that the sanctity of Indonesia's maritime borders and the country's food security are under threat (Syailendra 2017, p. 248). Although Indonesia has no direct territorial disputes with China over islands in the South China Sea, repeated incursions by Chinese fishing vessels into Indonesian waters have triggered strong protests in Indonesia, prompting President Jokowi to bolster his nationalist rhetoric and hold a limited cabinet meeting on board a warship around the Natuna Islands in 2016 (McRae 2019, p. 769). Though limited in scope and intensity, these symbolic acts can be seen as evidence that power rejection has also been part of Indonesia's foreign policy repertoire with China.

This mix of cooperative and confrontational strategies can also be observed in Indonesia's relations with the other great power, the United States. As mentioned above, the United States are of less economic significance to Indonesia than China, but they remain Indonesia's most important security partner. Military ties were particularly strong during the early New Order period when the United States, along with other Western states, backed Suharto's regime with substantial assistance for the Indonesian military. Defence cooperation was then suspended between 1991 and 2005 following an international outcry about gross human rights violations by Indonesian troops in East Timor, but since the resumption of military ties and the subsequent signing of a strategic partnership in 2015, Indonesia has once again looked to the United States for military equipment, assistance and training. According to the US Department of State (2020), 'the United States has $1.88 billion in active government-to-government sales cases with Indonesia under the Foreign Military Sales (FMS) system' and each year, the two states hold over 170 bilateral military engagements.

And yet, there is a widespread perception that these ties are not as close as they appear. Writing in July 2018, Harding & Natalegawa (2018, p. 1) opened a policy brief for the US-based think tank Center for Strategic and International Studies by saying that 'U.S.–Indonesia relations are not meeting their potential'. Other authors have labelled the security ties between the two countries 'superficial' (Purdey, Missbach & McRae 2020, p. 201). These assessments mirror those about the bilateral trade relationship, which Suoneto (2020) has described as 'underperforming'.

One obstacle to closer relations between the two countries is that US foreign policy has repeatedly targeted Muslims, be that through military interventions (Afghanistan, Iraq, Syria), executive orders (Donald Trump's infamous 'Muslim ban' in 2017) or other political decisions such as the moving of the US embassy in Israel. While Islam is generally not a prominent feature of Indonesian foreign policy, all these US policies reverberated deeply in Indonesia, forcing the government to respond to public pressure by going into power rejection mode. A second factor is the broader, relatively benign strategic environment in Southeast Asia, which has given neither side sufficient reason to lift security cooperation to the next level. For Indonesia, Purdey, Missbach and McRae (2020, p. 201) noted that 'without a pressing, direct threat to its security, Indonesia has had no incentive to compromise its autonomy in setting its foreign policy direction by drawing closer to the United States'.

2016, p. 3). In reality, however, ASEAN has fallen short in fostering meaningful collaboration on most of these issues and Indonesia, in particular, remains woefully unprepared for most non-traditional security threats. Covid-19 exposed this lack of preparedness most dramatically, but the country has also done little to lift its disaster relief capacity, improve the situation of irregular migrants passing through the country en route to Australia or tackle environmental degradation.

Arguably, the one exception where Indonesia has in fact acted decisively and efficiently is the fight against terrorism. Though initially reluctant to recognise the seriousness of the threat, Indonesia eventually reacted to the bombing campaign in the early 2000s by passing anti-terror legislation and setting up a special anti-terror unit and a National Counter Terrorism Agency (see Chapter 6). Regionally, it ratified the ASEAN Convention on Counterterrorism (ACCT) in 2012 and has pushed, though unsuccessfully so far, for an ASEAN-wide extradition treaty to better combat terrorism (Nasu et al. 2019, p. 101). To explain why Indonesia has invested more resources into the fight against terrorism than into lowering its carbon footprint or improving its healthcare system, at least three factors are worth noting. First, despite the transnational links of Indonesian terror groups, fighting terrorism and radicalism broadly fits into Indonesia's preoccupation with domestic security threats. Second, it is not only political elites, but also the general public which regards terrorism as one of the most serious threats to security in Indonesia (Gindarsah & Priamarizki 2015, p. 10). Politically, it is therefore imperative for the government to demonstrate responsiveness to the people's threat perceptions. Third, counterterrorism measures require fewer economic resources but can deliver quicker results than long-term investments in public health or climate change action.

Conclusion

All in all, this chapter has shown that Indonesia's regional leadership credentials are mixed at best. More than two decades after the fall of Suharto, the country is still constrained in its ambition to be a first among equals in Southeast Asia, due to the combined effects of limited military and economic capabilities and an 'inward-looking strategic culture' (Anwar 2020b) which tends to define domestic security threats as more serious than external ones. This strategic culture has been deliberately fostered by Indonesia's military establishment, but it has also been facilitated by the relatively benign strategic environment in which Indonesia has indeed not faced any direct threats from other states.

Whether the increasingly intense power rivalry between China and the United States will ultimately change this strategic culture remains to be seen. China is Indonesia's largest trading partner, but its growing assertiveness in the South China Sea and especially its incursions into Indonesian waters are a concern for the Indonesian government. So far, however, Indonesia has neither caved in nor openly challenged the Chinese government over these provocations. Instead, it has continued its hedging strategy by further diversifying its defence and development cooperation links. Current President Jokowi also appears to have rediscovered ASEAN as a tool to engage external powers after he had largely ignored this long-established cornerstone of Indonesian foreign policy for much of his first term in office.

As long as the balance of power between China and the United States holds, non-traditional security issues will remain the most serious threats to Indonesian lives and livelihoods. But the lack of action to tackle climate change and the ineffective response to the Covid-19 outbreak in 2020 showed that Indonesia is yet to treat such threats with the seriousness they warrant. If Indonesia wants to show leadership in the region, it will need to lift its game in dealing with these kinds of threats.

References

Abraham, I 2008, 'From Bandung to NAM: non-alignment and Indian foreign policy 1947–65', *Commonwealth and Comparative Politics*, vol. 46, no. 2, pp. 195–219.

Acharya, A 2014, *Indonesia matters: Asia's emerging democratic power*, World Scientific, Singapore.

Adiputera, Y & Missbach, A 2021, 'Indonesia's foreign policy regarding the forced displacement of Rohingya refugees: Muslim solidarity, humanitarianism, and non-interventionism', *Asia-Pacific Journal on Human Rights and the Law*, vol. 22, no. 1, pp. 69–95.

Anwar, DF 2020a, 'Indonesia and the ASEAN outlook on the Indo-Pacific', *International Affairs*, vol. 96, no. 1, pp. 111–129.

Anwar, DF 2020b, 'More continuity than change in Indonesia's security posture', *ASPI Strategist*, 30 January, viewed 21 December 2020, <https://www.aspistrategist.org.au/more-continuity-than-change-in-indonesias-security-posture/>.

Argama, R 2020, 'Major procedural flaws mar the omnibus law', *Indonesia at Melbourne*, 9 October, viewed 9 December 2020, <https://indonesiaatmelbourne.unimelb.edu.au/major-procedural-flaws-mar-the-omnibus-law/>.

ASEAN 1976, *Treaty of amity and cooperation in Southeast Asia*, 24 February 1976, viewed 9 December 2020, <https://asean.org/treaty-amity-cooperation-southeast-asia-indonesia-24-february-1976/>.

ASEAN Secretariat 2016, *Fact sheet – ASEAN political-security community*, ASEAN Secretariat, Jakarta.

Beeson, M 2014, *Regionalism and globalisation in East Asia: politics, security and economic development*, 2nd edn, PalgraveMacmillan, Houndmills, Basingstoke.

Bland, B 2020, 'Jokowi's foreign policy approach: look for friends with benefits', *Financial Review*, 28 August, viewed 9 December 2020, <https://www.afr.com/world/asia/jokowi-s-foreign-policy-approach-look-for-friends-with-benefits-20200824-p55ou6>.

Busch, M 2018, 'Economic policy in the Australia-Indonesia relationship: unbound potential, everlasting anticlimax', in T Lindsey & D McRae (eds), *Strangers next door: Indonesia and Australia in the Asian century*, Hart Publishing, Oxford, UK; Portland, OR, pp. 471–498.

Caballero-Anthony, M (ed.) 2015, *An introduction to non-traditional security studies: a transnational approach*, Sage Publications, London.

Center for Strategic and International Studies 2020, *Southeast Asia Covid-19 tracker*, viewed 21 December 2020, <https://www.csis.org/programs/southeast-asia-program/southeast-asia-covid-19-tracker-0>.

Chen, IT & Yang, AH 2013, 'A harmonised Southeast Asia? Explanatory typologies of ASEAN countries' strategies to the rise of China', *The Pacific Review*, vol. 26, no. 3, pp. 265–288.

Ciorciari, JD 2018, 'Indonesia's diplomatic and strategic position under Yudhoyono', in U Fionna, SD Negara & D Simandjuntak (eds), *Aspirations with limitations: Indonesia's foreign affairs under Susilo Bambang Yudhoyono*, ISEAS-Yusof Ishak Institute, Singapore, pp. 33–59.

Emmers, R 2005, 'Regional hegemonies and the exercise of power in Southeast Asia: a study of Indonesia and Vietnam', *Asian Survey*, vol. 45, no. 4, pp. 645–665.

Fitriani, E 2015, 'Yudhoyono's foreign policy: is Indonesia a rising power?', in E Aspinall, M Mietzner & D Tomsa (eds), *The Yudhoyono presidency: Indonesia's decade of stability and stagnation*, ISEAS-Yusof Ishak Institute, Singapore, pp. 73–90.

Fukuoka, Y & Verico, K 2016, 'Indonesia-China economic relations in the twenty-first century: opportunities and challenges', in YC Kim (ed.), *Chinese global production networks in ASEAN*, Springer, Cham, pp. 53–75.

Gayatri, IH, Veronika, NW & True, J 2020, 'Indonesia's UN Security Council drive for inclusive peace and security', *The Interpreter*, 2 September, viewed 18 December 2020, <https://www.lowyinstitute.org/the-interpreter/indonesia-s-un-security-council-drive-inclusive-peace-and-security>.

Gindarsah, I & Priamarizki, A 2015, *Indonesia's maritime doctrine and security concerns*, RSIS Policy Report, S. Rajaratnam School of International Studies, Singapore.

Haacke, J 2019, 'The concept of hedging and its application to Southeast Asia: a critique and a proposal for a modified conceptual and methodological framework', *International Relations of the Asia-Pacific*, vol. 19, no. 3, pp. 375–417.

Hameiri, S & Jones, L 2013, 'The politics and governance of non-traditional security', *International Studies Quarterly*, vol. 57, no. 3, pp. 462–473.

Harding, B & Natalegawa, A 2018, *Enhancing the US-Indonesia strategic partnership*, CSIS Brief, July 2018, Center for Strategic and International Studies, Washington DC.

Hatta, M 1953, 'Indonesia's foreign policy', *Foreign Affairs*, vol. 31, no. 3, pp. 441–452.

International Court of Justice (ICJ) 2020, *Application of the convention on the prevention and punishment of the crime of genocide (The Gambia v Myanmar), provisional measures, order of 23 January 2020*.

Karim, MF 2017, 'Role conflict and the limits of state identity: the case of Indonesia in democracy promotion', *The Pacific Review*, vol. 30, no. 3, pp. 385–404.

Karp, P 2018, 'Indonesia warns it will 'adjust' policies if Australia moves Israel embassy', *The Guardian*, 19 October.

King, A 2017, 'Major Asian nations join UN rebuke of US over Jerusalem', *Nikkei Asia*, 22 December.

Kuik, CC 2016, 'How do weaker states hedge? Unpacking ASEAN states' alignment behavior towards China', *Journal of Contemporary China*, vol. 25, no. 100, pp. 500–514.

Lindsey, T & McRae, D (eds) 2018, *Strangers next door: Indonesia and Australia in the Asian century*, Hart Publishing, Oxford, UK; Portland, OR.

McRae, D 2014, *More talk than walk: Indonesia as a foreign policy actor*, Lowy Institute Analysis, Lowy Institute, Sydney.

McRae, D 2019, 'Indonesia's South China Sea diplomacy: a foreign policy illiberal turn?', *Journal of Contemporary Asia*, vol. 49, no. 5, pp. 759–779.

Murphy, AM 2017, 'Great power rivalries, domestic politics and Southeast Asian foreign policy: exploring the linkages', *Asian Security*, vol. 13, no. 3, pp. 165–182.

Nabbs-Keller, G 2013, 'Reforming Indonesia's foreign ministry: ideas, organisation and leadership', *Contemporary Southeast Asia*, vol. 35, no. 1, pp. 56–82.

Nasu, H, McLaughlin, R, Rothwell, DR & Tan, SS 2019, *The legal authority of ASEAN as a security institution*, Cambridge University Press, Cambridge.

Natalegawa, M 2018, 'Indonesian foreign policy: waging peace, stability, and prosperity', in U Fionna, SD Negara & D Simandjuntak (eds), *Aspirations with limitations: Indonesia's foreign affairs under Susilo Bambang Yudhoyono*, ISEAS-Yusof Ishak Institute, Singapore, pp. 14–32.

Observatory of Economic Complexity 2020, *Indonesia*, viewed 9 December 2020, <https://oec.world/en/profile/country/idn>.

Poulgrain, G 1998, *The genesis of konfrontasi: Malaysia, Brunei, Indonesia 1945–1965*, Crawford House Publishing, Bathurst.

Purdey, J, Missbach, A & McRae, D 2020, *Indonesia: state and society in transition*, Lynne Rienner, Boulder, Colorado.

Rosyidin, M 2017, 'Foreign policy in changing global politics: Indonesia's foreign policy and the quest for major power status in the Asian Century', *South East Asia Research*, vol. 25, no. 2, pp. 175–191.

Rüland, J 2009, 'Deepening ASEAN cooperation through democratisation? The Indonesian legislature and foreign policymaking', *International Relations of the Asia-Pacific*, vol. 9, no. 3, pp. 373–402.

Rüland, J 2021, 'Democratic backsliding, regional governance and foreign policymaking in Southeast Asia: ASEAN, Indonesia and the Philippines', *Democratization*, vol. 28, no. 1, pp. 237–257.

Shimazu, N 2014, 'Diplomacy as theatre: staging the Bandung Conference of 1955', *Modern Asian Studies*, vol. 48, no. 1, pp. 225–252.

Simpson, B 2005, '"Illegally and beautifully": the United States, the Indonesian invasion of East Timor and the international community, 1974–76', *Cold War History*, vol. 5, no. 3, pp. 281–315.

Sugianto, D 2017, 'Peringkat kemudahan bisnis RI naik ke 72, Jokowi: tahun depan 50', *Detik Finance*, 1 November, viewed 9 December 2020, <https://finance.detik.com/berita-ekonomi-bisnis/d-3709379/peringkat-kemudahan-bisnis-ri-naik-ke-72-jokowi-tahun-depan-50>.

Sukma, R 1997, 'Indonesia's bebas-aktif foreign policy and the "security agreement" with Australia', *Australian Journal of International Affairs*, vol. 51, no. 2, pp. 231–241.

Sukma, R 2004, *Islam in Indonesian foreign policy: domestic weakness and the dilemma of dual identity*, Routledge, London & New York.

Sukma, R 2009, 'Indonesia-China relations: the politics of reengagement', in S Tang, M Li & A Acharya (eds), *Living with China: regional states and China through crises and turning points*, PalgraveMacmillan, Houndmills, Basingstoke, pp. 89–106.

Suoneto, N 2020, 'The five strategic challenges facing US-Indonesia relations', *The Diplomat*, 7 October, viewed 14 December 2020, <https://thediplomat.com/2020/10/the-five-strategic-challenges-facing-us-indonesia-relations/>.

Syailendra, EA 2017, 'A *nonbalancing* Act: explaining Indonesia's failure to balance against the Chinese threat', *Asian Security*, vol. 13, no. 3, pp. 237–255.

Trading Economics 2020, *Indonesia GDP annual growth rate*, viewed 14 December 2020, <https://tradingeconomics.com/indonesia/gdp-growth-annual>.

Tunsjø, Ø 2017, 'U.S.-China relations: from unipolar hedging to bipolar balancing', in RS Ross & Ø Tunsjø (eds), *The rise of China: power and politics in East Asia*, Cornell University Press, Ithaca, NY & London, pp. 41–68.

US Department of State 2020, *Factsheet: U.S. security cooperation with Indonesia*, US Department of State, Bureau of Political-Military Affairs, Washington DC, 30 November, viewed 17 December 2020, <https://www.state.gov/u-s-security-cooperation-with-indonesia/>.

Van Bruinessen, M 2012, 'Indonesian Muslims and their place in the larger world of Islam', in A Reid (ed.), *Indonesia rising: The repositioning of Asia's third giant*, Institute of Southeast Asian Studies, Singapore, pp. 117–140.

Widyaningsih, E & Roberts, CB 2014, 'Indonesia in ASEAN: mediation, leadership, and extra-mural diplomacy', in CB Roberts, AD Habir & LC Sebastian (eds), *Indonesia at home and abroad: economics, politics and security*, National Security College Issue Briefs, Nos 1-14, National Security College, Canberra, pp. 105–116.

World Bank 2020a, *GDP ranking*, viewed 9 December 2020, <https://databank.worldbank.org/data/download/GDP.pdf>.

World Bank 2020b, *Ease of doing business report 2020*, viewed 9 December 2020, <https://www.doingbusiness.org/en/rankings>.

13 Indonesia in Comparative Perspective

Introduction

When Indonesian President Jokowi won his first election in 2014, many observers of Indonesian politics breathed a sigh of relief. By defeating the controversial former general Prabowo Subianto, who during his campaign had repeatedly flirted with authoritarian fantasies, the seemingly humble and reform-minded Jokowi appeared to have provided a new impetus for the fading narrative of *reformasi*. *Time* magazine (2014) called his victory 'a new hope', while prominent scholars like Aspinall and Mietzner (2014) described the election results as 'democracy's close call'. Coming merely two months after Thailand had just experienced its latest military coup, the Indonesian election ushered in a brief period of positive democratic developments in Southeast Asia, a region where democracy has long struggled to gain a foothold. In 2015, for instance, Myanmar's powerful military decided not to overturn the election victory for Aung San Suu Kyi's opposition party, the National League for Democracy (NLD). Then, in 2018, Malaysia also recorded an extraordinary election result when the opposition defeated the once unassailable National Front and its dominant party, the United Malays National Organisation (UMNO), for the first time since independence.

By the time the Malaysian opposition took over the government, however, the democratic outlook for Indonesia had already changed. As described extensively in this book, under Jokowi, democratic quality gradually declined. Nor did the democratic resurgence in other Southeast Asian countries last very long. The Malaysian opposition-turned-government soon found itself back in opposition again, while things in Myanmar got much worse. On 1 February 2021, the military staged another coup d'état, ending all hopes for democratisation in the state with the longest history of military rule in Southeast Asia. Meanwhile, in Thailand, the monarchy–military alliance retained a stranglehold on power despite holding elections in 2019, while the Philippines descended into quasi-authoritarian rule under populist president Rodrigo Duterte. In short, Indonesia's democratic decline since 2014 is not the exception but the norm in Southeast Asia.

A comparative perspective may not alter Indonesia's track record against normative democratic benchmarks, but it can help to put the country's development into a broader context. This context has been widely documented, both globally and

DOI: 10.4324/9780429459511-13

regionally in Southeast Asia, for many years now. Scholars and think tanks have described it variously as democratic backsliding, regression, recession or decline. In order to understand how Indonesia fits into these broader trends, this last chapter will therefore look at the country's democratic track record through a comparative lens. By considering both global and regional trends as well as political developments in other Muslim-majority countries, the chapter will conclude that, compared to many other states in Southeast Asia and the Muslim world, Indonesia's democracy actually still holds up quite well. Nevertheless, there are abundant signs that Indonesia should no longer be regarded as a model Muslim democracy, if in fact that label was ever accurate at all. Rather than providing a blueprint for other states, be that in the Muslim world or elsewhere, Indonesia's development exemplifies the challenges and complexities of establishing and deepening democracy in a region without many historical precedents of democratic governance and at a time when the appeal of democratic governance is in decline around the world.

Before commencing the comparative analysis, the next section of this chapter will begin with a quick summary of the following key arguments developed in this book. First, Indonesia's democracy has to contend with massive historical baggage inherited from prolonged colonial rule and decades of authoritarian rule under Sukarno and Suharto. Second, since the onset of democratisation, Indonesia has defied the odds to develop a reasonably well-functioning institutional framework for democratic governance and elections. Third, the period when narratives about democratic reform dominated public discourse is long gone. Instead, Indonesia is now in the midst of ideational contestation between the last defenders of the *reformasi* narrative, proponents of repressive pluralism and adherents of Islamism. Fourth, democratic achievements in relation to the institutional framework and policymaking are gradually eroding under incessant pressure from entrenched elites, while long-existing democratic deficits that were never really resolved in the early post-Suharto years such as corruption, limits to freedom of religion and the weak institutionalisation of political parties not only persist but, at least in some cases, are becoming more and more serious. Fifth, Indonesia's trend towards illiberal democracy has negative implications for Indonesia's ability to tackle some of its most pressing policy challenges, with public health, gender equality, human rights and environmental protection all suffering from the consequences of democratic decline.

Legacies of the Past

We began the book with a brief historical overview that first sketched Indonesia's emergence as a nation-state after a long period of colonial occupation and then outlined the country's turbulent postcolonial journey from democracy to authoritarian rule and back to democracy. On this long and protracted road to democracy, Indonesia went through a range of distinct historical regimes that can be usefully divided into the colonial era, a brief period of constitutional democracy (1949–1957), Sukarno's Guided Democracy (1957–1966) and eventually Suharto's New Order (1966–1998).

All these distinct regimes have left important legacies with significant ramifications for contemporary politics. First, colonial rule not only laid the foundations for the territorial borders of the modern state, but also instilled a strong sense of nationalism and a deeply engrained suspicion against external interference in domestic affairs in Indonesia's national psyche. As highlighted in Chapter 12, this legacy of the colonial era continues to inform Indonesian foreign policy until today. Moreover, the colonial period was also the incubator of widespread resentment against Chinese Indonesians, a small minority whom the Dutch had bestowed with privileged access to economic positions and resources as part of their social stratification measures. This anti-Chinese sentiment has reverberated time and again in the years after independence and it remains prevalent among substantial parts of the Indonesian population.

Second, the most significant legacy of Indonesia's first democratic regime in the 1950s was the alignment of socio-religious cleavages with political parties and electoral politics. Back in the early 20th century, the Indonesian nationalist movement had comprised a broad array of groups who were united in their struggle for independence but divided over the future shape of the Indonesian nation-state. The sharpest dividing line ran between secular-pluralist nationalists and Islamists. In Chapters 2, 3 and 6, we outlined how political parties representing the interests of these two streams first dominated the 1955 election and how this cleavage then defied dealignment, fragmentation and personalisation of electoral competition to re-emerge as the main – some would say the only – ideological feature of Indonesian party politics today. Beyond electoral politics, religious divisions form the backbone of the socio-political polarisation that has eroded the foundations of Indonesian democracy in recent years.

Third, Guided Democracy paved the way for the armed forces to play a major political role in Indonesia. This political role was later institutionalised by the New Order regime, but it was Sukarno's abolition of constitutional democracy in 1957 that established the armed forces as a key political actor. Today, the military is ostensibly back in the barracks, but it remains an influential strategic group whose support no president can afford to lose. More than 20 years after the fall of Suharto, civilian control over the armed forces remains elusive and military personnel are once again participating in many essentially civilian tasks, for example infrastructure development.

Fourth, the New Order regime left an indelible mark on Indonesia, with multiple ramifications for contemporary Indonesian politics. Most chapters in this book have therefore dedicated some attention to the New Order legacy, highlighting the deep impact of this period on today's configuration of ideas, interests and institutions as well as Indonesia's contemporary policy challenges. Among the most consequential continuities from the New Order are the massive influence of entrenched oligarchs over processes of policymaking and interest articulation, as well as the ubiquity of informal practices like clientelism, patronage distribution and corruption. In the realm of ideas, meanwhile, Suharto's developmentalist ideas, which centred on the subordination of freedom and civil liberties for the sake of political stability and economic development, still resonate, as is evident in many of current President Jokowi's policies. At the same time, communism remains demonised just like in the New Order and no democratically elected president has yet dared to confront the traumatic events that brought Suharto to power in 1965–1966.

Indonesia Today: A Model Muslim Democracy?

Yet, despite these continuities, Indonesian politics today differs markedly from the time before 1998. As outlined throughout this book, the democratisation process that commenced after the fall of Suharto facilitated new ideas, transformed political institutions and enabled new actors to provide input into policymaking. During the first decade of the 2000s, Indonesia earned accolades from international observers for its successful transition in which democracy became the dominant narrative in public discourse, constitutional reforms led to a vastly changed institutional framework and civil society emerged as a strong bulwark against elite tendencies to slow down or wind back democratic reforms. And even though these trends began to stall and eventually reverse in the 2010s, Indonesia is not yet on the cusp of a return to authoritarian rule. For now, at least the basic foundations of democracy remain in place, including:

- Regular competitive elections that are largely free and fair and independently organised by professional electoral administration bodies;
- A strong record of political participation backed up by political rights such as freedom of association and freedom of expression;
- A stable system of horizontal checks and balances that includes not only the three arms of government, but also independent and semi-independent commissions.

Nevertheless, there are worrying signs that the quality of Indonesian democracy is declining. Two main trends can be distinguished. First, areas of strength like the ones mentioned above are gradually eroding and, second, existing democratic deficits that have plagued Indonesia since the formative years of the current regime persist and, in some cases, are becoming more and more serious. In the following section, we recap some of the main arguments developed in this book in relation to these regressive trends.

To begin with, elections remain one of the key strengths of Indonesia's democracy, thanks largely to the professionalism of the General Election Commission (KPU) and the Election Oversight Agency (Badan Pengawas Pemilu, Bawaslu), high and often enthusiastic voter turnout and the absence of systematic electoral fraud and election-related violence. Nevertheless, as we described in Chapters 3 and 4, the integrity of elections has been increasingly compromised in recent years, due to an exponential rise in vote buying, the discriminatory instrumentalisation of religious and ethnic identity for electoral purposes and the government's efforts to constrain opposition activities. Some of these problems like the explosion in vote buying have materialised as unintended consequences of electoral system change and could therefore be addressed through electoral reform, but others have deeper structural roots and will not be resolved easily through electoral engineering.

Another example of a former democratic strength being emasculated is the relentless campaign against the Corruption Eradication Commission (Komisi Pemberantasan Korupsi, KPK), Indonesia's most vigorous defender of horizontal accountability. Within Indonesia's complex institutional landscape, where checks and balances between the executive and legislature tend to be poorly enforced, the KPK has long been an island of integrity. But its impeccable track record drew the ire of the political elite and so in 2019, after several previous attempts to curtail the commission's powers had failed in the face of mass protests (see Chapter 7), the government eventually succeeded in its endeavour to clip the KPK's wings. The revisions to the KPK law, described in detail in Chapter 5, were a highly symbolic blow to the democratic reform narrative, not only because they hit the most effective institutional bulwark against the oligarchy but also because they demonstrated the decreasing efficacy of public protest in the Jokowi era.

Other important cornerstones of Indonesian democracy like freedom of association and expression are also under threat. As discussed in Chapter 7, Indonesia not only has a relatively free media but also a vivid associational landscape where myriads of organisations vie for public attention. However, not all organisations and certainly not all individuals enjoy equal rights to express their views. While intolerance and discrimination against minorities are not new in Indonesia, the increase in polarisation since the 2014 presidential election has heightened both tensions at the grassroots and repressive measures from the government against opposition figures and groups. All in all, the space for dissent in Indonesia has shrunk considerably during the Jokowi presidency, as we highlighted in Chapter 10.

In addition to these relatively new problems, Indonesia has also struggled to address more deeply rooted democratic deficits, including:

- Persistent failure to uphold the rule of law;
- Limited freedom of religion;
- Weakly institutionalised parties.

Endemic corruption in the judiciary and police force has long made a mockery of the rule of law in Indonesia. As discussed in Chapter 5, institutions like the KPK and the Constitutional Court were created to address this, but while these two have maintained high standards of integrity and competence, very little progress has been made in relation to reforming the courts or the law enforcement agencies. In addition, both the police and the courts have increasingly become tools for the government's illiberal agenda, as has been evident in recent crackdowns targeting a wide range of government critics, including Islamists, Papuan activists and detractors of the government's Covid-19 response.

Closely related to the absence of the rule of law is the failure to uphold the democratic principle of equality. In Chapters 9 and 10, we showed that members of religious, ethnic and sexual minorities continue to face intolerance, discrimination and persecution, especially if they are Chinese Indonesians or if their belief system or sexual orientation is regarded as deviant from established norms like the six legally recognised religions or heterosexuality. Public opinion surveys have repeatedly shown that many Indonesians have very low trust in Chinese Indonesians and hold extremely conservative views about religious and sexual norms, so discriminatory state policies, arbitrary police violence and vigilante action against minorities are often tacitly supported by the public.

Finally, a third persistent problem is the poor institutionalisation of Indonesia's political parties. Although we pointed out in Chapter 3 that the party system has become quite stable over the last three elections with similar parties winning seats in parliament every five years, this stability is more a reflection of restrictive party and election laws than of strong party identification among ordinary Indonesians. Furthermore, political parties suffer not only from low party identification, but also from programmatic shallowness, lack of access to properly regulated state subsidies, pervasive corruption and rent-seeking, oligarchic control and elitism, as well as a lack of meaningful engagement with ordinary citizens. Many of them are highly leader-centric at the top, but largely clientelistic at the grassroots. Perhaps unsurprisingly, public opinion polls regularly record political parties at or near the bottom of the list of trusted institutions in Indonesia. The parties' poor performance has not only damaged their public standing but also affected the broader trajectory of Indonesian democracy. As accountability remains poor and political agendas are increasingly set by non-partisan actors, the political soil has become enormously fertile for radical populists keen to undermine the democratic foundations of the post-Suharto regime.

Thus, as Indonesia approaches a quarter of a century under democratic rule, the trajectory of the post-Suharto regime is clearly pointing towards illiberal, rather than liberal democracy. And as we have shown in Chapters 8–11, this trend towards illiberalism has implications for Indonesia's ability to tackle some of its most pressing policy challenges. Nowhere has this been more obvious than in the government's ineffective response to the Covid-19 pandemic, which exposed the dramatic consequences of polarisation, corruption and populism for public health. Even before Covid-19 hit in 2020, however, democratic deficits such as poor law enforcement, corruption and the silencing of civil society already impacted on public policymaking, for example in the field of environmental policy where conservation efforts have been regularly thwarted by the collusion between entrenched oligarchic business interests and corrupt politicians and law enforcement agencies. Meanwhile, the struggle for gender equality and human rights is facing more and more obstacles as the space for critical voices shrinks in the face of executive aggrandisement and social conservatism.

Indonesia in Comparative Perspective

The picture of Indonesian politics we have painted in this book echoes other recent analyses of the country's democratic decline. Davidson (2018, p. 59), for example, concluded his assessment of 20 years of democracy in Indonesia by highlighting the state's failure to protect minorities, warning ominously that 'if the inadequate protection of *all* minorities is not addressed with requisite conviction and resources, Indonesia's democracy might be imperilled'. More recently, Power and Warburton (2020, p. 15) stated in the introduction of their edited volume on democracy in Indonesia that 'this volume argues that Indonesian democracy is at its lowest point since the fall of the New Order'. Clearly, close observers of Indonesian politics see the democracy glass as pretty much half empty. But this view contrasts with that of some comparativists who tend to see the Indonesian democracy glass as half full rather than half empty. By looking 'backward and outward' rather than 'forward and inward', Hicken (2020, p. 28), for example, maintains that 'there is much to be positive about' when analysing Indonesia's democratic trajectory.

Building on Hicken's reminder of the broader comparative dimension, we will now put our analysis of Indonesian democracy in a comparative perspective. While Hicken based his assessment primarily on data from the Varieties of Democracy (V-Dem) Project (http://www.v-dem.net), we will focus on data from two other well-known international democracy indexes published by Freedom House and the Economist Intelligence Unit (EIU). In doing so, we will compare Indonesia not only to global and regional Asian trends, but also to political developments in other Muslim-majority countries in order to eventually return to our initial question whether Indonesia is a model Muslim democracy.

Indonesia's Democratic Development in Numbers

To establish how Indonesia's democratic trajectory stacks up against developments in other countries, it is useful to first of all review how the most influential international democracy indexes have assessed Indonesia over time as these indexes provide a good basis for comparison with a large range of countries. The longest-running of these is the annual Freedom in the World index, created in 1972 and published since 1978 by the US-based and US government–funded NGO Freedom House. The reports are usually published at the beginning of a calendar year, with data and scores referring to events from the previous year (for example, the 2014 edition covers events from 2013). Freedom in the World divides countries into status categories called free, partly free and not free. Each country receives a numerical mark from 1 to 7 for a range of criteria in two categories (political rights and civil liberties), with 1 signifying the most free and 7 the least free. Moreover, since the 2014 edition, the report also provides detailed scores for each of the seven assessment criteria so that each country now also receives a score between 0 and 100 (see Table 13.1), which allows for better comparison with other indexes such as the EIU Democracy Index.

The British-based EIU Democracy Index is another ranking that has gained a strong reputation for assessing the state of democracy around the world. First published in 2006, but annually since 2010, this index measures civil liberties, electoral process and pluralism, the functioning of government, political participation

Table 13.1 Freedom House assessment criteria

Assessment category	Assessment subcategory	Maximum score
Political rights	Electoral process	12
	Political pluralism and participation	16
	Functioning of government	12
Civil liberties	Freedom of expression and belief	16
	Associational and organisational rights	12
	Rule of law	16
	Personal autonomy and individual rights	16
Total		100

Source: Freedom House (2021a).

and political culture. The EIU reports are best known for categorising countries into four regime types called full democracy, flawed democracy, hybrid regime and authoritarian regime. These four categories correspond with numerical scores from 1 to 10, whereby 10 is the highest possible score for a full democracy. In contrast to the Freedom in the World reports, the Democracy Index carries the year of coverage in its edition name, so the Democracy Index 2014 refers to events in 2014.

Figures 13.1 and 13.2 track the evolution of Indonesian democracy according to these two indexes. The first shows how Freedom House has assessed Indonesia's progress on political rights and civil liberties from the final year of the authoritarian New Order period to the year after Jokowi's re-election, with the years in the figure referring to the year under review, not the year the report was published. As can be seen, from the very beginning of the post-Suharto period until now, Indonesia has consistently upheld political rights better than civil liberties. This assessment is in line with the views of most Indonesia specialists who have long emphasised the relative integrity of Indonesia's electoral process while lamenting persistent religious intolerance and the weak rule of law.

Freedom House does not, however, share Power and Warburton's assessment that Indonesian democracy is 'at its lowest point since the fall of the New Order'. For the US organisation, political rights were more compromised in the years up until 2004 than today because the military still held seats in the legislature in those years and the president as well as local leaders were not yet directly elected. This assessment might be seen as an overemphasis on formal representative institutions at the expense of substantial political freedoms because despite the presence of an indirectly elected president and a military faction in the House of Representatives, significant reforms were passed during those early post-Suharto years and there were few restrictions on other political freedoms. By contrast, today's president, local leaders and parliaments are all elected freely, but democratic reform has stalled and political pluralism is under threat from growing polarisation.

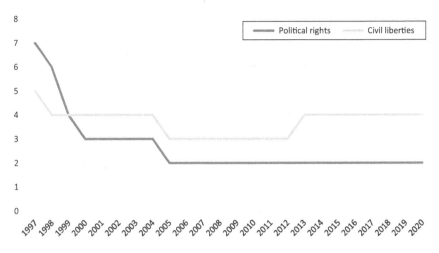

Figure 13.1 Indonesia's scores in the Freedom in the World surveys, 1997–2020

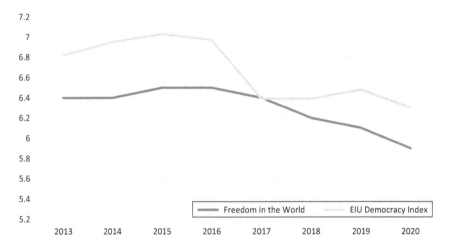

Figure 13.2 Comparing Indonesia's democracy scores – Freedom House vs. EIU

Overall, the impression from Figure 13.1 is that Indonesia's democracy is stagnant, but has not regressed since the country was downgraded from 'free' to 'partly free' in the 2013 report. But a closer look at the scores for the individual subcategories actually reveals a more nuanced picture, as is demonstrated in Figure 13.2. The dark line in that figure shows that Indonesia's aggregate score out of 100 – divided by 10 in the figure to enable a straightforward comparison with the EIU score – did in fact decline for four consecutive years between 2017 and 2020. And while the declines are small, they do certainly represent a regressive trend, just like many Indonesia specialists have argued in recent years.

Interestingly, the authors of the EIU index do not share this view. In contrast to the slow but persistent decline documented by many country experts and captured by Freedom House, the EIU index depicts a sharp fall in 2017 – to reflect the Islamist mobilisation against Ahok – but then the score somewhat surprisingly stabilises and, even more surprisingly, increases again slightly in 2019. Presumably this increase was a recognition of the relatively successful 2019 election, but it plays down the various illiberal measures taken by the Jokowi government in the run-up to that election. It is only in 2020 that Indonesia's EIU index score drops again, this time to its lowest ever score of 6.30. Arguably though, this dramatic shift is linked more closely to the government's decision to impose restrictions on movement and social activity in response to Covid-19 rather than the broader illiberal tendencies that underpinned Indonesian politics. Generally, it is striking that with the exception of 2017, the year when Islamist protestors mobbed Ahok out of office and into jail, the EIU analysts have always viewed Indonesia in a more positive light than their colleagues from Freedom House and dedicated country experts.

Despite the discrepancies, the two graphs confirm that there is a clear regressive trend that gives cause for concern. In both democracy indexes, Indonesia's 2020 score is much lower than the 2013 score. To be sure, Indonesia has never been a liberal or 'full' democracy, as the EIU index labels countries with a score greater than 8. It has, however, been consistently placed in the second category of 'flawed democracies' which is reserved for all countries with scores greater than 6, and less than or equal to 8. For a while, it was even right in the middle ranges of that category. Since 2017 though, its rank is closer to the 'hybrid regime' category, indicating a downward trend. This trend is even more pronounced in the Freedom in the World reports where Indonesia's status dropped from free to partly free in 2013 and the country's aggregate score has shown a slow but steady decline in recent years. In 2020, it dropped to under 60 – which in the EIU classification would relegate it to a hybrid regime.

This trajectory is symptomatic of a broader global trend of democratic regression (Diamond 2015, Levitsky & Ziblatt 2018) in which illiberalism, polarisation and populist post-truth politics are eroding the foundations of democracy around the world. The annual reports by Freedom House and the EIU have documented this democratic recession and captured its essence in headlines and titles such as 'Democracy in Crisis' (Freedom House 2018), 'Democracy in Retreat' (EIU 2010, Freedom House 2019), 'Democracy in Limbo' (EIU 2013) or 'Democracy under Siege' (Freedom House 2020). In their 2021 report covering events from 2020, Freedom House (2021, p. 1) wrote that the pandemic, economic and physical insecurity and violent conflict led to a '15th consecutive year of decline in global freedom'. Scores for political rights and/or civil liberties deteriorated in 73 countries, while improving in only 28. As shown above, Indonesia was one of those countries whose overall score declined, just as it had in the three previous years. The following sections will compare these scores with those of Indonesia's closest neighbours in Southeast Asia and those of other Muslim-majority states to establish just how serious Indonesia's democratic regression has been from a comparative perspective.

Democracy in Southeast Asia

Southeast Asia has long been resistant to the allure of democracy. Although several states held free elections in the early postcolonial period, by the 1970s the entire region was under authoritarian rule. When the 'third wave of democracy' (Huntington 1993) reached Southeast Asia, only the Philippines, Thailand and, somewhat belatedly, Indonesia began a democratic transition, whereas pressure for democratic reforms was suppressed by the regimes in Malaysia and Myanmar. Timor-Leste achieved independence in the early 2000s and with initial assistance from the United Nations established democratic rule. While Thailand was unable to sustain its democratic gains of the 1990s after two military coups in 2006 and 2014 (Chachavalpongpun 2020), the other three countries – the Philippines, Indonesia and Timor-Leste – have upheld democratic rule until today. Only Timor-Leste, however, has defied the trend of democratic regression and managed to stabilise its democratic regime in recent years (Croissant & Sharkh 2020). By contrast, political developments in the Philippines have resembled those in Indonesia, with populism, polarisation and utter disregard for the rule of law manifesting as key features of the Duterte presidency that began in 2016 (Deinla & Dressel 2019).

Meanwhile, the two countries that fended off pressure for democratic reform in the 1990s, Malaysia and Myanmar, made some modest democratic gains in the 2010s. In Myanmar, the military regime cautiously allowed some reforms from 2011 onwards, granting civilian politicians and non-government organisations more space and eventually holding relatively free and fair elections in 2015 (Bünte 2021). These noteworthy achievements, however, were offset by persistent allegations of genocide against the Rohingya minority and in 2021, a military coup ended all advances towards a more open political regime.

By comparison, the changes in Malaysia appeared less dramatic but no less important in the context of the country's democratic trajectory. In 2018, the opposition managed to win a general election for the first time ever since independence (Ostwald & Oliver 2020), seemingly ushering in a new era of electoral politics in which the outcome of elections is actually uncertain. But the new government collapsed merely 21 months after winning office, handing power back to the old regime and leaving Malaysia in a situation of precarious instability (Ufen 2021).

Such political upheaval has been inconceivable in the other five Southeast Asian states. Singapore, Cambodia, Brunei, Vietnam and Laos have all been under the same regime for decades, with no realistic prospect for change. While Singapore under the rule of the People's Action Party (PAP) at least allows limited political competition and civil liberties, Cambodia, Vietnam and Laos are all effectively one-party states with high levels of political repression. Brunei, finally, is an authoritarian sultanate that does not hold elections at the national level, restricts civil liberties and implements a strict version of the sharia penal code.

All in all then, it is clear that Southeast Asia as a region has not been a particularly fertile environment for democracy. This is reflected in Figures 13.3 and 13.4

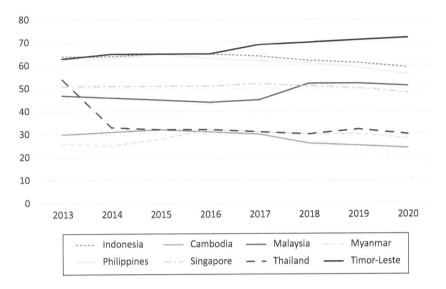

Figure 13.3 Freedom in the World, Southeast Asia, 2013–2020

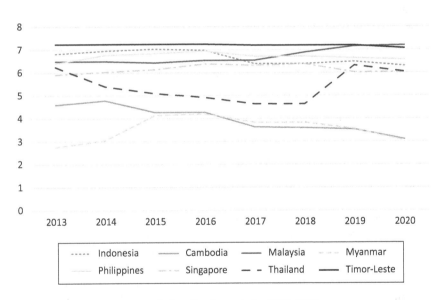

Figure 13.4 EIU Democracy Index, Southeast Asia, 2013–2020

which capture the region's democratic development in the scores of the Freedom in the World and EIU indexes. The figures cover all Southeast Asian states except Brunei (no data in the EIU index) and the communist one-party states of Vietnam and Laos.

These figures reveal some significant discrepancies in the assessments of countries like Malaysia or Thailand as well as some minor but still noteworthy differences for countries like Timor-Leste and the Philippines. Malaysia and Thailand both get significantly higher scores in the EIU Democracy Index than in the Freedom in the World reports, echoing the trend that was visible in the Indonesia data. Of particular note is the drastic upgrade in Thailand's score in 2019, whereas Freedom House only recorded a minuscule improvement that year. Timor-Leste tops the ranks in both indexes in most years, but while the EIU index notes hardly any changes in Southeast Asia's most democratic state, Freedom House has documented a steady improvement in Timor-Leste's democracy. With a net gain of six points, this small state thus clearly defies the broader trend of democratic regression in Southeast Asia. By contrast, the Philippines' political developments under President Duterte have earned the country a notable decline in the Freedom in the World report. Somewhat oddly though, this decline is not reflected as clearly in the EIU index.

Seen through this regional comparative lens, Indonesia's democratic development may appear a bit more positive than the single-country focus of this book has suggested. Despite the declines in the last three years, Indonesia still ranks highly among Southeast Asian states in both leading democracy indexes. Its trajectory of decline is mirrored in the Philippines and was, for several years, eclipsed by Thailand. But recognising this comparative context is not to say that the situation in Indonesia should be no reason for concern, especially given that some democratic gains have in fact been made in the region, even in the midst of a global democratic recession. Ironically, it is now Timor-Leste, the small country once occupied by Indonesia and the only Southeast Asian state that is not a member of ASEAN, that leads the way in Southeast Asian democratic development. This is a sobering conclusion for those who like to see Indonesia as the trailblazer of democracy in Southeast Asia.

Indonesia and the Islamic World

As discussed in Chapter 12, the main period when Indonesia sought to leverage its democratic credentials in ASEAN was during the Yudhoyono presidency. Under current President Jokowi, democracy features less prominently in foreign policy rhetoric, but Indonesia still likes to highlight that it is one of only a few Muslim-majority states in the world that upholds the main principles of democracy. That is particularly noteworthy because Indonesia is in fact the most populous Islamic country in the world, accounting for about 13 percent of the entire Muslim population in the world, according to a Pew Research report (2009) on the global distribution of Muslims. Other countries with large Muslim populations are located in South Asia (Pakistan, India and Bangladesh), northern and central Africa (Egypt, Nigeria, Algeria and Morocco) and the Middle East (Iran and Turkey).

A closer look at these ten countries suggests that very few are democratic. India, the only one of these countries where Muslims are not the majority, may be widely known as the largest democracy in the world, but under current Prime Minister Narendra Modi, the country has gone through a period of 'democratic decoupling' (Ding & Slater 2021) whereby elections continue to run smoothly but civil liberties are increasingly restricted. Significantly, the country's large Muslim minority has been among those most seriously affected by Modi's radical Hindu-nationalism. Still, apart from Indonesia, India was the only of these countries to land in the 'flawed democracy' category in the 2020 version of the EIU Democracy Index, while all others were either hybrid or authoritarian regimes. Freedom House, meanwhile, labelled all of these ten countries either partly or not free in their 2021 report covering developments in 2020, with India dropping into the partly free category for the first time. Figures 13.5 and 13.6 illustrate the trajectories of these states since 2013.

Once again, there are some significant discrepancies in the assessment, which raise questions about the assessment criteria and how they were applied. Morocco, for example, improved its score quite noticeably in the EIU rankings, but dropped in the Freedom in the World reports. Bangladesh also declined quite dramatically in the Freedom in the World reports, while improving its score in the Democracy Index in the last three editions. Nevertheless, despite these oddities, the reports do concur in a few key trends. First, compared to other large Muslim-majority countries, Indonesia's track record looks strong. Second, the EIU's assessment of Morocco aside, none of these countries have made significant democratic gains in recent years. Rather, most regimes are relatively stable in their hybridity or authoritarianism. Where there is change, it is usually for the worse, with Turkey being the most dramatic example.

Thus, compared to other large Muslim-majority states, Indonesia's democratic trajectory looks remarkably solid. Nevertheless, there are some states in the Islamic world who have better track records than Indonesia. For the EIU, these are only Malaysia and Tunisia, but Freedom House also ranked Senegal,

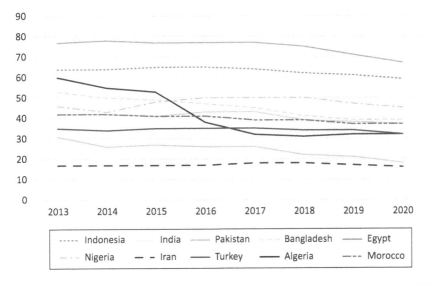

Figure 13.5 Freedom in the World, countries with large Muslim populations, 2013–2020

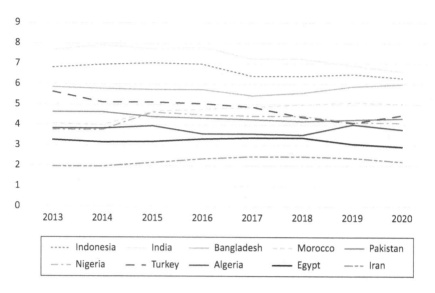

Figure 13.6 EIU Democracy Index, countries with large Muslim populations, 2013–2020

Albania and Sierra Leone higher than Indonesia. West Africa was in fact a very dynamic region for democratic development in the early 2000s and 2010s, but more recently the democratic recession also reached this part of the world (Temin & Linzer 2020). Generally, rankings for several countries have stagnated or declined, leaving Tunisia as the only 'free' Muslim-majority country in the world in the 2021 Freedom in the World report. Somewhat oddly, Senegal received the same overall score as Tunisia, but was only ranked as 'partly free' since the exclusion of important opposition figures from the 2019 presidential election. Table 13.2 lists the ten most democratic Muslim-majority states in 2020, as recorded by Freedom House and the EIU.

Table 13.2 Most democratic Muslim-majority states in 2020

Freedom House	*Score*	*EIU*	*Score*
Senegal	71	Malaysia	7.19
Tunisia	71	Tunisia	6.59
Albania	66	Indonesia	6.3
Sierra Leone	65	Albania	6.08
Indonesia	59	Bangladesh	5.99
Burkina Faso	54	Senegal	5.67
Kosovo	54	Morocco	5.04
Malaysia	51	Sierra Leone	4.86
Niger	48	Kyrgyzstan	4.21
Nigeria	45	Nigeria	4.10

Sources: Economist Intelligence Unit (2020); Freedom House (2021b).

Conclusion

Indonesia made noteworthy democratic advances in the first ten years after the end of the authoritarian New Order. A period of democratic stagnation without any meaningful reforms followed and, as it turned out, soon morphed into democratic regression. Today, Indonesian politics still features democratic elections and its institutional framework remains reasonably robust, but demands to address deficits in the institutional setup through institutional and structural reforms are increasingly drowned out by populist strains of nationalism and Islamism. The *reformasi* narrative of the late 1990s and early 2000s is in urgent need of revival.

Compared to other states in Southeast Asia and in the Muslim world, Indonesia's track record may look a bit more positive. Hicken (2020, p. 43) called Indonesian democracy 'imperfect, as all democracies are, but generally healthy when compared with its neighbours, and with many other democracies around the world'. But since Hicken wrote these words, things have only deteriorated further. As shown in this last chapter, Indonesia's scores on the Freedom in the World and EIU Democracy Index have just reached their lowest points since 2013 and prominent country experts have raised alarm bells that Indonesian democracy is at its lowest point since 1998.

As demonstrated throughout this book, we share these concerns about Indonesian democracy. While a comparative lens offers important contextual insights into broader global and regional trends, it should not dilute our assessment that Indonesia's political trajectory is heading in a worrying direction. Irrespective of developments in other countries, Indonesia's democratic decline is particularly noteworthy, not only because the country had defied so many odds when it democratised in 1998, but also because it has continued to defy these odds and managed to hold on to its democracy for a remarkably long period of time.

It is ironic then that these achievements have come under such intense pressure during the presidency of Jokowi, the man whose first election victory back in 2014 had inspired widespread hope that democracy would not only persist in Indonesia, but that it would thrive. Sadly, these hopes remained unfulfilled. Under Jokowi, democratic values such as freedom and equality have become so compromised that illiberal democracy appears to be the most appropriate label for Indonesia's current regime. And an illiberal democracy is hardly a model democracy.

References

Aspinall, E & Mietzner, M 2014, 'Indonesian politics in 2014: democracy's close call', *Bulletin of Indonesian Economic Studies*, vol. 50, no. 3, pp. 347–369.

Bünte, M 2021, 'Ruling but not governing: tutelary regimes and the case of Myanmar', *Government and Opposition*, online first, pp. 1–17, <https://doi.org/10.1017/gov.2020.38>.

Chachavalpongpun, P (ed.) 2020, *Coup, King, crisis: a critical interregnum in Thailand*, Monograph No. 68, Yale University Southeast Asia Studies.

Croissant, A & Sharkh, RA 2020, 'As good as it gets? Stateness and democracy in East Timor', in A Croissant & O Hellmann (eds), *Stateness and democracy in East Asia*, Cambridge University Press, New York, pp. 204–232.

Davidson, JS 2018, *Indonesia: twenty years of democracy*, Cambridge University Press, Cambridge.

Deinla, I & Dressel, B 2019, *From Aquino II to Duterte (2010–2018): change, continuity – and rupture*, ISEAS-Yusof Ishak Institute, Singapore.

Diamond, L 2015, 'Facing up to the democratic recession', *Journal of Democracy*, vol. 26, no. 1, pp. 141–155.

Ding, I & Slater, D 2021, 'Democratic decoupling', *Democratization*, vol. 28, no. 1, pp. 63–80.

Economist Intelligence Unit (EIU), various years, *Democracy Index*, EIU, London.

Economist Intelligence Unit (EIU) 2020, *Democracy Index 2020: in sickness and in health?*, EIU, London.

Freedom House, various years, *Freedom in the world*, Freedom House, Washington DC.

Freedom House 2021a, *Freedom in the world 2021 methodology*, Freedom House, Washington DC.

Freedom House 2021b, *Freedom in the world 2021: Democracy under siege*, Freedom House, Washington DC.

Hicken, A 2020, 'Indonesia's democracy in a comparative perspective', in T Power & E Warburton (eds), *Democracy in Indonesia: from stagnation to regression?*, ISEAS-Yusof Ishak Institute, Singapore, pp. 23–44.

Huntington, SP 1993, *The third wave: democratization in the late twentieth century*, University of Oklahoma Press, Norman.

Levitsky, S & Ziblatt, D 2018, *How democracies die*, Crown, New York.

Ostwald, K & Oliver, S 2020, 'Four arenas: Malaysia's 2018 election, reform, and democratization', *Democratization*, vol. 27, no. 4, pp. 662–680.

Power, T & Warburton, E 2020, 'The decline of Indonesian democracy', in T Power & E Warburton (eds), *Democracy in Indonesia: from stagnation to regression?*, ISEAS-Yusof Ishak Institute, Singapore, pp. 1–20.

Temin, J & Linzer, I 2020, 'West Africa's democratic progress is slipping away, even as region's significance grows', *Freedom House Perspectives*, 19 March, viewed 10 April 2021, <https://freedomhouse.org/article/west-africas-democratic-progress-slipping-away-even-regions-significance-grows-0>.

Time Magazine 2014, *A new hope*, 16 October.

Ufen, A 2021, 'The downfall of Pakatan Harapan in Malaysia: coalitions during transition', *Asian Survey*, vol. 61, no. 2, pp. 273–296.

Index